Becoming John Wayne

Becoming John Wayne

The Early Westerns of a Screen Icon, 1930–1939

LARRY POWELL *and*
JONATHAN H. AMSBARY

McFarland & Company, Inc., Publishers

Jefferson, North Carolina

ALSO OF INTEREST AND FROM MCFARLAND: *The Films of John G. Avildsen: Rocky, The Karate Kid and Other Underdogs* by Larry Powell and Tom Garrett (2014); *Black Barons of Birmingham: The South's Greatest Negro League Team and Its Players* by Larry Powell (2009)

LIBRARY OF CONGRESS CATALOGUING-IN-PUBLICATION DATA

Names: Powell, Larry, 1948– author. | Amsbary, Jonathan H. (Jonathan Howard), 1956– author.
Title: Becoming John Wayne : the early westerns of a screen icon, 1930–1939 / Larry Powell and Jonathan H. Amsbary.
Description: Jefferson,, North Carolina : McFarland & Company, Inc., Publishers, 2018. | Includes bibliographical references and index.
Identifiers: LCCN 2018001221 | ISBN 9781476664132 (softcover : acid free paper) ∞
Subjects: LCSH: Wayne, John, 1907–1979—Criticism and interpretation.
Classification: LCC PN2287.W36 P69 2018 | DDC 791.4302/8092—dc23
LC record available at https://lccn.loc.gov/2018001221

BRITISH LIBRARY CATALOGUING DATA ARE AVAILABLE

ISBN 978-1-4766-6413-2 (print)
ISBN 978-1-4766-2994-0 (ebook)

On the cover poster art from *The Lawless Frontier,* 1934 (Monogram Pictures/Photofest)

Printed in the United States of America

McFarland & Company, Inc., Publishers
Box 611, Jefferson, North Carolina 28640
www.mcfarlandpub.com

The authors would like to thank
Coleman McPherson
for his research assistance on this book.
His contributions are greatly appreciated.

Table of Contents

Introduction

Becoming John Wayne explores the early Westerns of John Wayne, from his first starring role in the 1930 epic *The Big Trail* up to and including his breakthrough role as the Ringo Kid in John Ford's 1939 classic *Stagecoach*. This book argues that it was during these 1930s Westerns that Marion Michael Morrison transformed from a prop man for the movie studios into the John Wayne film persona that became world-famous. He did that by using the decade to improve his acting skills, developing his ability to handle stunts, and becoming an expert horseman. Moreover, he became perhaps the most recognizable and iconic movie star of the studio age, if not all time. He also helped to transform the Western and action movies of the studio era.

The book provides plot summaries of these Westerns. Many fans have never seen these movies, and previous books about John Wayne have hurried through these productions. Most other books devote only a handful of pages to the movies themselves. In many books, most of these films are never mentioned at all. We have tried to correct those omissions.

After the box office failure of *The Big Trail*, Wayne was relegated to B Westerns where he honed his craft. He started the transformation by working in Westerns with Tim McCoy and Buck Jones, where his acting was often awkward and overstated, like that of a stage actor instead of a movie star. That was followed by a stint in a series of six Warner Brothers Westerns in which he shared billing with a horse named Duke; all six were remakes of earlier films by Ken Maynard. His acting started getting better, particularly in action scenes, but he was still awkward when working with his female leads.

Wayne then moved to Poverty Row, churning out Westerns for Monogram–Lone Star in which he developed an understanding of stunt work. His acting skills continued to improve, as did his stunt work. He and Yakima Canutt started developing the basic elements of on-screen fighting, in which one person would swing with a near-miss blow, while the other reacted as if they had been hit. Between his improving acting, stunt skills and horsemanship, Wayne became a cowboy hero in those B Westerns. His only setback was his brief, unsuccessful casting as a singing cowboy.

After a stint with Universal, he became a regular in Republic's Three Mesquiteers series. By then, he was a full-fledged cowboy hero star, and his on-screen persona was well defined. His acting, riding and stunt skills were finely tuned. Not surprisingly, it was during this latter stint, he was picked by John Ford to play the Ringo Kid in *Stagecoach*. By the end of 1939, Marion Michael Morrison had completed the transition, becoming John Wayne both on and off the screen.

His early Westerns are largely forgotten by the viewing public, but they played a major role in developing his film persona. During those early films, he changed his name and worked on his acting skills. In the process, he quit being Marion Michael Morrison, or "Duke" Morrison as his friends called him, and gradually invented his new on-screen personality: John Wayne. In essence, it was during those early formative years— from 1930 to 1939—that John Wayne became John Wayne.

His son Ethan Wayne recalled that his father's years of training went well beyond his acting skills. He described his father as "a consummate professional who hones his craft and became not only the biggest Western actor, but also the best horseman and gun handler on the big screen."[1] John Wayne took pride in his horsemanship, noting that he "never used a mechanical horse in my life."[2]

His riding skills were apparent in a scene from the 1966 movie *El Dorado*. Facing the family of a man that he had just killed, Wayne backs his horse away from the ranch house, constantly keeping his eyes on the family that might want to shoot him. That maneuver took an expert horseman. Despite some critics who disparaged the way he sat on a horse, he had come a long way from the young actor who needed Yakima Canutt to double for him in nearly every riding scene.

Appropriately, his career started in Westerns. His first job was handling props for a Tom Mix Western. His first starring role was in a Western, Raoul Walsh's *The Big Trail*. When that didn't work out, he turned to the Poverty Row studios and worked his way back to stardom—again by playing a cowboy hero.

Fred N. Cavinder noted that the link between Wayne and Westerns was an appropriate one: "[I]t was, in retrospect, a moment of fate as inevitable as any showdown, as certain as the cleverest cutoff at the pass, as classic as the cattle drive. Wayne helped mold the Western movie and it, in turn, shaped him into a star."[3]

If Westerns shaped John Wayne, he also helped to shape the Western. As Helen Akitt wrote, "For many people, no one epitomizes the Western like John Wayne. With towering stature and steely gaze, Wayne dominated his movies like a national monument dominates the land. His image was a metaphor for America itself, its strength, its determination, and its reliability."[4]

His name is now iconic, and he gladly accepted the new moniker. It seems like an easy decision now, but—if anything—it could be criticized for being too common for a cowboy. That issue was discussed for humorous effect by Jackie Chan and Owen Wilson in the 2000 movie *Shanghai Noon*. When asked his name, Chan's character replies, "My name is Chon Wang." Wilson's character, misunderstanding the response, says, "John Wayne.... That's a terrible cowboy name."

Still, by the end of the '30s, when Duke starred in *Stagecoach*, he had accepted the new name and developed the acting skills and persona that would make him a star. He then become famous. In most of those latter films, he simply played John Wayne—the persona he spent ten years developing.

There were a few exceptions. He played two historical characters, rancher John Chisum in *Chisum*, his 1970 version of the Billy the Kid story, and Davy Crockett in Wayne's own 1960 production *The Alamo*. In both cases, though, his interpretation of the characters were based on his longtime on-screen persona.

The only true exceptions were the two movies in which he portrayed Rooster Cogburn, *True Grit* (1969), for which he won as Oscar, and its sequel *Rooster Cogburn* (1975). The original performance was truly superb, but echoes of his John Wayne persona kept creeping into his 1975 reprise.

The Duke was born in Winterset, Iowa, in 1907 as Marion Robert Morrison. His mother soon legally changed his middle name to Mitchell. Duke didn't like the new moniker and started going by Marion Michael Morrison.[5] He gained his nickname at an early age, taken from his favorite dog[6]; he spent so much time with the pet that the family started calling him Little Duke.[7] He attended college in California as a football player before easing into the movie industry.

He served as a prop boy in Tom Mix Westerns.[8] Wayne got his start in uncredited roles starting in 1926. His first credited role came in a 1929 quickie, *Words and Music*, where he was billed as Duke Morrison. He played Pete Donohue, a young musician competing in a songwriting contest while courting a young girl.

His next credited role had the potential to be a big break: He was selected to star in a major film. Duke Morrison was renamed John Wayne and starred in *The Big Trail*, an epic directed by Raoul Walsh.[9]

Walsh would become a major director in his prime, but he wasn't ready to direct a major Western in 1930. When the film bombed, Duke became a B-movie actor. Most but not all of his early B-films were Westerns.[10] At least one had a budget so small that they could only afford one horse, which the various characters took turns riding.[11]

During this time, Wayne became arguably the first singing cowboy. He played "Singing Sandy" in a couple of those B Westerns, although the singing was done offstage by someone else. Those films were typical of the movies in which he labored for years. The genre of B Westerns and serials became his training ground.

Those movies employed simple and repetitive plots. As Bobby Copeland wrote, "The cowboy hero had the fastest horse, quickest draw, fanciest clothes … and he possessed a heart of purest gold. Even on his worst day, he could beat the daylights out of the meanest bad guy."[12]

Many were directed, and sometimes written, by Robert Bradbury. Bradbury's films were considered actor-proof, because the focus was on action rather than dialogue. What dialogue there *was* is usually mundane and uninspired.

The plots typically followed a standard formula. Wayne comes to the rescue of an old codger and his daughter (or niece), stops the bad guys from taking their ranch or money or mine, and reveals the mastermind of the criminal scheme to be a respectable rancher or banker or businessman.

Along the way, Duke is often accused of being a criminal himself and sometimes arrested, necessitating that he clear his name. Dave Kehr noted that the plots employed by these films were not particularly specific to the Western genre and were "frequently interchangeable with those of the crime movies that Republic also made in vast quantities, with the cowboys taking the roles of state or federal marshals investigating specific crimes."[13]

Each film was made in a week on a budget of around $28,000 with Wayne usually getting $2500 a film. As with many Wayne films of the era, the cast often featured a stable of actors that included George Hayes, before he became known as "Gabby" Hayes,[14] and character actor–stuntman Yakima Canutt,[15] a veteran rodeo rider.[16]

For Duke, it was a training ground in which he learned to act. Gabby got a chance to develop his classic sidekick character.[17] Canutt would become the greatest stuntman in the history of the movies. As Ethan Wayne recalled, "My father really looked up to Harry Carey Sr. And Yakima Canutt."[18]

Canutt is the one individual who was most responsible for developing the concept of stunt work in films. Lee Simmons once called Canutt "the first action hero" because of his early stunt work.[19] Together Canutt and Wayne developed the modern technique of on-camera fighting. They used near-miss swings and camera angles to give the audience a sense of two men fighting, even though no blows were landing.[20] Prior to their work, on-screen fights were pretty lame events. The stuntman's acumen in the business allowed Wayne to become the first cowboy hero to use tables and chairs in a film fight.[21]

During the 1930s, Canutt seemed to be Wayne's only stunt double. (Later in Wayne's career, other stuntmen would get the call to double for him, including the legendary Jock Mahoney.) Unfortunately, as George N. Fenin and William K. Everson noted, "[Canutt] was often very carelessly photographed: e.g., the director would offer a medium close-up of Canutt leaping into the saddle, seconds later the audience realized that it was supposed to have been Wayne. The last reel often found Canutt, doubling for Wayne, chasing himself!"[22] Canutt's work as a stuntman continued for years and his influence can be seen in many movies made after he had retired with one of the most recognizable tributes appearing in *Raiders of the Lost Ark* when Indiana Jones leaps from a horse onto a Nazi truck.[23]

Although the films were weak, they served as a training ground for the Duke and were crucial in the development of film stunt work. Students of film history will enjoy some of their primitive techniques, particularly the use of a single stationary camera to film each scene, a rolling splice of film to shift between scenes, and the use of a swift camera pan to reflect the passage of time between two scenes.

Some of the movies included work with child actors, a common casting technique in B Westerns.[24] Child actor Sammy McKim, who worked with both Wayne and Gene Autry, really liked Wayne. "Autry didn't seem to warm up to kids and was rather cool in his off-camera relationships," McKim once said. "Wayne was good-natured."[25]

Overall, Marion Michael Morrison became John Wayne—both in name and in terms of his on-screen image. His Westerns reflected this image and his life. Indeed, as he wrote in his unfinished autobiography, "The cowboy appeals to a basic emotion—heroic tradition."[26]

Michael Goldman noted, "Over the years, Wayne wore the stereotype of being a 'cowboy star' as a badge of pride."[27] He made a total of 84 Western films. Even his final film, 1976's *The Shootist*, was a Western that presented his impending death from cancer as an allegory of his own life—on and off the screen.

He even acknowledged how he carefully crafted the screen persona that became John Wayne. "When I started, I knew I was no actor, and I went to work on this Wayne thing," he once said. "I figured I needed a gimmick, so I dreamed up the drawl, the squint as a way of moving meant to suggest that I wasn't looking for trouble but would just as soon throw a bottle at your head as not. I practiced in front of a mirror."[28]

John Wayne was not unique in creating a persona. Many actors of the day tried to do the same thing. But, as Terrence Rafferty noted, "Wayne was unusual in the simplicity of his rugged-individualist persona—he was a living reproach to the very idea of complexity—and in the ease with which he wore it, like that battered, funky-looking old cowboy hat he sported in picture after picture."[29] He continued:

> And that ease is really quite an achievement, especially considering that for at least the three decades of his screen life Wayne was representing the essence of American masculinity to the entire free world: a burden that would probably make most guys a little tense.[30]

Indeed, he worked on the image until he became John Wayne. As his son Ethan later wrote, "[A]ll his life he adhered to the timeless code of the West: self-sufficiency, quiet nobility, and the willingness to help those who can't help themselves. This set of values drove him to perfect his craft and become Hollywood's defining cinematic cowboy."[31]

This book chronicles the change from Duke Morrison to John Wayne. It started with changing his name in 1930, but it didn't reach full expression until John Ford directed him as the star of *Stagecoach*. Through the decades of the 1930s, John Wayne worked through his initially awkward acting style to become an international icon of the silver screen.

1

1930: *The Big Trail*

What was John Wayne's first major film role? It was not *Stagecoach* (1939), but rather the epic *The Big Trail* (1930).

Wayne was 22 years old when, after only five B films, he got the starring role in the Raoul Walsh Western, co-starring Tyrone Power, Sr., and Marguerite Churchill.[1] It turned out to be the first and only talking film for Power Sr., who died the following year.

A presidential decree inspired the movie. Herbert Hoover had called on the nation to celebrate the 100th anniversary of the first wagon train to traverse the Oregon Trail.[2] That group of pioneers departed from Independence, Missouri, on April 10, 1830. Fox Film Corporation decided to celebrate the event by releasing a movie about the trek.[3]

The script was done by committee. It had a story provided by Hal G. Evarts, while the dialogue was a patchwork provided by writers Marie Boyle, Jack Peabody and Florence Postal. Shooting started on location in Yuma, Arizona, and problems immediately arose. Away from the confines of studio control, Walsh lost control of many of the actors. The cast and crew consumed so much alcohol in Yuma that Walsh said "that the name of the movie should have been 'The Big Drunk.'"[4]

After Yuma, shooting moved to the Sacramento River area in California for a river scene, and then to Wyoming (Grand Teton Pass; Jackson Hole; Yellowstone National Park), Utah (St. George; Springdale; Hurricane Bluffs in Zion National Park), Oregon and Montana (Moise-National Buffalo Range). Other locations included the Grand Canyon in Arizona and in Imperial County, Sequoia National Park and the Buttercup Dunes and Sacramento, California. The action and dialogue of the script was often altered to fit the locations used. The film was shot in 16 different locations and in six different states, an approach that was unusual and expensive. The final budget was estimated to be two million dollars, a huge financial commitment for the time. As for Walsh, Ronald

L. Davis noted that he considered the experience "a nightmare from start to finish."[5]

Wayne got the role because Walsh had trouble filling it. Walsh's first choice, Tom Mix, was already working on another film. His second choice was Gary Cooper, but he was under contract to Paramount and they refused to loan him for Walsh's film.

Wayne, who was working in the prop department at the time, eventually got the part because Walsh spotted him unloading furniture from a truck. Some sources credit John Ford with pointing out the future star to Walsh.[6] Others credit Walsh with spotting him, noticing both his muscular body and a face that would appeal to movie audiences, but credit Ford for vouching for the Duke's work ethic.[7] Mark Eliot wrote that Walsh approached Wayne and asked if he could act. Duke said he could not. "Maybe you could learn," said Walsh.[8]

Wayne took that statement too literally and immediately made a mistake. He hired a drama coach to teach him the basics of the craft. Unfor-

John Wayne (right) with Ian Keith and Marguerite Churchill in *The Big Trail* (1930).

tunately, he chose a tutor who worked with stage actors, not those who worked on films. The result was a Duke who used exaggerated and grand gestures. Walsh had to pull him off the set and spent two weeks to get him to tone down the movements before he could use him. Many of those exaggerated movements appear in the film.[9]

Wayne got the part despite early problems in his auditions. He didn't get along with the studio's acting coach, an eastern veteran of stage work who told him, "You'll never be an actor in a hundred years." He stumbled in his audition scene until becoming angry and snapping back at the other actors. And his voice was too nasal; Walsh made him scream until he was hoarse, and tested him again.

Finally, it went well, perhaps due to Wayne's perseverance. Michael Goldman argued that Wayne "finally won the day with gumption"[10] because he improvised during a scene when the other actor went off script and tried to throw him off with a series of questions. Wayne responded with improvised criticism of the actor for having soft hands and not being ready to hit the trail to Oregon. The Duke won the part and also got a salary of $75 per week, a major payday during the Depression.

His first duty after being hired was to learn how to throw a knife. He went to expert Steve Clemente who taught him how to throw one so that it completed one revolution every 12 feet, and he used that skill on-screen in the movie.

The movie itself was an epic ahead of its time, the first to use a widescreen technique as it explored the mythology of Western migration. Greg Santoro wrote that it was "shot on eye-popping locations and painstakingly 'authentic' from its ox-drawn wagons to its pioneers' food supplies."[11] Andrews arris summarized the director's approach: "The Walshian hero is less interested in the why or the how than in the what. He is always plunging into the unknown, and he is never too sure what he will find there."[12] That approach perfectly captures the essence of *The Big Trail.*

Wayne played Bret Coleman, a scout who leads a wagon train west over the Big Trail, better known today as the Oregon Trail. Along the way, the settlers contend with snowstorms, Indian attacks, raging rivers and rugged cliffs, challenges faced by the real pioneers who traveled the Oregon Trail.[13] When they become discouraged, Coleman implores them to continue with a patriotic speech. Meanwhile, he courts a girl (Churchill) and looks for the "two skunks" who killed a friend.

His first on-camera scene turned out to be a difficult one. His job was to ride a horse alongside a wagon. Veteran character actor Tully Marshall was supposed to ride up beside him and offer Duke a drink of whiskey. The problem occurred when it turned out that Marshall really was drunk. Duke accepted the offer and took a big swig from Marshall's bottle, which turned out to be pure rotgut, not the water or tea Duke was expecting. But he swallowed gamely and kept the scene going.[14] The scene of him drinking from the bottle never made it to the screen.

But his lack of acting experience showed, particularly in the love scenes with Churchill. As Eliot wrote, "the uptight Wayne had absolutely no idea how to approach her."[15] Further, Duke is sometimes awkward in reciting his lines, and his reactions when responding to others are often overblown.

By modern standards, the film starts slow and takes a long time to introduce its cast before starting the trek westward. Wayne's acting is occasionally awkward, but also shows glimpses of charm. The plot offers plenty of opportunities for other cast members to comment about him. An enemy refers to him as "that young buck … with no hair on his face," while a settler describes him as "the breed of man who would follow a trail to the end." The most apt summary comes from a young girl saying her prayers at bedtime. She asks God to look after all the people she loves, but leaves out Wayne's character because he "can take care of himself."

Wayne has his own choice lines too. He dismisses advice from the unkempt wagon master about crossing a river: "What does he know about water? He never took a bath in his life." Wayne is also Walsh's spokesman for his view of the Western spectacle. "There's trees out there—big tall pines—just a-reachin' and a-reachin', as if they wanted to climb right through the gates of Heaven," he says.

Some dramatic scenes were also included, with the settlers having to find inventive ways to cross some of the terrain. Clark noted this: "Visually, this wagon-train Western is staggering and unique. During a flooded-river crossing and another spectacular scene in which crude pulleys transport wagons down a mountainside, it's as if we're watching some settler's superbly shot home movies."[16]

The Big Trail was released in California on October 2, 1930, with the tagline "The most important picture ever produced." It reached New York City on October 24. It was released nationwide on November 1. Its release to European theaters was spread out over two years, starting on December 26 in London and lasting until February 29, 1932, when it reached Spain.

Wayne found himself in the uncomfortable position of having to go on a publicity tour. He was sometimes billed as a "football player turned actor" or as a "cowboy turned actor," although the latter billing was undermined when one newspaper pointed out that the cowboy was wearing a new watch.[17]

John Wayne (left) with Tyrone Power (center) and Ian Keith: *The Big Trail* **(1930).**

Many observers expected *The Big Trail* to launch his career as a major star. It became, instead, the only Wayne film to be a financial flop, a combination of a $2 million production, movie houses which were not equipped to show its big-screen grandeur, and a release date that was only a few months into the Great Depression. The studio adjusted by re-cutting portions of the film for the standard format, but that also destroyed much of its original grandeur.

The film also had silent screen overtones. This was back in the days when studios were still learning how to make movies with sound. They didn't always know how to use sound and would let some scenes go silent.

They also often added frames of text to explain the action. Further, microphones were not well enough developed to get sound on a lot of exterior shots. For example, one caption reads, "Ten weary miles a day. There is no road, but there is a will, and history cuts the way." Another reads, "The last outpost, the turning back place for the weak; the starting place for the strong." Another notes, "Prairie schooners rolling west, praying for peace—but ready for battle."

From a camera's perspective, Walsh sometimes used "the slightly elevated angle of a lost child in the big world."[18] That approach may have overwhelmed some audiences.

There were plenty of other production problems, some resulting from the six different versions that were shot. There was a standard 35mm version that was shot for most theaters, while a 70mm version, using a process developed by Fox called Grandeur, was made for major theaters. In addition, four additional 35mm versions were shot in four different languages—French, German, Italian and Spanish—often using a different set of actors.

Fenin and Everson wrote that the German version of *The Big Trail* "was especially well put together. Dialogue taking a second place to action, the sequences that had to be re-shot, on the original sets, of course, were relatively few and comparatively simply. Although German audiences were deprived of John Wayne except in the long shots, Germany's exhibitors had a much more profitable product."[19]

Still, it got confusing, perhaps because there is such little emphasis on a plot. As Ricci, Zmijewsky and Zmijewsky wrote, "The plot itself is sparse, but the movie moves with such breathless sweep and with such climaxes that the story is relatively unimportant."[20]

The heavy reliance on production, and on the Grandeur process in particular, meant that "the impetus for *The Big Trail* was visual, not narrative."[21] Similarly, Eliot wrote that the movie had "too much vista, too little vision."[22] Clark concluded that it should be viewed "as a photographic revelation. If, that is, it's seen in its 70mm 'Grandeur' version that few Depression-era theaters could afford to show."[23] In fact, at the time of its release, only two theaters—one in Los Angeles and one in New York—had installed the Grandeur technology.

The movie did little to promote Wayne's career, perhaps because, as Smith wrote, it was "not a typical Wayne movie."[24] All in all, what you got is not great by modern standards, although it was impressive for its day.

Eyles argued the movie was going to do little for Wayne's career simply because of the way it was filmed. "In any case," he wrote, "the film did not rest so much on Wayne as on its spectacular highlights and the painstaking recreation of the hazards of pioneering."[25]

Clark wrote, "Wayne was green and awkward, but you can see potential not tapped until 1939's *Stagecoach*."[26] According to Eliot, director Walsh "was, at this point in his career, still directing with an actor's eye rather than a director's, and it limited his ability to construct a convincing *mise-en-scene*."[27]

Still, there were some pluses for Duke's career, not the least of which was that he got his screen name John Wayne. The film's executives changed it from Marion Michael Morrison to make him sound more macho. They got several suggestions, but the idea for "John Wayne" came from Walsh himself. Walsh suggested the last name Wayne because he had been reading about the Revolutionary War general "Mad" Anthony Wayne. The studio chose the first name John, although its possible that Duke chose it himself as a tribute to John Ford.[28] Regardless, Eyles noted that Wayne "sensibly welcomed the name thrust upon him" and wore it proudly after that.[29]

The B Western studios kept the name, promoting him as the star of the Western, and Duke returned to the quickie productions to hone his skills for another nine years. That led to his fine performance in *Stagecoach* and to his stellar career. However, Smith saw something positive in Wayne's work in *The Big Trail*. As he wrote, the movie "demonstrates how remiss [John] Ford was in using Wayne to no great effect for some years after *Stagecoach*."[30] Walsh later worked with Duke again in the 1940 film *Dark Command*.

Overall, *The Big Trail* may have actually hurt Wayne's career. Prior to taking the role, one of Duke's friends in the industry was John Ford. But after Wayne got the starring role in this Walsh film, Ford went five years without speaking to Duke. Walsh later said, "It's my belief that Ford felt if anyone was going to discover this new star, it was going to be Ford. Instead, it was me."[31]

According to John Carradine, who starred in *Stagecoach* with Wayne, "From the time Duke starred in *The Big Trail,* Ford didn't do a thing to help him. He sort of kept him in his place until he really needed John Wayne."[32] In fact, the movie was actually a double blow against Ford, since it not only gave Wayne his film debut, but also his stage name. As Eliot wrote, it was during filming of *The Big Trail* that "Duke Morrison crossfaded into John Wayne."[33]

Further, the movie helped to pave "the way for the boom period in 'B' Westerns from 1932 to 1942."[34] Other than that, though, *The Big Trail* did nothing positive for Duke's career. At the time, Duke was understandably disappointed. In retrospect, though, it may have been best for his career. Wayne later acknowledged, "I was totally unprepared to handle the consequences if the picture *had* launched me as a big star."[35]

Instead, Wayne started polishing his craft in B movies. As Munn wrote, "Cast into oblivion by that film's failure, he made his way through the Depression with large parts in tiny films and tiny parts in large films."[36]

2

1931: *Arizona* and *The Range Feud*

In 1931, John Wayne started toiling in cheaply made B movies, a career move that came because of his starring role in *The Big Trail*. As Davis noted, "Fox's publicity blitz for *The Big Trail* had made Wayne an attractive addition to the Columbia roster, and the studio's action films seemed well suited to his talents."[1]

Wayne landed in six productions. Two were Westerns, *Arizona* and *The Range Feud*. The non-Western films were *Girls Demand Excitement, Three Girls Lost, The Deceiver* (in which he played a corpse) and *Maker of Men*—most under a contract that paid him $75 per week.

In *Girls Demand Excitement,* Duke played the male lead, Peter Brooks, a college student who doesn't think women should attend college. Virginia Cherrill played socialite Joan Madison, who convinces Duke to reconsider his outdated views. Marguerite Churchill, his *Big Trail* co-star, was also in the movie. Wayne has frequently noted that this was the worst film he ever made.

Girls Demand Excitement was released by Fox on February 8, 1931. It was quickly followed by *Three Girls Lost*, a non–Western mystery. Architect Gordon Wales (Wayne) flirts with a young woman (Marsha Tallant) who is locked out of her apartment. When she is murdered, suspicion lands on Duke. He teams up with the girl's roommate to identify the real killer. The cast also included future Academy Award winner Loretta Young, who became a lifetime friend to Wayne[2] and godmother to his first child.[3] Fox released the film on April 19, 1931.

The plot of *The Deceiver* revolves around actor Reginald Thorpe (Ian Keith), stabbed in the back and found dead in his dressing room. Duke's role was simple: He played Thorpe's dead body. It was arguably his best acting job to that point in 1931. The movie, produced under the working title of *It Might Have Happened,* was released on November 21.

14

Maker of Men, a college football story starring Jack Holt, focuses on a player who is so bad that he's rejected for the college team by the college and the college's coach—his own father. He tries to redeem himself by playing for another team, one of the college's rivals. Wayne plays a supporting role as Dusty Rhodes, another football player. Much of his job is simply to react to the words and actions of others, a technique that Wayne used effectively after he became a star. Columbia released it on December 18, 1931.

Arizona and *The Range Feud* were Duke's two Westerns for the year. *Arizona,* released on June 27 by Columbia, was a remake of two silent movies (1913 and 1918) with the same title. Both were based on a play by Augustus Thomas that was first presented in Chicago in 1899. The 1931 *Arizona* was directed by George B. Seitz, and Robert Riskin provided the dialogue. The 70-minute feature has also shown up under its working title of *Men Are Like That.*

Wayne plays Bob Denton, a football star and ladies' man at West Point. (The film is enhanced by some stock footage of an Army-Navy football game.) Wayne's character is also the protégé of his father figure, Colonel Frank Bonham (Forrest Stanley), the commander of a remote outpost in Arizona. Duke knows that he will be assigned to the fort when he graduates.

He has a problem on campus in the form of Evelyn Palmer (Laura LaPlante, who got top billing in the film). LaPlante is perhaps better known for her work in *The Cat and the Canary* (1927) and *Show Boat* (1929). Evelyn, is beautiful, but Bob enjoys dating a lot of women around the area. That doesn't work out. Bob tells her he has no intention of marrying her and completes his tenure at West Point without Evelyn at his side. Evelyn gets her revenge by traveling West to romance and marry Colonel Bonham—knowing that Bob will soon be assigned to the fort.

Our hero graduates, is commissioned a second lieutenant in the Army, and heads westward to begin his career, elated at the idea of working with his mentor, Colonel Bonham. But Evelyn is there too, playing her dutiful role as the colonel's wife. That situation, of course, is bound to cause problems.

The good news is that Evelyn's sister Bonita, or Bonnie (June Clyde) as she is known to most, also lives at the fort. Bonnie's personality is more attuned to that of our hero, who quickly loses interest in any other girl but her. Even the colonel encourages the relationship. After all, he is unaware of the history between Bob and Evelyn. He is happy to see the potential of his protégé marrying into the family. Bob and Bonnie are so happy together that they secretly marry.

Evelyn sees an opportunity to get even with Bob when the colonel is away from the fort. She makes an advance at Bob, but he's happy with Bonita and appalled at both Evelyn's persistence and her lack of fidelity to his mentor. Evelyn manipulates Bob into a compromising situation. That leads to two problems. First, Evelyn uses the situation to try and break up Bob and Bonita, unaware that the two are married. From Evelyn's perspective, she's getting revenge while also protecting her sister from developing a relationship with a man who has a bad attitude toward women.

The second problem: Colonel Bonham asks for Bob's resignation. Bob manages to solve both problems, gets his revenge on Evelyn, and—more importantly—gets to stay with Bonnie.

As the reader can perhaps tell, *Arizona* is more of a romantic drama than a true Western. Dickerson aptly wrote, "[T]his is what they used to call a 'woman's picture.' …It's as close to a *Cruel Intentions* as you're going to get in 1931."[4]

The movie was re-released twice, once under the title *Men Are Like That* and later as *The Virtuous Wife*. Both of the latter releases emphasized the romantic angle, not its Western locale. That's one reason that Dickerson wrote, "For John Wayne fans, it's bound to be extremely disappointing."[5]

It does include one memorable, non-romantic scene, but Duke's not featured in it. The scene revolves around an auction in which Evelyn tries to outbid the colonel for the team football, signed by everybody (including Bpb).

Waltz wrote, "Some lavish sets make this appear to be higher budgeted than it probably was, while the direction of George B. Seitz (who later directed some of Judy Garland's early films) speeds up the film once the plot takes off."[6]

Regardless, this film did little to enhance Duke's career—other than sending his character out west to Arizona.

The Range Feud is actually a Buck Jones Western. Jones, who started his Western career in the silent era and was billed in this movie as "The Screen's Greatest Outdoor Star," plays Sheriff Buck Gordon.[7] Duke plays a supporting role as local rancher Clint Turner, who works his cattle with his father (Will Walling) The duo are in competition with another rancher, John Walton (Ed LaSaint). Turner is courting Walton's daughter Judy (Susan Fleming).

The Columbia film, directed by D. Ross Lederman and written by Milton Krims, was filmed on location at Vasquez Rocks County Park in

Los Angeles and at the Walker Ranch in Newhall, California. It hit theaters on December 1. European audiences got to see it in June of the following year. The original 64 minutes was cut to 57 minutes when the film was released to television.

Both the Turners and Walton face an immediate problem: Rustlers are stealing their cattle. Both ranchers blame each other for their losses. Their feud is well-known, and they subsequently end up in a public argument. Soon afterwards, John Walton is found shot to death. Duke's character ends up arrested for the murder.

Clint's close friend Sheriff Buck doesn't believe that Clint could commit such a crime, and races to identify the real villain. Clint, meanwhile, waits in jail with his scheduled hanging approaching. Sheriff Buck grows increasingly desperate in his attempts to find the real killer, knowing that his friend's life could literally hang in the balance. But he succeeds, and that person turns out to be another rancher who is a longtime enemy of Clint Turner's father. (Seeing no reason to waste a good plot, this movie got remade in 1934 as *The Red Rider*. The second version again starred Buck Jones.)

Clint's role involves little action or heroism. As Eyles wrote, "Wayne found he wasn't working much, although still receiving his salary under contract, and the films he did get didn't give him any chance to excel."[8] It was truly a supporting role, but Wayne comes off well. As Ciopron wrote, "Wayne had a generic playfulness (as a serene country lad, sure of his good looks), and there is a large stream of underplayed irony in his early roles, perhaps a kind of a superiority complex, as he felt superior to what he was doing."[9] Fenin and Everson noted that this was one of the Buck Jones film made by Columbia that "deserve to be rated above the 'assembly line' category."[10]

Duke's only chance to learn something about being a Western hero was to watch Buck Jones in action. Otherwise, its only contribution to Duke's career is that it puts him behind bars, a plot element that will frequently occur in many of his 1930s Westerns.

In fact, this film may have actually worked against Wayne's career. After *The Range Feud*, Wayne's roles with Columbia gradually grew less prominent, "due to a conflict with the legendary Harry Cohn, head of the studio."[11]

3

1932: *Texas Cyclone* to *Haunted Gold*

In 1932, John Wayne was busy, appearing in a dozen different films, mostly on Poverty Row with Monogram,[1] who was known for a "constant flow of micro-budgeted genre pictures."[2] The studio eventually changed its name to Allied Artists in 1953 in an attempt to improve its image. As Wayne himself described the period, "fights, falls, stunts in five- and six-day Westerns filled my summers. Hunting and fishing in Mexico filled my winters."[3]

He started the year in the adventure serial *The Shadow of the Eagle*. His other non–Western films from the year were *The Voice of Hollywood No. 13*, *Running Hollywood*, *Lady and Gent*, *The Hollywood Handicap* and *That's My Boy*. Tucked in between the movies was another serial, *The Hurricane Express*.

His Westerns during the year were *Texas Cyclone*, *Two-Fisted Law*, *Ride Him, Cowboy*, *The Big Stampede* and *Haunted Gold*. However, in the first two of these, Wayne's role was limited to a supporting role while somebody else (Tim McCoy) was the real hero. It took him a little longer to get into the lead role himself.

The Shadow of the Eagle is the story of the Eagle, a villainous pilot who uses skywriting to make threats against a corporation. Pilot Craig McCoy (Wayne) goes looking for the Eagle. It was shot at three California locations, Griffith Park, Antelope Valley and Lancaster. The plot was spread over 218 minutes in 12 episodes. Mascot Pictures released the first installment on April 1, 1932. After Duke became a star, it was re-released in 1949. *The Shadow of the Eagle* marked the first time that Duke worked with the great stuntman Yakima Canutt, someone who would have an important impact on his career.[4]

The Voice of Hollywood No. 13 was a 12-minute short, directed by Mack D'Agostino, about a radio station (S*T*A*R) that featured a number of variety acts. Some big name stars were featured, including Gary Cooper, Jackie Cooper and Thelma Todd. Wayne played the station's emcee. It was released on January 17. *Running Hollywood* was a 20-minute comedy two-reeler, directed by Charles Lamont, in which Wayne again played an emcee. Charles "Buddy" Rogers was the lead performer. A Thalians Club production, it was released on January 27.

Lady and Gent was an 84-minute feature film in which Duke played Buzz Kinney, a young boxer who defeats an over-confident veteran. By the end of the film, Duke's character is a worn-out veteran himself, complete with a cauliflower ear and a broken nose. Eyles wrote, "It is the most extreme form of makeup ever applied to Wayne's features and consequently both grotesque and disturbing to see today."[5] Charles Starrett, who would later gain fame as the movies' Durango Kid, had a major supporting role. It was shot at Paramount and released on July 15.

In *The Hurricane Express*, a 12-episode serial directed by J.P. McGowan and Armand Schaefer, a villain wrecks trains. Tully Marshall was the serial's star and Wayne appeared as Larry Baker, the hero who hunts down the villain after his father is killed in one of the wrecks. The entire Mascot serial ran for 227 minutes. It was later edited down to a 79-minute feature version.

The Hollywood Handicap was a 20-minute two-reeler comedy-musical, directed by Charles Lamont, in which Wayne played an unnamed character. The star of the production was Marion Byron. The Thalians Club production was released on August 10.

That's My Boy is a college football story that features the 1931 national championship team of the University of Southern California. Richard Cromwell and Dorothy Jordan played the leads. Uncredited, Wayne appears as an unnamed football player.

As mentioned earlier, Duke had supporting roles in two Tim McCoy Westerns in 1932.[6] *Texas Cyclone* features McCoy as the hero and Shirley Grey as the female lead. Duke has a supporting role as Steve Pickett. A young Walter Brennan also appears in the film as Sheriff Lew Collins. Duke and Brennan later worked together again, most memorably in the Howard Hawks classic *Rio Bravo* in 1959.[7]

Texas Cyclone was directed by D. Ross Lederman from a screenplay written by Randall Faye. The story was provided by William Colt Mac-Donald, who is perhaps better known for creating the Three Mesquiteers—one of the most popular B Western series of all time.

McCoy plays cowboy Texas Grant, who rides into Stampede, Arizona, and is surprised to discover that all of the locals believe he is a guy named

Jim Rawlings. The problem is that Rawlings is supposed to be dead. McCoy's character decides to stick around and see if he can figure out what's going on and also help the pretty widow hold onto her ranch. Eventually, McCoy's character takes a blow to the head and realizes he really *is* the missing Jim (I never said it was actually realistic).

The good news is that Wayne got to see the great Tim McCoy operate on the set. It was shot on location in Santa Clarita and in the Chatsworth area of Los Angeles—two locations that Duke would eventually find familiar. Santa Clarita is a picturesque valley north of downtown Los Angeles.[8]

Perhaps Wayne learned a few things in the process. Most audiences, though, likely didn't even realize he was in the film, which was released on February 24.

The highlight of the film was Duke's supporting performance. As Simpson called it "fun and, at times, funny. John Wayne as Steve is worth the whole 58 minutes. Tim McCoy overacts like nothing I've ever seen and the whole movie is simply enjoyable."[9]

In fact, it was so much fun that the movie was remade three times, as *The Mysterious Avenger* (1936), *One Man's Justice* (1937) and *The Stranger from Texas* (1939) with Charles Starrett getting the starring role in all three remakes before he became known as the Durango Kid.

Wayne got his second chance to work with McCoy in *Two-Fisted Law*. Alice Day was the female lead. (Morrison criticized her performance, writing that she "is the least capable of the cast, but even she brightens up as the story progresses."[10]) McCoy plays a rancher who loses his ranch to a shady money lender and turns to prospecting to make a living. He ends up charged with murder. Eyles summarized Wayne's participation: "He was simply a pal of the star with only a handful of lines to speak."[11]

The 64-minute film was shot on location in Santa Clarita and in the area of Newhall, California and released on June 8. Wayne plays a character named "Duke," with no last name. Walter Brennan again appeared in a supporting role. When the movie went to television in the early 1950s, the names of Wayne and Brennan moved up to second and third on the credit listings (compared to eighth and ninth originally), since they were both better known by then.

Two-Fisted Law was the last film Wayne made for Columbia, ending a turbulent relationship between him and studio head Harry Cohn. Cohn blamed Wayne for interfering with an advance that he made to a pretty young actress. Actually, Wayne hadn't been involved in the incident, but

Cohn didn't believe that. He kept putting Wayne in small roles as a result. By leaving Columbia, Wayne would finally get a shot at some roles as a Western hero, even if those roles were with smaller companies.

Ride Him, Cowboy was Wayne's first starring role in a Western film since *The Big Trail* in 1930. It was also the first of ten films he made for Warner Brothers. Fenin and Everson praised these ten Warner movies, noting that many were similar in spirit to the silent films of Fred Thomson.[12] The problem for Wayne was that, even though the movies made money, Warner Brothers was "a studio that viewed Westerns as a social disease."[13] As a result, Wayne gained experience but little respect from his bosses.

For Wayne, *Ride Him, Cowboy* provided an opportunity to understand the positive role of humor in an adventurous Western. And maybe he learned something about being a hero.

The first six of these films were remakes of Ken Maynard silent Westerns.[14] Warners obtained the rights to these movies when the studio acquired First National studios. As Eyles noted, the films gave Warners "a series to compete with those being made at other studios by such stars as Fox's George O'Brien and Paramount's Randolph Scott."[15]

This one was the first of six straight films that Fenin and Everson described as "a remarkably good series of Westerns produced for that company by cartoon-maker Leon Schlesinger."[16] Schlesinger is better known today for his work with the Warner Brothers cartoon division, which gave the world such characters as Porky Pig, Daffy Duck and Bugs Bunny.[17] The idea was to make six cheap films by using "as much footage from the original silent Maynard films as possible and substitute an actor for close-ups and dialogue scenes."[18] *Ride Him, Cowboy* was a remake of Maynard's 1926 film *The Unknown Cavalier*.

Warners chose Wayne for the starring role, then dropped the idea of using him after hearing a report that Wayne was "a drunken womanizer."[19] Wayne heard about the rumor and went to his agent Al Kingston. Wayne blamed the rumor on Harry Cohn, who had a bitter relationship with Wayne when he was under contract with Columbia. When Kingston passed that information on to Warner, Duke was back to starring in the films.

Duke played hero John Drury. Duke's first name was "John" in each of the first six films, prompting Eyles to suggest that the studio was likely trying to "merge the actor and the part in audiences' minds to help build up a following so that it was John Wayne up there on screen rather than an actor in a role."[20]

Ruth Hall played the female lead. Others in the cast included Henry B. Walthall, Otis Harlan, Harry Gribbon and Frank Hagney. Six-foot-five Glenn Strange, better known for his TV roles as Butch Cavendish on *The Lone Ranger* and Sam the Bartender on *Gunsmoke,* served as an uncredited stunt double for Wayne. Fred Allen was the director. The film, which sometimes shows up under the title *The Hawk,* was released to theaters on August 27, 1932.

Your first impression of this entry is that it seems a little far-fetched. Maybe that's because it opens with a horse on trial for attempted murder. The judge is determined to try the horse. The horse's owner is fearful of the trial. Her father tries to calm her down. "Honey, Judge Parker is a fair man," he says. "He'll give Duke [the horse] a fair trial." Sure 'nough, Duke the horse is saved when Duke the cowboy rides into town and offers to ride the renegade. "Where I come from, we don't shoot horses when they get ornery," Drury explains, "we tame 'em."

That leaves Duke (the cowboy) and his new equine friend free to track down the real villain, a mysterious piece of slime known only as "The Hawk." This Hawk feller has been attacking ranchers, running off their cattle, and generally making life miserable in the community. Even worse, he framed Duke (the horse) because it was the only one who knew he was the real villain.

Unfortunately, Duke (the horse) turns out to be smarter than Wayne. The four-legged Duke soon realizes that the Hawk is none other than the innocent-acting rancher serving as their guide. Duke (the cowboy) doesn't figure that out until the Hawk leaves him to die in the desert and frames him for the Hawk's own dastardly deeds. Duke (the horse) saves the cowboy, but Wayne must face trial on the trumped-up charges.

Light humor is provided by the small town judge (Gribbon) who presides over Wayne's trial. "Being as we ain't got any Bible, and nobody here's ever seen one anyway, the jury will not be sworn in," he declares. And he adds, "Henry Sims, the court appoints you persecuting attorney."

Don't worry. The girl (Ruth Hall) proves Wayne's innocence, and the Hawk is finally brought to justice. Unfortunately, Wayne comes out of this one looking like a cowboy who has chased one too many dogies. The Hawk gets the drop on him with Duke's own gun, ties him up in the desert, and even whups him in the climactic fight. It is Duke the horse who identifies the villain, saves the cowboy, and even kills the villainous Hawk.

There's a little mix-up here and there. When Duke the horse unties Duke the cowboy in the desert, the knot that the horse is working on changes several times. In one instance, the horse actually reties the knot. I told you it was far-fetched—John Wayne playing second banana to a horse named Duke.

Regardless, among amateur reviewers, Smith liked it, describing it as "a good series opener with little obvious use of stock footage."[21] Connors was more critical, noting that the movie "swipes its most exciting material" from the original Maynard film.[22] Doyle's verdict: "Surprisingly good, unpretentious little Western that winds up its tale in less than an hour. ... Easy to note how Wayne's acting skills became vastly improved over the years."[23]

Contemporary critics overlooked the plot. As Davis wrote, "Reviews were kind, especially to Duke; the critics agreed that he was a dashing figure of a man. The consensus was that John Wayne made a splendid hero, even with a threadbare plot."[24] Miller noted that, as the first leading role in Wayne's B Westerns, "it was a clever start. Not especially innovative, but clever."[25]

Regardless, it was lots of fun. And fans get to see Wayne pretend to play a harmonica, letting loose on "Comin' 'Round the Mountain."

Actor Paul Fix had a small role. He would become Wayne's unofficial acting tutor. Fix is better known to Western fans as Marshal Micah Torrance on the ABC-TV series *The Rifleman* (1958–63) with Chuck Connors. Fix was an accomplished actor who was perhaps the man perhaps most responsible for helping Duke Morrison invent John Wayne.

The Big Stampede features Wayne as John Steele, a deputy marshal assigned by Governor Lew Wallace (Berton Churchill) to bring peace to the New Mexico territory. Other cast members included Noah Beery, Paul Hurst and Mae Madison. Iron Eyes Cody had a small, uncredited role. Miller noted that Beery provided "a villainous adversary of ripe vintage … who rose to the occasion imposingly."[26]

Tenny Wright directed the film, which was based on a story called "Land Beyond the Law" by Marion Jackson. Kurt Kempler wrote the screenplay. The film was a remake of Maynard's 1927 silent titled, appropriately, *Land Beyond the Law*. Also receiving credit in the movie was Duke, the trick horse that Wayne rode. Duke was the same horse who saved Wayne's skin in his previous entry, *Ride Him, Cowboy*. The 54-minute film was shot on location at the Miller and Lux Ranch near Dos Palos and the Warner Ranch near Calabasas, California. It was released on October 8, 1932.

Wallace, who really was the governor of New Mexico and also a Civil War general,[27] is better known today as the author of the novel *Ben-Hur*.[28]

John Wayne and his horse Duke in *The Big Stampede* (1932).

He wrote that book while serving in New Mexico. For purposes of the film, though, he wants to show President Rutherford B. Hayes that he can handle the job.

The biggest problem is Sam Crew (Beery), a major rancher in the state who built up his herd by encouraging wagon trains to come to the area and then stealing the settlers' cattle. When the law tries to interfere, Crew simply kills the lawman.

There is another rustler in the area, an intimidating bandit by the name of Sonora Joe (Luis Alberni). Sonora Joe is an imposing figure. In one scene, he and his men enter a saloon. Their presence immediately causes all talking to stop. "Why all this silence?" Joe asks. "Is this a saloon or somebody, she's dead?"

Governor Wallace wants to stop the lawlessness in the area, so he meets with our hero and explains the problem. Steele volunteers to handle the job and starts by drifting into town and posing as a drunk. Also new in town: a wagon train led by settler Cal Brett (Lafe McKee). The settlers ask Crew for help, but Crew and Sonora Joe have their eyes on the prize cattle.

Crew has his gunman, a rascal named Arizona (Paul Hurst), kill Brett to ensure that he can steal the cattle. That's enough for Duke to target Crew as the real problem in the area. He convinces Sonora Joe to join him in his effort to bring down the rancher.

The marshal meets and falls for local beauty Ginger Malloy (Mae Madison), who came west on the recent wagon train. Her major job is raising her younger brother Patrick (*Our Gang* actor Sherwood Bailey), an obnoxious kid who spends most of his time annoying people with his slingshot.

The climactic showdown involves Duke and Sonora Joe taking on Crew's gang. Part of the fight is a big stampede (hence the title of the film). Fortunately for Duke & Co., the studio didn't bother to shoot this scene. They simply used footage from Maynard's silent version of the story.

If this plot sounds familiar, it's probably because much of the plot seems based upon the real Lincoln County War that exploded in the New Mexico territory in 1878. That war included a big rancher (John Chisum), a lawman and an outlaw who were thought to be friends (Pat Garrett and Billy the Kid) and a lawman who was killed in the fight (Sheriff William Brady).[29] *The Big Stampede* simply switches the roles of some of these characters around, making the big rancher a villain. John Wayne would later portray the big rancher in his version of the Billy the Kid saga, the 1970 film *Chisum*. The plot was later reused in *Land Beyond the Law* (1937) with Dick Foran in Duke's role.

Contemporary reviewers were more impressed by the stock footage that came from the original Maynard Western. As Eyles noted, "The film's climax was all that its title promised, thanks to Ken Maynard's work in the silent version."[30] Davis wrote, "Reviewers commented more on the five thousand head of stampeding cattle that added thrills to the final reel than on the performance of the actors."[31]

Did Duke learn much from this film? That's hard to say, because his acting was awkward at best. As Smith wrote, "Wayne's inexperience really shows In this film."[32] At one point, he instantaneously transitions from a drunk to a lawman with no explanation for the shift. In one scene he's a drunk. When he appears the next time, he is a sober and serious lawman. Still, it was his second consecutive Western and he was on his way to becoming identified with the genre.

Wayne did meet some cast members who would play a major role in his later career. Berton Churchill, who appeared as Lew Wallace, joined Duke in the cast of *Stagecoach*. In the latter, Churchill played Gatewood, the banker who embezzled from his own bank and joins the passengers to escape with the money.

Another cast member also became a longtime friend. Paul Hurst played Arizona, one of the key members of Sam Crew's band of rustlers. Hurst is probably better known for his performances in gangster movies, but he also appeared with Duke in *Angel and the Badman* and *Big Jim McLain*.

One of the most important new co-workers on this film was Tom Bay. Bay had a small, uncredited role in the movie, but he was also a stunt-man that Wayne once described as "one of the toughest men I ever met."[33] Wayne credited Bay with refining the technique of on-screen fighting in which camera angles and near-misses allowed for the creation of realistic

John Wayne with Sheila Terry in *Haunted Gold* (1932).

fight scenes. The technique reached near perfection in some later movies directed by Robert Bradbury.

In *Haunted Gold*, Duke the cowboy once again co-starred with a horse named Duke. Once again, Duke the horse saves the day for Duke the cowboy. Naturally, Duke the horse got second billing—above the title and ahead of female lead Sheila Terry. Mack V. Wright directed the film, using a script written by Adele Buffington. The eerie ghost town camerawork was handled by Nick Musuraca, who later worked on RKO's horror classic *The Curse of the Cat People*.

Haunted Gold was filmed on location at the Iverson Ranch near the Chatsworth area of Los Angeles. The Iverson Ranch was a 500-acre ranch in the Simi Hills. Studios started filming movies there in 1912.[34] More than 3500 productions (movies and TV episodes) were shot there, including the opening scenes of *High Noon* (1952). It was a staple shooting location for *The Roy Rogers Show, The Lone Ranger* and *The Gene Autry Show*. Autry purchased the property in 1953 and renamed it Melody Ranch.[35]

The 58-minute *Haunted Gold* was released December 7, opening at the Strand Theater in New York.[36] The opening title is enhanced by animated owls provided by producer Leon Schlesinger. (As mentioned above, Schlesinger was better known as the head of Warners' cartoon division, i.e., the Looney Tunes and Merrie Melodies unit.) *Haunted Gold* was the third of six remakes of Ken Maynard films, this one based on his 1928 movie *The Phantom City*. Both films are essentially Western versions of *The Cat and the Canary*.

Haunted Gold is the closest thing that Duke ever did to making a horror film. The plot is an interweaving of a Western with a ghost story, and the sense of a horror film is evident. Eyles wrote that the film "made rather eerie use of the paraphernalia of the mystery chiller: sliding panels, sinister shadows, and hooded figures."[37]

The film opens with John Mason (John Wayne) and Janet Carter (Sheila Terry) both getting a strange letter telling them to visit an abandoned mine in a ghost town called Ghost City. Mason is intrigued because he inherited half of the mine, named the Sally Anne, from his father. Janet returns out of curiosity, since her father was cheated out of his half to a villain named Joe Ryan (Harry Woods).

Mason arrives in town with his cook, a black man named Clarence (Blue Washington). Janet is already there—and so is Joe Ryan and his outlaw gang. And there's somebody, or something, else: a mysterious entity known only as "The Phantom."

Ryan is looking for gold that he believes is hidden somewhere in the mine or nearby. Officially, Ryan and Mason are co-owners of the mine, but Ryan is there to share in the gold with anybody. Two more characters show up, the mine's former manager Tom Benedict (Erville Anderson) and his servant Simon (Otto Hoffman), men who were lured by a similar letter apparently sent by The Phantom. They join the spooky housekeeper Mrs. Herman (Martha Mattox), who adds to the atmosphere. We see "The Phantom" peeking out from behind secret panels as he follows the activities of his guests. Adding to the spooky setting are a dark cemetery, the lights going out mysteriously in the villain's cabin, even a howling wolf.

Mason quickly figures out that his partner is up to no good. He tries to take on the bandits while also working on a plan to get Sheila's half of the mine back under her ownership. It's not easy. A lot of the action occurs underground, either in the haunted mine or in a maze of tunnels under the ghost town. To defeat the villains, Mason must deal with a series of secret passages and trap doors. This is all done while the audience listens to creepy organ music. Mason's goal is to prove that Ryan is an outlaw. If he can do that, perhaps he can force him to return his share of the mine to Janet.

That plan actually works, but the good times don't last long. The Phantom, who has been helping Duke most of the time, causes him to get distracted. Our hero ends a prisoner of the gang. He has to escape from his captors, battle the villainous Ryan and save the day for Janet.

Comedy relief is provided by Blue Washington in the role of Clarence Washington Brown. Washington played the same role in the Maynard version of the movie. His work is funny, but demeaning to blacks by modern standards and based on black stereotypes of the time. Even his lines in the script followed that stereotype ("Lordy boss, a spook, the Phantom himself done snitched it").

The way Clarence is treated by the other characters is also offensive. The movie was shot in 1932, two years before the implementation of Hollywood's Production Code. As a result, there were no limitations on the use of racial slurs. Clarence is sometimes referred to as a "darkie," "Sambo" or "boy" (the latter by Wayne himself), while the outlaws talk about his "watermelon accent."

Clarence wasn't exactly invited to the town. In fact, his boss Mason had ordered him to stay at the ranch. The superstitious cook wants to help his boss, and he follows him there. But he's too superstitious to be of much help.

The climactic scene is considered a classic for early Westerns. It starts with our hero escaping from a mine by climbing up a mine shaft as the shaft crumbles around him. Fenin and Everson noted that the sequence required an "elaborate set construction and many bizarre and effective camera angles."[38]

That scene features a fight between Mason and one of Ryan's henchman and involves a key performance by Duke the horse. As Fenin and Everson described it, the scene has "Wayne and the villain battling it out in a large ore bucket, suspended over a yawning chasm. The bottom falls out and the villain tumbles to his death; Wayne is left dangling on a rope to be saved only by the intervention of his horse."[39] Yes, indeed. Duke the horse saves Duke the cowboy again.

In the end, the true identity of "The Phantom" is revealed: He turns out to be Janet's father. After being released from prison, he moved back to the mine and gradually put together a fortune in gold. As Ricci, Zmijewsky and Zmijewsky wrote, "Wayne's arrival in the nick of time prevents the outlaws from stealing the gold."[40] That means that Mason and Janet get to stay together as co-owners of the mine. At the end, they seal their partnership with a kiss. That scene may look familiar. The two will similarly lock lips at the end of *'Neath the Arizona Skies* (1934).

The movie has several other interesting components that are worth noting. Duke doesn't sing in this one, but he does play a harmonica. It was just one song, "She'll Be Comin' Round the Mountain," but you can count it as an overlooked talent for Wayne. Another interesting scene has Sheila Terry playing "Sweet Genevieve" on the organ. Written in 1869 by Henry Tucker, the tune is also used as part of the score at the end of the film. But that's not what makes the scene interesting. Look carefully and you'll spot a statue of the Maltese Falcon on top of the organ. This prop was previously used in the 1931 version of the movie by the same name. And—why waste a good name?: Wayne had the moniker John Mason again in his 1935 movie *The Dawn Rider*.

Haunted Gold usually gets good reviews from fans for a B Western. Massey wrote that it was "very entertaining and just plain fun!"[41] Vogel agreed, noting that "the 'supernatural' elements in this film make it worth watching!"[42]

Miller wrote that it was "the most entertaining in the Warner set; it is fast, fervent, finely photographed by Nick Musuraca, and has a mystery angle, which seldom fails to garnish any Western"[43]

How did this influence Wayne's future career? It had one of the more inventive plots that he would find early in his career, and it is arguably the best of the six Maynard Westerns he did for Warners. Further, Duke is showing himself to be a quick study at the craft of acting. His acting still needed work, but he was not as stiff in this movie as he was in the first of the Maynard remakes. He was beginning to get used to playing the hero, but he had yet to establish the on-screen swagger that is generally associated with John Wayne.

4

1933: *The Telegraph Trail* to *Sagebrush Trail*

In 1933, Wayne appeared in 11 films, although two (*Central Airport, College Coach*) featured him in small, uncredited roles. Of the nine others, four (*The Life of Jimmy Dolan, His Private Secretary, Baby Face, The Three Musketeers*) were not Westerns. The five oaters of 1933 were the most he had made in the genre up until that time. They were *The Telegraph Trail, Somewhere in Sonora, The Man from Monterey, Riders of Destiny* and *Sagebrush Trail*. Goldman described work on the movies as "backbreaking, with little reward beyond learning the movie business."[1]

Central Airport is the story of a pair of daredevil pilots; Wayne has an uncredited role as the co-pilot of a wrecked plane. The film was directed by William "Wild Bill" Wellman.[2] Wellman's son later recalled that there "was so much protest at showing the crash of a commercial airliner that the scene was struck from the picture."[3]

In *College Coach*, Duke had another uncredited role as a student in a crowd. Again the director was Wellman, who brought back Duke for another small role. Wayne later worked with Wellman again, this time as the star of the movie, in 1954's *The High and the Mighty*.

In *The Life of Jimmy Dolan*, a boxer accidentally kills someone at a party. The film starred Douglas Fairbanks, Jr., and Loretta Young. Duke has a small role as Smith.

His Private Secretary was made by a small production-distribution company called Showman's Pictures. It starred Wayne as Dick Wallace, a young man who wants to marry. Dick's father opposes the union and insists that Duke stay in the family business. The girlfriend handles the problem by getting a job in the company, using it as a chance to demonstrate that she is worthy of marrying the son.

Baby Face with Barbara Stanwyck and George Brent told the story of a woman who uses her femininity to get ahead in the world. Duke had a supporting role, playing a character named Jimmy McCoy Jr. Eyles described the role as "one fairly important opportunity to act outside the Western field in a main feature."[4] Still, Warners only used him after that for Westerns or for small roles in other films.

In the action-adventure serial *The Three Musketeers*, Lt. Tom Wayne's (Duke) job is to rescue three other members of the French Foreign Legion so they can join him in tracking down the villain of the piece.

Also in 1933, Wayne made the first of 16 Westerns that Wayne for Monogram's Lone Star Productions unit. Five of those 16 came in 1933.

Warners' *The Telegraph Trail* was the fourth remake of a Maynard silent for Duke. In this case, the original film was Maynard's *The Red Raiders* (1927). The white stallion named Duke the Wonder Horse again gets second billing, ahead of Frank McHugh and female lead Marceline Day. Tenny Wright was the director, using a script by Kurt Kemplar. The film was originally 60 minutes, but was cut when sold to television. It was released on March 18, 1933, in New York. In Germany, it was released under the title *High Wolf,* the name of a major Indian character.

Like others in this series, this movie was enhanced by using footage

John Wayne in *The Telegraph Trail* (1933).

from the Maynard original. In this case, there were some impressive shots of an Indian war dance that really stood out.

The plot was simple: The telegraph is coming to a Western town, but not everyone is happy. Bad guy Gus Lynch (Albert J. Smith) has been making a lot of money with a store that overcharges for essential supplies. If the telegraph gets through, he fears he'll lose his stranglehold on the local economy (exactly how that would occur is never mentioned). He convinces the nearby Indians, led by Chief High Wolf (Yakima Canutt), to wage war against those stringing the wire toward the town. After all, a telegraph could lead to more soldiers which could lead to more white men which could mean that these Indians might be wiped out.

Sounds like a surefire plan to stop progress, but there's a catch. Before he is killed by Indians, a soldier telegraphs enough of a message back to the fort for the good guys to know something is afoot. They turn to cavalry scout John Trent (John Wayne) and his trusty sidekick Corporal Tippy (Frank McHugh), knowing that the murdered soldier was a friend to both men. Their job is to complete the final section of the telegraph, find out what's going on, and to get supplies through to the settlers.

Meanwhile, villain Lynch has his eyes set on beautiful Alice Keller (Marceline Day). She tries to throw off Lynch's advances by telling her uncle (Otis Harlan) that she is already engaged to Duke. Our hero has to go along with the ruse and falls for the young lady for real.

Meanwhile, Lynch becomes concerned that Trent, Tippy and their co-worker Lafe (Lafe McKee) might actually succeed in finishing the telegraph line. That calls for drastic action, and he convinces Chief High Wolf to launch a massive attack on the workers' camp.

The plot is less than unique for Western movies, where you can find plenty of scripts in which an evil white man tries to arouse Indians into fighting other white men. What makes this one a little different is that it is played with a touch of humor. In one scene, two soldiers are fully intoxicated when they are attacked by the Indians. At one point, they convince themselves that a single bullet killed eight Indians.

Some of the humor appears unintentional. In one scene, Wayne climbs a telegraph pole to send a message to the fort. As he works there, with little protection against attack, a group of Indians ride up. Duke draws his gun, shoots the leader, holsters his gun and tries to continue sending his message as if he is in no further danger.

Naturally, this doesn't work. The other Indians return fire, knocking him off the telegraph pole. He's not really dead, but he pretends to be. That works, and the other Indians leave him there on the ground. After they leave, Duke gets up and removes the chieftain headdress from the Indian that he shot. He then removes his shirt, dons the war bonnet and rides off in Indian disguise.

Still dressed in that manner, he joins the body of Indians who are attacking a wagon train positioned in a defensive circle. He somehow manages to jump into the circle without getting shot by the settlers. Once inside, he removes the war bonnet, puts on a leather shirt and starts fighting alongside the settlers. Eventually Duke saves the day, although he needs help from Marceline Day and his steady mount, Duke the Wonder Horse. But Duke the man needs help from Duke the Horse in all of these Warner Westerns. Anyway, he first gets help from the pretty girl. She overhears the villains talking about an ambush. She makes sure that Duke gets the information so he can take appropriate action.

Duke the Horse has his fine moment too. In something of an unusual scene, the Wonder Horse is in a tent when he spots the outline of some Indians silhouetted against the wall of the tent. Smart horse that he is, he simply kicks those pesky Indians through the wall of the tent.

The final major fights features hundreds of extras. Much of that footage was recycled from Ken Maynard's original version of this story. And, of course, the plot is resolved in the same way as that of the Maynard film, i.e., the cavalry rides to the rescue. Notice that the tracks of the camera car are visible when the Indians are attacking and when the cavalry charges to the rescue.

Wayne and McHugh work well together. McHugh might have made a good Western sidekick, but his level of talent meant that he would soon be elevated to A movies. This is the only film in which he worked with John Wayne.

Hausner really liked the humor in the film, particularly the "comedy by both Frank McHugh and Otis Harlan.[5] In their funniest scene, they get drunk while the Indians are attacking and they are bleary-eyed enough to think one bullet fells as many as eight Indians. ...The scene itself, in the middle of a battle in which many are killed, indicates director Tenny Wright did not direct with a heavy hand."[6] Smith rated it as above average and noted: "Not the best of Wayne's Warner Bros. films but better than most of the Poverty Row Lone Star Westerns which followed this series."[7]

Eyles saw growth in Wayne's acting skills. He cites one scene in particular in which Wayne hears about the death of his friend, noting that when Wayne reacts, "he snarls with choked rage, his face tightening, the skin shining and his eyes narrowing to slits."[8]

In the 1933 film *Footlight Parade*, James Cagney's character is shown a talkie film to explain why he's facing unemployment as a silent star. The film they show is *The Telegraph Trail.* Also, in the 1940 short *You Ought to Be in Pictures,* a poster of the movie is on Leon Schlesinger's desk.

This film is unique among Wayne Westerns in that he wears a pair of guns, not just one, and both guns are worn butt forward. This latter technique was used by both Wild Bill Elliott in his Western movies and by Guy Madison as TV's Wild Bill Hickok. But it wasn't used by Wayne in other films. Maybe he was trying to start a trend.

Anyway, did John Wayne get anything out of this movie that helped him become a star? Absolutely. This was the first Western in which he got to work closely with Yakima Canutt, the stuntman who would redefine stunt work in Hollywood. They became lifelong friends, and Yakima was Wayne's stunt double in many future movies. Further, he played a major role in teaching Wayne the basics of fighting, riding and other things that are all part of a Western movie.[9]

That means, of course, that this movie played a major role in John Wayne becoming John Wayne.

In *Somewhere in Sonora,* Wayne plays John Bishop in his fifth remake of a Ken Maynard film. In this case, it's a 1927 film of the same name.

The hero uncovers a plot to rob a silver mine that belongs to his girlfriend's father. To spoil the plot, Wayne infiltrates the gang that's planning the robbery. The film was directed by Mack V. Wright, using a Joseph Anthony Roach script that was based on a story by Will Levington Comfort. The film was shot on location around Sonora, California, and in the Alabama Hills near Lone Pine, California. It was released on May 27, 1933. Once again, Duke the Wonder Horse got second billing. Frank Rice and Billy Franey provide comic relief as Wayne's sidekicks, who constantly fight with each another.

The movie opens with two young ladies, Mary Burton (Shirley Palmer) and Patsy Ellis (Ann Faye), visiting Bob Leadly's (Henry B. Walthall) ranch near Twin Forks, Arizona. John Bishop (Wayne), Leadly's foreman, is scheduled to drive a stagecoach in a race at a local rodeo.

At the start of the race, John makes a silly remark about his competitor's wagon falling apart. That remark becomes a problem when the man's buggy wrecks and nearly kills him. John gets blamed for the accident, which was really the work of local gamblers who had bet heavily on John. The sheriff arrests him and puts him in jail.

He gets out of jail with the help of his sidekicks Riley (Frank Rice) and Shorty (Billy Franey). Once out, he learns that his Leadly's son Bart (Paul Fix) is running with an outlaw gang near Sonora.

In real life, Duke and Paul Fix were truly good friends. Davis described Fix as being "Duke's friend and acting coach."[10] Wayne also credited Fix with helping him "develop his so-called rolling gait walking style [after] Wayne told him he was uncomfortable with how he walked on the big screen."[11] Davis argued that Fix was the person who taught Wayne to walk with his toes pointed inward, while giving Yakima Canutt credit for helping Wayne develop the rolling swagger that became one of Wayne's most distinctive features."[12]

Fix worked in more films with Duke than any other actor. This was the second film in which they worked together. The last came 40 years later: *Cahill, U.S. Marshal* (1973). Fix was the father-in-law of Harry Carey, Jr., another regular in Duke's films.

In *Somewhere in Sonora*, Fix plays a misguided young man who has taken up with a gang, the Brotherhood of Death, headed by Monte Black (J.P. McGowan). Even worse, membership in the gang may be permanent, since nobody has ever escaped it alive. John and his two friends journey to Sonora to find the missing son.

The name of villain Monte Black was an inside joke at Warner Brothers. Monte Blue, one of the studio's stars during the silent era, got stuck playing supporting roles after the advent of sound. He had minor in some classic films, including *Casablanca* (1942) and *Key Largo* (1948).

The trio arrives in Sonora where John meets Mary and Patsy again, this time in a Mexican cantina that features a band playing "Lady of Spain." The duo are standoffish toward Duke, remembering his arrest. They change their minds when they lose control of their buckboard and John saves them. His two sidekicks tell the girls what really happened in the race.

It turns out that the girls are in Sonora to visit Mary's father. John finds out that the Black gang is planning to rob that mine in nearby Paloma. Mary's father learns the location of the gang's hideout, using information provided by a captured gang member. John rides to the hideout to join the gang, posing as an escaped prisoner. He plans to rescue Bart Leadly and also to keep the villains from robbing Mary's father. John fights and beats several members of the gang in the local cantina.

As a member of the gang, Duke gets to find Bart and tell him that he has been sent by the boy's father. Their chance to escape comes when the villainous Black sends John ahead as part of the gang's plan to rob the mine. He arrives there early and stops the robbery by sounding alarm bells at the mine. Some of the gang members escape, and they capture both John and Bart. The climax includes recycled footage from the Maynard film, although one memorable scene here has villain Black trying to aim at our hero.

As usual, Duke the Wonder Horse plays a major role in saving the day at the end. This time he does it by leading the Mexican authorities to the gang's hideout in time to save John and Bart.

If that sounds a bit weak, it is. The script is not one of the best, and Duke's acting still needed a lot of work. The biggest gain that Wayne got out of the movie was a chance to work closely with Paul Fix, who became his mentor.

As Wayne fan Michael Elliott wrote, the movie "features a plot that never really makes too much sense…. The film has action, wannabe drama, laughable romance and some really bad comedy but all of this is what you'd expect to find. [It's] for Wayne die-hards only."[13] Connors wrote that it was simply a "sloppily pieced together remake of an older silent…. The best thing to be said about Wayne's [acting] may be 'he was still learning his craft.'"[14]

Smith noted that *Somewhere in Sonora* was "arguably the weakest of the six WB features. Wayne's inexperience in the acting department really shows here."[15] Elliott agreed, writing that Wayne "certainly hadn't gotten his acting chops down yet as there are many scenes here where he comes off rather poorly."[16]

Eyles, who had some positive comments, also saw problems: "Wayne is extremely capable in handling the lighter moments (such as joking with his girl) or in issuing orders or recruiting the townspeople, though he seems unsure of himself as an actor when called on to do nothing much but stand around or when displaying intense emotion."[17]

Indeed, Wayne's idea of romantic dialogue is to merely say his lines in a lower voice. He would quickly recover from that mistake, of course. But credit that lesson as an important part of him becoming a star.

The Man from Monterey was the last of the six Ken Maynard Westerns that John Wayne did for Warner Brothers, and it is arguably the worst of the bunch. This one is a remake of Maynard's 1928 release *The Canyon of Adventure*. Wayne's version was directed by Mack V. Wright, using a screenplay provided by Leslie Mason. As with the other five remakes, Duke the Wonder Horse gets second billing, ahead of female lead Ruth Hall. The 57-minute movie was released on July 15, 1933. Davis noted that it was "a costume picture rather than a traditional Western, since it takes place in the era of the sword rather than the six-shooter."[18] The movie opens in 1848, just after the U.S. acquired the territory of California as a result of the Mexican War.

The feds send Captain John Holmes (Wayne) into the territory on a

John Wayne with Ruth Hall in a poster for *The Man from Monterey* (1933).

mission: convince the Spanish landholders in the territory to register their property with the government. Those lands that are not registered within three days will be declared part of the public domain. In other words, register or lose your land. But Don Jose Castanares (Lafe McKee) is reluctant to comply.

A villainous Mexican, Don Pablo Gonzales (Francis Ford), tries to convince Castanares not to register. (Francis Ford was the brother of John Ford, who became Duke's mentor and made him a star in *Stagecoach*.) Gonzales has ulterior motives: If Castanares doesn't register the land, the evil Don knows he can buy the property cheaply on the open market. He wants both the land and Castanares' beautiful daughter Dolores (Ruth Hall) for his son Luis (Donald Reed).

Our hero's first stop is the Castanares' hacienda. On his way there, he chances upon what looks like a holdup. He intervenes and saves Dolores, unaware that it's a fake robbery. The evil Luis staged the attack so that he could ride to the rescue and save Dolores. John's intervention kept him from appearing to be a hero.

Luis responds by trying to rob John. John responds by not taking the robbery seriously; instead, he keeps flirting with Dolores while Luis continues to grow even angrier.

After meeting with the Castanares family, Duke convinces Don Jose to register his land. That plan is foiled, however, when Don Pablo's men kidnap Don Jose on his way to handle the paperwork. Dolores agrees to marry Luis if he will free her father.

John finds an ally when he visits a local saloon. Local singer Felipe (Luis Alberni) finds himself in a confrontation with Luis over Felipe's girl friend Anita (Nena Quartero). John intervenes on Felipe's behalf and gains a partner in the process. Soon afterwards, the duo get a third ally. Duke and Felipe help an American bandit named Jake Morgan (Slim Whitaker). Morgan had planned to take control of Castanares' unregistered land too, but he eventually teams with John and Felipe.

As Luis prepares to marry Dolores, John and Felipe plot to break it up. Felipe's girlfriend Anita dons the wedding dress and stands in for Dolores, while Felipe dresses in drag to disrupt the wedding ceremony.

The duo team up to free Don Jose, with Duke using a sword in the resulting fight. This may have been a learning experience for the young actor. He was so bad with a sword that he never did it again. Maybe he figured that out during this movie.

John is taken prisoner by the villains. The U.S. Cavalry tries to come to his rescue, but John relies on Duke to go to Morgan's camp to lead the bandit back to help him. Morgan rides to the rescue, the land is saved, and John gets to marry Dolores. Thanks, of course, to Duke the Wonder Horse.

One unusual feature of the film is that included more music than was typical of Westerns of the era. Eight musical numbers are featured, including a pair ("Basilada," "Mexican Dance") written by Xavier Cugat.

Reviews of the film were not positive, even among John Wayne fans. Amateur reviewer Abrams noted, "The acting and script are, for the most part, pretty bad but that's part of the charm."[19] Smith was more direct, describing the acting as "uniformly awful."[20] Some of this is due to the speed in which it was filmed, with many lines being missed. That little problem didn't slow down production, though; they just kept on filming. According to Chris Stone, "*The Man from Monterey* has virtually nothing to offer the movie fan, not even the John Wayne completist. Its story is hackneyed, its actors mostly amateurish and their character's boring."[21] Miller wrote that Wayne "was stuffed into some uncomfortable military uniforms and fancy below-the-border duds, and was ill at ease."[22]

Stone saved his only positive comments for one actor: "Luis Alberni gives a comic performance that, while not especially funny, seems positively inspired compared with the rest of the cast." Abrams also liked Alberni's performance, writing that he "has to be one of the great unsung character actors in Hollywood history."[23]

One exception to the negative reviews came from Lovell. He noted that Wayne "gets at least one positively badass moment where he enters a guy's house through the window and smoothly strikes up a conversation.... The Duke just has that air of coolness about him that you welcome him into your home whether he comes through the door or the window."[24]

The film marked the end of Wayne's contract with Warners and the end of Duke's pairing with Duke the Wonder Horse. Eyles wrote, "Warners handling of Wayne in the last three films seems nearly as insulting as the treatment meted out to him at Columbia,"[25] It was also the end of Warner Brothers' effort at B Westerns until later in the decade when they tried again using Dick Foran as their cowboy star, while also using the old Maynard films to enhance the productions.

In the spring of 1933, John Wayne signed a contract with Lone Star Productions, a company whose films were distributed by Monogram, where Trem Carr was in charge of production. Monogram, Davis noted, "was considered a step up from Mascot, although the company rented most of its sets and aimed its product at unsophisticated audiences paying admission prices of twenty-five cents or less."[26]

Monogram took advantage of their new star by casting him a number of Westerns. As Miller wrote, "Though the budgets were low, Wayne's star rose higher with the Monograms. His youthfulness, ability, leisurely manner of speech blended to make him a Western favorite. Their slapstick was amusing, but interrupted the flow of the narrative."[27]

His first movie with the company was *Riders of Destiny*. It was produced by Paul Malvern, a person that Davis described as an "unsophisticated filmmaker [who] had grown up reading dime novels and pulp fiction."[28] The movie co-starred Gabby Hayes and Cecilia Parker. Gabby would go on to become perhaps the greatest sidekick in Western movie history.[29] Parker would later get more visibility as the older sister in Mickey Rooney's Andy Hardy movies.

Al "Fuzzy" St. John, a nephew of Fatty Arbuckle, has a supporting role. He would later grow a beard and become a well-known sidekick for a number of B Western cowboys including Lash LaRue and Buster Crabbe.[30] Miller complained that the movie "contained some misplaced comedy" simply because St. John and another comic, Heinie Conklin, were in the cast.[31]

Robert N. Bradbury was the director and also provided the story. His biggest innovation in the film was the idea of a singing cowboy, Singing Sandy, with Duke in the role. Green noted that *Riders of Destiny* "was planned as the first of a singing Western series, but Sandy sang in only the first of these productions, and the character of Singing Sandy was not used again."[32] There had been some music in earlier Westerns, but all were in big-budget films. At the time, "it was a novel addition for such cheap pictures as Monogram planned."[33]

The 53-minute film was shot on location at the Andy Jauregui Ranch near Newhall, California. Newhall was near Los Angeles, but required that the cast and crew arrive early in the morning so they could build a fire to warm up the cameras for the day's shooting.

Other location shooting was done at sites near Kernville, Lancaster and Palmdale and on the Trem Carr Ranch near Newhall. Kernville was a small Western town outside of Los Angeles that is now underwater, a result of a dam in the area. The movie was released on October 10, 1933. Duke's first Western for Lone Star, it marked the first of 15 times that Wayne was teamed with Gabby Hayes in a Western.

Although the film has few exceptional moments, this is the one from which anthologies about Wayne invariably choose to illustrate the early phase of his career as Singing Sandy, the movies' first singing cowboy. Never mind that Duke couldn't sing. They simply dubbed his voice (probably by Smith Ballew) with lyrics from songs such as "A Cowboy's Song of Fate," and the sound quality was pretty bad too.

Still, Gabby said he "could listen to that all night." The really amazing thing about the line, though, is that he sounds like he means it.

More importantly, *Riders of Destiny* contains a number of classic scenes, including the most famous Singing Sandy scene of all: Duke facing down a bad guy with the lyrics to "A Cowboy's Song of Fate" turning more ominous. The scene cuts to an onlooker who hears the song and identifies him as "Singing Sandy, the most notorious gunfighter since Billy the Kid." Duke then tells villain Slip Morgan (Earl Dwire), "Make it fast, Slippery, this is your last draw."

The plot is a bit above-average, but nothing spectacular. Duke plays Sandy Saunders, a Washington Secret Service agent sent to end a cowboy dispute over water rights. It opens with Duke coming upon a wounded sheriff, who immediately deputizes him. He then stumbles upon a holdup. The bandit turns out to be a beautiful blonde (Cecilia Parker) who convinces him that she is not really an outlaw.

Wayne loans her his horse to escape, and he sneaks inside the stagecoach for a ride into town. There he overhears the driver when the real robbers arrive, and he realizes that some form of conspiracy is afoot. In town, Cecelia returns his horse and invites him to meet her father (Gabby). Gabby, in turn, lays out the dynamics of the water fight.

Big rancher Kincaid owns the water rights to the only river in the valley, something which happened when Lost Creek dried up. Gabby has the only supplemental supply of water, a well from which he can provide drinking water but little else to the others in the valley. Kincaid wants to buy up Gabby's ranch, along with all the rest of the land in the valley. If the owners refuse, he plans to cut off all water from their ranches. Standing in the way is Duke, so Kincaid tries twice to kill him. After the second failure, he tries to buy off the lawman.

Duke agrees, but lets the other townspeople in on his plan. They sign an agreement with Kincaid, but add a provision that his land becomes public property if he fails to deliver water to them. Duke, meanwhile, convinces Kincaid to eliminate his final opposition by blowing up Gabby's well. The resulting explosion unlocks the water flowing beneath Gabby's ranch, restoring water to Lost Creek. Kincaid's water supply is depleted.

What follows is a shootout scene that director Bradbury borrowed from one of his earlier films, 1932's *Man from Hell's Edges*.[34] The film's climax is Kincaid's death in a major stunt, a horse diving head-first over a cliff and into a lake. Yakima Canutt handled this stunt chore. This dramatic stunt became stock footage in the Lone Star library and was subsequently edited into another of Duke's early movies, *Paradise Canyon* (1935). Yakima also performs a great stunt in which a stagecoach drives over him. He would perform this stunt for a wider audience in 1939 on *Stagecoach*.

Except for the singing, Wayne comes off pretty good in this one. As Doepke wrote, "Wayne is quite engaging as the good guy, looking every inch the part."[35] Roberts and Olson noted that the movie "showed that Wayne was not a singing cowboy, but the film did demonstrate that he was a cowboy actor."[36] Roberts and Olson added that the movie was "a surprisingly good B Western. Although the script is poor and predictable, Bradbury movingly portrays the importance of water to the thirsty West."[37]

Morton called it his favorite among Wayne's Lone Star Westerns and added that it had "some truly exciting stunt work, and a remarkably lyrical climax that I don't think Robert N. Bradbury ever came close to emulating again. ...It's so good that you'd almost believe that Ingmar Bergman had seen this film and been inspired by it as he started on *Virgin Spring*."[38]

It's not perfect, mainly because of the singing. Most of that occurs early, which is one reason that Wayne fan Walker wrote, "Please don't judge this film by the first ten minutes."[39] Still, if you look for mistakes, you can certainly find them. The most obvious is the presence of power poles in some scenes—poles that are too modern to pose as telegraph poles.

When Duke first appears, he is riding his horse, playing a guitar and "singing." When he loans his horse to Faye Denton so she can escape, the guitar has disappeared. And one character changes clothes and height in the middle of a chase scene.

But those items are no big deal. Singing Sandy remains the biggest problem. Still, the idea of a singing cowboy was started. Green credits Bradbury with coming up with the idea, writing that the director "clearly foresaw a market niche for a singing cowboy, although he did not pursue it with particular vigor beyond directing a great many such Westerns in a long career."[40]

That premise of a singing cowboy, though, was not for Wayne. That's a lesson he learned well in this film. Unfortunately, he did continue to lip-synch some tunes in later movies.

John Wayne (left) with Slim Whitaker (right) and Yakima Canutt in *Sagebrush Trail* (1933).

Sagebrush Trail is an above-average B Western that features Wayne as John Brant, a man falsely accused of murder who escapes to the West. It was the first of a series of productions that came to be known as the Lone Stars, i.e., the name of the production company. The movie was directed by Armand Schaefer from a script by Lindsley Parsons. Parsons did double duty for Lone Star, also serving as the company's West Coast publicity director.[41]

Female lead Nancy Shubert plays Sally Blake. Lane Chandler has a major role as Joseph Conlon (aka Bob Jones), while Yakima Canutt plays outlaw gang leader Ed Walsh. Slim Whitaker also appears in an uncredited role as a henchman.

Yakima was also Duke's stunt double in the film. Jack Jones and Eddie Parker also did stunts. The movie was a remake of the 1931 Tom Tyler film *Partners of the Trail*. Armand Schaefer was the director; this was one of the few Wayne–Lone Star Westerns not directed by Robert Bradbury. Schaefer worked with a script provided by Lindsley Parsons. The 54-minute film was shot on location at the Bronson Caves in Griffith Park, the Trem Carr Ranch and in Kernville. Bronson Caves is one of four tunnel entrances in the horseshoe-shaped Bronson Canyon (Stier, 2006).[42] The movie was released on December 15, 1933.

The movie opens with the publication of a newspaper extra announcing that a prisoner has escaped. That cuts to a train pulling into a station where a sheriff awaits to look for the fugitive, John Brant, who was in jail for the murder of George Wagner in Baltimore.

Brant spots the sheriff searching the train, jumps off, climbs on a horse and tries to escape. The sheriff and his deputy take off in pursuit. Our hero escapes by jumping off his horse into a small lake. He uses a reed to breathe under the water while the sheriff searches fruitlessly for him.

This entire incident is witnessed by "Jones," a cowboy hiding nearby. When Brant surfaces, Jones takes him to the hideout (actually Bronson Caves) he shares with an outlaw gang, introducing him as his new friend Smith.

The gang leader (Yakima) is skeptical of Brant but lets him work as the cook for the group. After Duke cleans off the table following dinner, the guys start playing cards. One is caught cheating, and a fight erupts. Duke tries to interfere to help Jones, but gets knocked out when one of the men hits him over the head with a chair.

Cut to a scene with the sheriff and deputy examining a wanted poster for Brant. The sheriff posts it on a bulletin board next to one for Joseph

Conlon, who is obviously Bob Jones. The sheriff notes that it might be a problem if Conlon and Brant get together, since the murder victim had been with Conlon's wife.

Back at the hideout, Conlon offers to pull a job with Brant to show that he can be trusted. Their target is the safe at the local post office. The duo ride into town and enter the store that also houses the post office. Brant stops to talk with Sally, the pretty girl behind the counter. Conlon goes to talk to the postmaster, her dad, and asks when the mail will be coming in.

Brant places a large order with the young lady and also secretly writes a message to her on a nearby package. When Conlon returns to Brant, he sees the load of groceries and orders the same thing.

While Sally gathers the order, he breaks the eggs that Brant carries, and they run down the side of his clothes. Sally offers to sell them a new hatband each, but they say that can wait until next time. Duke tells Sally his friend will pay for both orders, and, as they leave, he breaks the eggs in Conlon's arms. A short time later, Sally spots writing on the package that reads, "Your safe will be robbed." She makes an excuse to re-wrap the item and shows the note to her father. They arrange to have the sheriff waiting that night, with the lights out, to see if someone breaks in.

That night, Brant and Conlon approach the store. Brant notes that no lights are on, and he considers that bad news. Sure enough, when they open the door to the store, Brant is shot in the shoulder. He and Conlon run off, and the sheriff sees no reason to chase them in the dark.

The next scene is in a saloon hosted by a barkeep called "Blind Pete." Conlon approaches Pete, who tells him the afternoon stage will be carrying a payroll for the mine. Conlon goes to the back room, where Brant has been recovering from his wound. He notices that Brant is sporting a new hatband, and then tells him about the imminent holdup.

When Conlon leaves, Brant mounts his horse and heads toward the stagecoach. He finds a spot in the trail and covers himself with sagebrush. When the coach rolls over him, he grabs it on the back, pulls himself to the top, and robs the guards without ever pulling his guns. They toss the payroll off the coach and never stop.

Brant hides the money in a hollow tree. When Yakima's gang tries to rob it further down the road, they get nothing. As they try to find the yahoo who stole their money, Conlon finds a hatband in the sagebrush on the road and recognizes it as Brant's.

Brant rides into town to see Sally. He tells his story of his time in jail, tells her where to find the payroll, and says he needs to stay with the gang to find the man who can prove him innocent. As they finish, Sally realizes that his hatband is gone; she gets him another.

Conlon returns to Blind Pete's saloon, and Brant arrives soon afterwards. Conlon sees Brant's hatband and reconsiders his suspicions. The duo start talking about Sally, but they both decide that neither is good enough for her.

Conlon uses the moment to talk about finding his wife with another man, killing the guy and living as a fugitive ever since. Brant realizes that Conlon never knew that he had been arrested for the crime. He suggests that they both get a drink and give up their current line of work. "It'll lead us both to a rope necktie someday," he adds.

Both men are back at the hideout when Yakima announces that a load of bullion will be shipped the next day. The haul will be enough for the gang so that they'll never have to pull another robbery. Brant hears the announcement and goes into another room where he starts dressing. When asked where he's going, he says he's going shopping "for eggs."

Conlon spots a bucket of eggs nearby, and tells Yakima that he too is suspicious of the new henchman. He plans to follow Brant; if he sends him back to the hideout alone, that will be the signal that he should be killed. By now, Brant is in town, peeking through the store window for Sally, when he spots the sheriff. He gives a note to a man and asks that the man give it to Sally. The note asks Sally to meet him at Blind Pete's Saloon.

Inside the store, the sheriff shows Sally posters of Conlon and Brant. She says she doesn't recognize either, but the sheriff suspects she knows more than she's telling. When she mounts a horse and races out of town, the sheriff and deputy follow her. Meanwhile, Conlon is still following Brant. He trails him to the saloon, saying that he came to help him "carry back them eggs."

Sally rushes in to warn Brant about the sheriff, but the lawmen arrive before the hero can escape. A broken mirror provides enough of a distraction for the men to escape, but the lawmen pursue. When Conlon's horse is shot, Brant picks him up and the two men avoid capture. Once they're safe from the sheriff, Conlon convinces Duke to take their remaining horse and ride to the hideout alone while he returns to town.

In town, Conlon finds Sally and tells her she will never see Brant again. Sally then explains who Brant was and how he was trying to help his friend go straight. "I'm a bigger sap than I thought I was," Conlon says.

He races toward the hideout to save Brant, while Sally goes to the sheriff and tells him about the planned ambush at the abandoned mine.

Conlon arrives before the shooting starts, warns Brant. They hide behind a stagecoach while shooting it out with the gang. (By the way, no explanation for the presence of the stagecoach is provided.)

Brant gets on top of the stage and drives it into the mine shaft and out the other side. The outlaw gang mounts their horses and take off in pursuit. With Conlon driving, Brant grabs a low branch of a tree and waits for the three remaining villains to pass below him. He drops down on the last one, knocks him off his horse and chases down the other two.

Conlon has been shot. Brant races after the stage and jumps on it to save his friend. But the reins are on the ground and Duke has to jump between the horses to retrieve them. As he does so, the coach breaks from the horses and wrecks. Brant rides the horses like a *Ben-Hur* chariot driver and returns to find Conlon. When the sheriff arrives, Conlon confesses to killing George Wagner before he dies. Yakima, under arrest by the posse, says, "I always told Jones that Smith wouldn't make good as a bad man."

Nobody pays much attention to that. Brant and Sally are walking away, pausing only to kiss as the movie ends. This scene is one that caused Roberts and Olson to write that the Monogram movies were "one-kiss movies. Audiences learned that when the female lead kissed Duke, the movie was over."[43]

Overall, this movie features an above-average plot and some interesting scenes. Lane Chandler, as Conlon, is particularly effective. There is one obvious error, an editing mistake in which Brant and Conlon are riding into town. They enter a store, and Brant gives a note to the proprietor. Then, for no apparent reason, the film cuts back to the previous scene of Brant and Conlon riding into town.

Amateur reviewer Tippett noted that the movie was different from most B Westerns in that "it half-heartedly explored the reasons why some guys joined these gangs—bad raps, wrongful imprisonment, bad choices that left them nowhere else to go and so on, so that even some of the villains elicited sympathy."[44]

Smith liked it because it has "plenty of action, imaginative settings and lots of hard ridin.'"[45] Chance (2007a) considered it the best of the Lone Star Westerns, adding that it was "a great introduction to, and high watermark of, 1930s Westerns!"[46]

The emergence of John Wayne as a star was still years away, but he was already getting ready for it.

5

1934: *The Lucky Texas* to *'Neath the Arizona Skies*

The year 1934 marked a major turning point in John Wayne's career. He made just nine films, but all were Westerns: *The Lucky Texan, West of the Divide, Blue Steel, The Man from Utah, Randy Rides Alone, The Star Packer, The Trail Beyond, The Lawless Frontier* and *'Neath the Arizona Skies.* That meant the young actor was spending more and more time around real cowboys, men who were hired by the studio to work with their horses off the sets. Those cowboys, many of whom had rodeo experience, played an important role in increasing the authenticity of Westerns.[1] As Davis wrote, "Duke picked up on their memories, respected the cowboys, and absorbed much of their culture."[2]

Wayne was beginning to establish his screen persona as a Western hero. He was paying for it, however. He once noted that "the longest hours and hardest work in those years [during the 1930s]. One day I staggered home after working 26 straight hours."[3]

In *The Lucky Texan*, a Lone Star production, Wayne and Gabby play partners in a ranch and blacksmith shop who discover gold. Barbara Sheldon is the female lead. The 55-minute movie was shot on location around Kernville, California, and on the Trem Carr Ranch near Newhall. It was released on January 24, 1934.

With the help of his dog Friday, Wayne spots gold in a quartz pebble he removes from a horse's hoof, leading to the discovery of a rich gold claim. After that, Gabby gets framed for attempted murder, and Duke has to prove him innocent. Then Gabby gets shot and dog Friday saves him. Duke gets arrested for Gabby's murder, and Gabby has to save him. He does it by planning a surprise for the villains at Duke's trial.

Wayne plays Jerry Mason, a young college student who returns to Gabby's ranch after graduation. Gabby plays Jake Benson, the rancher who helped raise Mason.

John Wayne (middle) surrounded in *The Lucky Texan* (1934).

By the time Duke returns to the ranch, there's not much left. The old man tells him that all the cattle are gone, stolen by rustlers. Other than the ranchland, his only remaining asset is a blacksmith shop in town. The only good news is that his granddaughter Betty (Barbara Sheldon) is also off at college, but she will also soon return. Meanwhile, Duke and Gabby could reopen the blacksmith shop.

Duke responds by surfing down a flume on a log, landing in a lake. The stunt was actually performed by Yakima Canutt. Director Robert Bradbury later reused the footage in the movie *Trail of Terror.* In the latter movie, the stunt was performed by Bradbury's son, Bob Steele. Duke also used it again in *The Lawless Frontier.*

The most humor in the film comes in its climax when Gabby dresses as an old woman to see that Duke is set free in court. He engages in chitchat with those outside and makes fun of Duke's big feet when the sheriff leads him in. Gabby and Betty take seats on the front row.

Before the proceedings get started, Gabby asks to speak to the court. Still dressed as an older woman, he says he has known the defendant for a long time and that he knows who really shot Jake because he saw the whole thing happen. Gabby is told to take the stand and be sworn in as a witness. As he steps forward, his skirt falls off, and the crowd in the courtroom roars with laughter.

Not bothered at all by the ruckus, Gabby reveals that he's really Jake Benson and he points out "the two coyotes who shot me." The two villains escape by crashing through a window; Duke grabs a horse and takes off in pursuit. Gabby hops in a car and does the same.

The villains soon abandon their horses and switch to an automated railroad cart. Gabby chases in his car, crossing the railroad in front of the cart on three different occasions. Duke eventually catches up with the villains on his horse. He jumps onto the cart and knocks Yakima off. Meanwhile, Gabby stops his car on the tracks in front of the cart and corners Harris. Both men fight their respective villain. Both win, although Gabby is aided by hitting Harris on the head with a stick a couple of times.

The final scene is the wedding of Jerry and Betty. The wedding photographer has worked a long time to set up in the right spot. He tells the three participants—the couple and Gabby—to hold their positions as he takes the shot. Instead, Duke and Betty kiss. The frustrated photographer packs his equipment and leaves as the final scene fades out.

Female lead Barbara Sheldon receives two awkward kisses from Wayne (one through the bars of a jail cell). Two Yakima Canutt stunts stand out: a humorous scene of Yakima wresting with the burro (and losing) and his incredible slide down a water flume (as Wayne) on a tree branch. Film fan Miller wrote that the movie "is notable for the foreshadowing of the comedic talents of George Hayes, heretofore utility man of the indies. …Here he does the sidekick number, preparing himself, doubtless unknowingly, for a long tenure of lovable horseplay in the future."[4] Gabby provides some comic relief when he dresses as a woman. Pritch wrote, "Gabby Hayes is a laugh riot in drag in the courtroom scene and Canutt's 'Injun Joe' escape (through the open window of the courthouse) had me rolling. I loved this film."[5]

Another Duke fan, Smith, had a similar opinion, calling it "a cut above the average."[6] He added that Gabby Hayes, "who played many different characters in this series, plays Jake Benson very close to his eventual 'Gabby' character, which he had not fully developed at this time."[7]

Raskin also liked it, writing: "Gabby Hayes' irascible sidekick performance and Yakima Canutt's excellent stunt work make this one quite watchable. …With likable characters and a plot that keeps moving, this one is quite professional and on a par with a good Lone Ranger episode two decades later."[8] Doepke really liked Duke's performance, writing, "Note how loose and relaxed he is; he's having fun out there in LA's outskirts with all his buddies in the crew and cast. He's just perfect for these matinee specials."[9] Wayne was indeed learning to be likable on camera, and that skill would play a major role in his future success.

Slocum may have given the most apt appraisal: "Lone Star did well with Wayne once they retired the singing cowboy shtick and worked humor more directly in his films, like here. *The Lucky Texan* actually goes pretty far in this direction,"[10]

The Lucky Texan also holds an unusual place in modern television history. On a Saturday afternoon in 1996, a fire broke out in the studios of WNBC in New York, the parent station of the NBC television network. As the building was being evacuated, a staffer for the station quickly put a tape of *The Lucky Texan* in the station's tape player. The movie ran two consecutive times, creating confusion for some viewers at home.

West of the Divide is full of coincidences. Duke and Gabby Hayes are discussing the evil men who killed Duke's father and stole his little brother when a man stumbles toward them, collapses and dies at their feet. The poor dead guy drank from a poisoned waterhole and made it to within a few feet of Duke before dying. He urns out to have been an outlaw who is almost a dead ringer for Duke himself. He even carried a wanted poster of himself, sort of an early form of an ID card.

By coincidence, the dead outlaw carries a letter of introduction to the very villain who killed Duke's dad. Recognizing a stroke of luck when he sees it, Duke takes the letter, impersonates the outlaw and goes undercover as a member of the villain's gang.

Robert N. Bradbury again serves double duty as director and writer. The 54-minute film was shot on location near Kernville, California, and released on February 15, 1934. Miller noted that the plot of a hero searching for a family member was "a Bradbury stock-in-trade that he usually reserved for his offspring, Bob Steele, with little discernible variation."[11]

As an "outlaw," Duke's first assignment is to run off or kill a local rancher who has a parcel of land and a daughter (Virginia Faire Brown) whom the villain covets. Duke takes the job, steals the rancher's cattle, but fakes the planned murder.

Duke and the rancher set a trap for the bad guys. When they spring it, the big bad man is mistakenly killed by his own gang. While all of this is happening, there are a number of good stunts, and most come courtesy of the legendary Yakima Canutt. These start with a dramatic horse chase with two bad guys chasing the heroine, missing their leap, and knocking each other off their own horses. Later, Duke tries to stop a runaway wagon. He leaps on the team of horses and grabs the reins, and the wagon disintegrates behind him. The horses continue running full speed, pulling him like a skier while he rides the traces. There is also a marvelous scene with Duke's character leaping off a horse and through a window while his horse runs in full stride. Impressive. This was offset by one poor gunfight scene in which Duke shoots a gun out of the villain's hand. Unfortunately, Duke's gun is pointed at the ground when he makes this spectacular shot.

Duke is assisted in this adventure by a 12-year-old kid named Spud, played by Billie O'Brien. Somewhat like an early version of the *Home Alone* kid. Spud spends part of the movie outsmarting the bad guys, like when he takes the lead out of their bullets and reloads their guns.

There are some mistakes. The first occurs during a fight scene when Duke takes on a villain and Spud yells, "Come on, Ted." Actually, Duke is still impersonating outlaw Gat Ganns at that point. Only later does Spud learn that his real name is Ted. In another scene, the villain appears without a cigarette, with a cigarette, and then without one again—in the same scene. And a battery-powered torch is used in one scene, even though it wasn't invented until 1899. Somewhat surprisingly, this film was condemned by the Catholic Legion of Decency, apparently because of its violence.

Most of the available reviews of this film come from modern fans. Raskin didn't like this film at all: "It has all the bad elements of the series, bad acting, convoluted and dull plot, anachronisms (telephones, automobiles and women in 1930s clothes. Only the stunt work is excellent."[12]

Eyles disagreed, citing some of Wayne's scenes: "It is revealing to find in Wayne's performance moments of the same intensity of feeling as he brought to later work."[13] He added, "He was clearly a *working* actor, making the most of his lines instead of just reading them, and building up a useful reservoir of technique for later use."[14]

And Wayne did gain some valuable experience from this film that would help him in 1939. This film was shot entirely on location in and around Kernville, an area north of Bakersfield, California. The same location was used by John Ford for the final chase scene between the Apaches and the stagecoach in *Stagecoach*.[15]

Still, the good news is that Duke prevails. And, you might not believe this, but Spud turns out to be Duke's long-lost little brother.

Gee, what a coincidence.

Blue Steel is a standard B Western that will never qualify for classic status. But for Wayne, the movie "shows the same appealing sense of youthful sincerity that marked the less intense moments of *West of the Divide*."[16] It's also a pretty good yarn, even if I never did figure out where they came up with the title. Perhaps director Robert Bradbury had the answer, since he also wrote the screenplay for this Lone Star production.

The 54-minute film is a remake of 1931's *A Son of the Plains* with Bob Custer, also written and directed by Bradbury. It was shot at seven different locations in California—the Walker Ranch and Trem Carr Ranch near Newhall, the Alabama Hills near Lone Pine, Santa Clarita, Big Pine, Kernville and the General Services Studios in Hollywood. Big Pine, which is the Owens Valley about 40 miles north of Lone Pine, was not frequently used in Wayne's movie, but the setting was a good one for *Blue Steel*.[17] The movie was released on May 10, 1934.

The story has Duke (as U.S. Marshal John Carruthers) and Sheriff Jake (Gabby Hayes) chasing the same villain, the Polka Dot bandit. Gabby begins to wonder if the bandit might be Wayne himself. Gabby sets aside his suspicion when the two team up to help a town in trouble.

Eleanor Hunt plays the female lead. She loses her father to a gunman early in the film, is almost seduced by the villain, but stumbles upon the plot in the process.

Meanwhile, our heroes uncover the town's real villain (Ed Peil), who turns out to be a respected rancher. The rancher wants to force the others off the land because he has discovered gold in the area. (This hidden-asset plot frequently appears in B Westerns.)

This idea of a successful rancher or businessman actually being a villain is a typical theme in many of Wayne's 1930s Westerns. Nevins described it as reflecting "the social and legal crises of the Great Depression" where capitalism was often seen as a villain that took advantage of the common person.[18] Matheson called the themes scathing portrayals of obese capitalists engaged in perpetuating social injustice and economic exploitation."[19] McGhee wrote, "These stories portray economic disaster as a result of deliberate strategies by capitalists to rob after reducing people to desperate need and mass hysteria."[20]

The Polka Dot Bandit is played by stunt legend Yakima Canutt. Duke identifies him using a spur broken during a robbery. Gabby's suspicions that Duke is the bandit increase, though, when he finds a polka dot handkerchief in Duke's saddlebags.

The film opens with a older man (George Cleveland) in charge of a hotel, nodding off in a chair while a storm rages outside. A rain-soaked Wayne enters softly and slips past him to hide in a closet.

Sheriff Gabby soon follows, shaking the rain off his coat, but he goes over to awaken the hotel host. Gabby is looking for a place to spend the night, but he also wants to keep an eye on the lobby because he's on the

John Wayne in *Blue Steel* (1934).

trail of the Polka Dot Bandit. Hank sends Gabby upstairs to a special room with two beds and a peephole that provides a view of the lobby. Wayne settles down in the closet.

The rain appears to be good for business, since Hank soon has three other customers. First is a matronly woman, and she's soon followed by a pair of nervous newlyweds. Hank offers them the bridal suite for two dollars a night. It is, he assures them, the best room in the hotel. But he warns them to be quiet because the man in the room beside them gets up at five in the morning.

This series of scenes apparently took several shots to complete. The guest book for the hotel changes positions several times as the scene progresses.

One final guest arrives, a stage driver (Hank Bell) carrying saddlebags with $4000 in payroll money for the nearby mine. Hank puts the money in his safe and says, "It'll be safe here. They'll have to take away the safe to get it." What Hank didn't notice is that Danti (Yakima Canutt), a.k.a. the Polka Dot Bandit, was outside watching him through an open window as he turned the combination on the safe. When the innkeeper goes upstairs, Yakima enters the room, opens the safe, and takes the money. In the process, he loses a rowel from his spur.

The noise of the robbery awakens Duke, who finds the rowel. By this time, Gabby is also awake. He peers through the hole in the floor, spots Duke at the safe, and believes he has found the Polka Dot Bandit. Gabby rushes downstairs, but too late to confront Wayne, who has already disappeared into the storm. Gabby pledges, "I'm gonna run him down if it takes me ten years."

Cut to the next morning. Wayne is inside a shack when he hears a noise approaching. He slips out through a window just before Gabby enters through the door, gun drawn. Gabby looks around, moves to the window and peers outside. Wayne enters through the door and gets the drop on Gabby, who surrenders his gun. Now Duke invites the sheriff to join him for a dinner of beans. He disarmed Gabby, he explains, because he was "just being careful. Why you might have been the Polka Dot Bandit."

Cut to a scene in Yucca City, where the townspeople are discussing their problem: They may be forced to sell their land because bandits are stealing all the supplies headed into the area. The town's leaders have written the governor in Sacramento, asking for assistance, but they have heard nothing. The townspeople suspect a traitor ("a skunk," in their terms), but they don't know who it might be. The camera does, though, because it shows us a nervous-looking man who seems to fit the bill.

We quickly learn that a rancher named Malgrove (Ed Peil) is the leader of the villains. He tells Yakima, "You know what to do," and adds that no harm should come to "the girl."

On the open range, the Mason family—father Dan (Lafe McKee), son Tom and daughter Betty (Eleanor Hunt)—are leading a mule train of supplies, while five outlaws chase them. The bandits shoot the father and son. Cut back to Duke and Gabby in the shack. Gabby sees Duke turn his back to him, and draws his gun. Before he can make an arrest, though, gunshots get their attention. They race outside, mount their horses and take off to save the people being attacked. One of the villains' shots hits Gabby's horse, causing Gabby to fall off a cliff into the river. Duke dives in save the sheriff, making the bad guys believe they have killed both men.

Betty rides into town to tell the locals that her father and brother were killed by bandits and the supplies lost. Malgrove steps up, promising to take care of Betty and inviting her to live at his ranch. Cut to the plains again, where Duke and Gabby hunch over the body of Dan Mason as several of the townspeople approach. The group takes the two bodies into town.

In town, Malgrove and Yakima draw their guns in an attempt to arrest Duke and Gabby. The two men protest their innocence, to no avail, but they're cleared when Betty walks up and declares them heroes.

Since supplies failed to make it through again, Malgrove offers to buy all the local ranches for $100 each. Duke and Gabby step in, promising to deliver the needed supplies. Malgrove offers to pay for $1000 in supplies if they can bring the cache through. While he speaks, Duke spots a rowel missing from one of Yakima's spurs and knows he has found the Polka Dot Bandit. He tells Gabby to keep an eye on Danti for a surprise in the near future. Gabby notes that he may have a surprise for Duke too.

Cut to Malgrove's ranch, where he is hosting a shy Betty. He again offers to make the ranch her home. Before she can answer, Yakima rides up and Malgrove goes out to meet him. Betty slips behind a fence where she can hear their conversation. She learns that Malgrove is trying to starve out the small ranches because their properties sit atop a massive gold field. A worker comes out of the house and alerts Malgrove to Betty's presence near the fence. He grabs her, pushes her to Yakima and tells him to take her to the hideout "until the town is deserted."

Duke tells Gabby he will go to Malgrove's ranch to get the order of supplies. Once he leaves, Gabby mounts his own horse and follows at a distance. Duke rides up to a bunkhouse with a sign on the door: "Danti. Keep out." Ignoring the sign, he goes inside, finds it empty and starts searching Danti's items. Inside a set of saddle bags he finds a polka dot scarf and money wrappers from the "Lost Lode Mine." He takes the saddle bags.

Malgrove spots him near the bunkhouse and sends two of his henchmen after Duke, saying, "Now's your chance. Remember, no shooting." That puts the two bad guys at a disadvantage. Duke enters a barn, climbs to the loft and lassos one by his legs. He pulls that gent up toward the ceiling, ties the rope and runs to the other end of the barn. There he spots the other villain below. He jumps down and begins fighting with him. The first bad guy pulls himself into the loft using the rope around his ankles. He goes to the other side, spots Duke and his partner fighting below, and begins to cut a rope holding a bale of hay. Before he can cut through the rope, Gabby rides up and shoots him. Duke finishes the other one off with a knock-out blow.

Malgrove apologizes for the actions of his hands, saying they had standing orders to stop strangers on the ranch. He seems not to notice that one of his cowboys has been shot. Duke and Gabby get the supply order and say they'll leave and return by dawn before the bandits can learn that they've left.

When the heroes depart, Malgrove tells his henchmen to be ready. When he finishes speaking, the partially cut rope at the top of the barn unravels and the bale of hay falls on Malgrove and the other villain.

Instead of leaving immediately, Duke and Gabby hang around nearby while Duke wonders what happened to Betty. When Malgrove leaves the ranch, Duke follows him to the bandits' hideout. Gabby wakes up soon afterwards, rummages through Duke's saddle bags and finds the polka dot scarf. His belief that Duke is the bandit seems firmly set.

Malgrove arrives at the hideout with Duke close behind. He enters the shack, talks to some of the bandits and finds out that Betty is imprisoned in a storeroom. Duke learns this while listening from outside, and quickly heads to the storeroom. Betty tells Duke that Malgrove is the leader of the bandits. Duke tells her he will return before dawn to help her escape. Instead, he heads back to camp to fill Gabby in on the news.

The duo rise early the next day and head to the bandits' camp, but one of the bandits sees them leave. At the hideout, Malgrove tells two of his henchmen to guard the girl, while the others go with him to attack the supply wagon they expect Gabby and Duke to be driving. The departure of the bandits give Duke a chance to rescue Betty.

Gabby finds a wagon and horse, plus a bonus: a cache of supplies. Gabby simply recovers the stolen supplies from the thieves and loads them onto the wagon rather than trying to get a new shipment into town. Meanwhile, the villain who saw our heroes head toward the hideout intercepts the rest of the bandits and tells them to return to their home base.

Duke helps Gabby load supplies. A guard, asleep during all the commotion, wakes up and runs to keep Betty from escaping. Betty screams, Duke races to help, and the bandits keep racing back toward the hideout. Betty spots the gang, but Duke and the villain are in a fight by now. Betty runs to tell Gabby that the bandits are returning. Duke finally knocks out the villain. Gabby races to get one last box from the cache of supplies—a box of dynamite. After all, he notes, "It might come in handy."

What happens next is one of those three-way chases that Lone Star was so fond of. Betty grabs a horse and races toward town. Gabby drives the wagon while Duke (actually, Yakima) does a running-mount stunt and rides his white horse ahead of the wagon. Bringing up the rear are the bandits, desperate to stop the heroes before they can reach town.

Duke backtracks to the wagon and starts throwing sticks of lit dynamite in the path of the bandits. After a few tosses, Gabby stops the wagon, and both men place some dynamite at strategic points. The ensuing blast seals the pass and makes the bandits back off.

But not for long. The bad guys regroup, ride down a steep cliff, and race their horses down a shallow river. Gabby and Duke stop the wagon again, retrieve some more dynamite, and aim to detonate it with shots from their guns so that the bandits will be buried in the rubble. "Don't miss your mark," Duke tells Gabby. "It means the lives of everyone in town." They don't miss.

Betty arrives in town, telling the locals that Duke and Gabby are following with supplies. They soon arrive, with Duke telling everyone, "Your troubles are all over." He leaves Gabby to tell the rest of the story, while he chases after Betty and tells her that he's a government agent who has to go to Santa Fe next. He adds, "You don't know it, but you're going to go with me." Gabby arrives on the scene to arrest Wayne as the bandit, but Betty identifies him as a U.S. marshal. The movie ends with a slight twist on the cliché of riding off into the sunset. In this case, Duke and Betty ride off together, holding hands.

The fact that all of these events occurred in California, and Santa Fe is east of that, doesn't seem to bother them at all. In the case of *Blue Steel,* the sun always sets in the east.

Doepke cited the work of Hayes, noting, "This looks like an early stage in the evolution of Hayes' unforgettable 'Gabby' character. He's not called that, still the crusty old coot is definitely coming out."[21]

Despite the film's mundane status, modern Wayne fans generally like it. Raskin noted, "There is also the only risqué double entendre that I've seen in a Lone Star film when a newlywed husband comes back downstairs from his bridal suite and announces, 'I can't find it.'"[22]

Reid liked the camerawork.[23] He wrote, "Photographer Archie Stout, a specialist in location work, is also most at home with awesome vistas of wide open plains, ringed by rugged mountains and fleecy clouds in the Alabama Hills, California."[24]

The film is enhanced by excellent stunt work. In the early chase scene, when Gabby is shot from his horse and falls off a cliff into a river, Wayne leaps from his horse and jumps into the river to save him. The only problem is that a modern bridge is visible in the background when Duke's character makes his jump. This shot worked so well that the studio used the same location (and shots) for Duke's next film, *The Man from Utah*.

That's not the only repetition in the film. The ranch house appeared again in *The Star Packer* (1934) and *The Desert Trail* (1935). And the entire plot is essentially used the following year for *Lawless Range*.

The best stunt is saved for the gun battle near the end of the film. The scene has Gabby racing across the plains in a wagon, while Duke and Betty race ahead on individual horses. A stray bullet knocks Eleanor off her horse, and she falls into the path of the oncoming wagon. Duke's character leaps from his horse onto the wagon tongue between the two front horses. When the racing horses reach Betty, Duke reaches down, picks her up (presumably a life-size dummy, given how light she seems to be) and puts her on his own horse. She grabs the reins and again races toward town. This stunt was performed by Canutt, not Duke. Yakima's character gets killed by a stray bullet from his own gang a few minutes before this stunt is executed. A stray bullet was not a dramatic way for the Polka Dot Bandit to meet his end.

Duke no doubt learned a great deal about stunt work while working on this one.

The Man from Utah was again scripted by Lindsley Parsons. Wayne is a singing cowboy named John Weston (he only sings in the opening scene, thank goodness) who looks for a job, stumbles upon a holdup, saves the marshal's (Gabby Hayes) life, gets arrested and takes an undercover job investigating a rodeo scam. Polly Ann Young and Anita Campillo have the top female roles. Young was the older sister of the more famous Loretta Young.[25] Robert Bradbury was the director. The movie was shot in the Alabama Hills and Owens River areas around Lone Pine, California. It was released on May 15, 1934. Originally 55 minutes, it was cut to 52 minutes for television.

Duke's job is to identify the killers of rodeo riders who are on the verge of winning money. With potential winners getting killed, the eventual winners are all the same riders (all part of the villain's gang). Duke is so good at riding that he does well on the rodeo circuit. Too well for the villains, of course, who try to kill his chances by placing a poisoned needle in Duke's saddle—the same technique used to kill the other riders.

It doesn't work. Duke ends up with a girlfriend (Polly Ann Young) who is the daughter of the local banker and foils the bandits' attempt to steal the bank's money.

If you keep a sharp eye out, you'll spot a wanted poster for Gat Ganns, a character from Wayne's 1934 movie *West of the Divide*. After all, why waste a good poster?

The film is padded with stock rodeo footage, much of which has little to do with the plot but does include some fine trick roping by Jack Hollister. And it has some unnecessary scenes, such as a canoe ride which only serves to fill time.

Generally, these B Westerns were shot in one week, with little extra time for extravagant scenes and plots. With this one, though, you get the feeling that they cut one, maybe two days from the filming schedule. Maybe that's why the film gets lackluster reviews from Duke's modern fans. Smith pointed out that Yakima Canutt played "the chief bad guy and once again [proved] that as an actor, he made a great stuntman."[26] Chance agreed that the best part of the film was Canutt's stuntwork.[27] Slocum advised fans to "pass this one by."[28]

Most complaints involve the interweaving of stock footage. But Haynie liked it, writing: "Those old rodeo scenes are exciting because they are real."[29]

The plot was different from other early B Westerns—so different that it was used multiple times, thus making some extra money for Parsons. It would be remade as *Trouble in Texas* (1937, starring Tex Ritter and Rita Hayworth), *Frontier Town* (1938, again starring Ritter), *Mesquite Buckaroo* (1939, Bob Steele), *The Utah Kid* (1944, Hoot Gibson and Bob Steele) and *Lawless Cowboys* (1951, Whip Wilson).

The film's contribution to Duke's career: not much. The singing cowboy approach just wasn't his thing, and the rodeo riding was all stock footage. But Wayne did get to work with a Parsons screenplay, and that's was a plus.

Randy Rides Alone is a movie with three distinguishing characteristics: (1) a script that was the epitome of a Lindsley Parsons story, (2) a noticeable lack of dialogue, and (3) George Hayes in a dual role, in one of them using a precursor of the walk he used as sidekick Gabby Hayes.[30]

Silent screen star Alberta Vaughn co-starred. Vaughn's career soon went downhill. She appeared in one other Western, *The Laramie Kid* (1935) with Tom Tyler, and finished her career later that year with a role in *Live Wire*. After that, her life disintegrated. Ankerich wrote that she "lived long enough to feel the chill of a cold, cruel Hollywood."[31] Others in the cast included Yakima Canutt, Earl Dwire, Artie Ortego and Tex Phelps. Unfortunately, as Reid noted, "Aside from Hayes, and perhaps Canutt, the support cast is totally uninteresting."[32] Harry Fraser served as director. The 53-minute film was shot on location at Santa Clarita, California.

An investigator walks into a murder scene, gets arrested for the crime, and then teams with the local heroine to reveal the real killers. It is full of action, stunts and shootouts, but short on dialogue. It is highly representative of the Lindsley Parsons type of story. Parsons liked to open his scripts with unusual, intriguing scenes. *Randy Rides Alone* fits that formula perfectly. It begins with Duke entering the Half-Way House, a building at a remote watering hole, and finding all of its inhabitants dead. The owner is draped over a bar, while unlucky customers are scattered around the room in various positions. Miller wrote, "It's still the bloodthirstiest but most intriguing beginning of any low-budget Western."[33]

The picture on a wanted poster on the wall has bullet holes instead of eyes. A note tells the meaning of the message: "Lay off Sheriff, or you'll get the same thing and it won't be no picture." Duke is arrested and charged with murder. The niece (and remaining owner of the Half-Way House) helps him escape so he can help identify her father's killer and discover who is trying to steal the $30,000 in cash left to her.

Gabby Hayes plays a dual role as a local store owner, "Matt the Mute," and the leader of the outlaw gang. As the outlaws' boss, he hides his troops in an elaborate hideout behind a waterfall. As Matt the Mute, he wears a mustache, walks with a hunchback gait, and communicates with everyone by writing notes.

Duke stumbles (literally) upon the hideout after he escapes from jail. Pursued by the sheriff, he (actually Yakima Canutt) leaps from his running horse as it crosses a bridge, landing in the water below. The current takes him to the waterfall.

The gang, knowing he is running from the law, skeptically accepts him as a new member. While with the villains, Duke compares the handwriting of the two characters and realizes that Matt the Mute and the outlaw leader are the same person. Duke sneaks out of the hideout to recover Alberta's hidden money and replaces the cash with dynamite found at the outlaw camp. When Duke later reveals the hiding place of the strongbox, Gabby slips away during a shootout to recover it. He blows himself up when he tries to open the box by shooting into it.

Overall, this film is pretty good. Smith warned viewers, though, that "John Wayne was in the midst of learning his craft in this series" of Lone Star Westerns.[34] Eyles thought Duke actually took a step backwards in this one, perhaps because he was working with a new director. At least that's the explanation that Eyles gives when he wrote that Wayne "does deliver some of his lines clumsily in this one."[35]

The one exception is when Wayne stumbles upon the villains' hideout in a cave behind a waterfall. When the bad guys inquire how he got there, Eyles noted that Wayne replies, "I fell in!," adding that he snaps the line "as though daring any of them to make something out of it."[36] Doepke liked the script, writing, "Lindsley Parsons did several scripts for Wayne and Lone Star, but this one's arguably his best."[37] Miller noted that the movie "indicates how Monogram, with limited resources, did make an attempt to inject some novel situations into their range product."[38]

Gabby's Matt the Mute has a number of similarities to the sidekick Gabby later developed for Hopalong Cassidy and Roy Rogers.[39] Much of Gabby's communication, though, is done with written messages. That contributes to a story that is remarkably short on dialogue. The opening scene alone goes for more than three minutes without anyone saying a word, as Duke surveys the carnage around him.

There are some continuity problems. Matt the Mute scribbles his notes quickly on a notepad that he carries with him. When the camera shifts to a close-up of the writing, though, his hand is always moving slowly. Also, Matt the Mute appears to be using 3x5 note cards in the long shots. When the camera moves to a close-up, he's using square pieces of paper.

In a stunt in which Duke leaps from a wall onto the back of his horse, he gets shorter in mid-jump. That results from an abrupt cut from Duke's leap to Canutt actually doing the jump. But Wayne seems to be making progress in some of the other areas related to being a Western star. As Eyles noted, "Wayne's walk in this film has a lazy air of increasing confidence, and he is seen twirling his six-shooter with professional ease."[40]

These are minor problems, though. This one is worth viewing for the plot and seeing Gabby develop a couple of traits of his most famous character.

The Star Packer co-stars Verna Hillie in a story which presages *The Lone Ranger*. Wayne is John Travers, a wandering marshal known as "The Lone Rider" who travels with an Indian sidekick named Yak (Yakima Canutt). Wayne comes to rescue a group of cattlemen terrorized by a bandit called the Shadow (a young George "Gabby" Hayes). Others in the cast included Bill Franey, Eddie Parker, Earl Dwire and Thomas G. Lingham. The 53-minute film, written and directed by Robert N. Bradbury, was filmed at the General Service Studios in Hollywood and on location in Santa Clarita, Kernville and Newhall. It was released on July 30, 1934.

John Wayne (center) and George "Gabby" Hayes (right front) support Thomas G. Lingham as Verna Hillie and others keep watch in *The Star Packer* (1934).

The movie opens with Duke and his white horse camped beside a river. An Indian (Canutt) approaches his campsite rowing a canoe. Duke helps Yak get the small boat out of the river. We quickly learn the rendezvous was planned, and Yak provides some information about an imminent stage robbery. Duke says they'll have to stop that, causing Yak to smile and say in his best Tonto-like fashion, "More trouble. More fun."

Cut to the town where a local leader named Matlock (Gabby) introduces the new sheriff to the townspeople. He then turns to the sheriff and updates him on the dastardly villain known as the Shadow. Cut back to Duke and Yak, where Duke plans to start his job by first robbing the stagecoach. It's a fake holdup, of course, merely done to prevent it from actually being robbed by the real villains.

Duke pulls it off by racing in front of the stage, grabbing a low tree limb and pulling himself up into the tree. When the stage passes beneath him, he jumps on top of it and demands the money from the driver and shotgun rider. He grabs the money bags and jumps off the stage, and Yak arrives with his horse.

When the real robbers arrive soon afterwards, they leave empty-handed, but not before shooting the stage driver. The shots spook the horses and places a fair maiden in distress. Duke rescues the leading lady Anita by chasing down the stage.

Wayne takes the stagecoach into town. A crowd gathers to see what has happened, and Duke gets some help in taking the wounded driver to a doctor. Included in the crowd is the new sheriff, but he doesn't hold the job long: He's shot and killed from ambush by an unknown sniper while the crowd watches. His death puts the locals in a funk, figuring that nobody will take the job now.

Not so. Duke volunteers for the job, not bothering to tell folks that he is already a marshal. His first duty: recovering the stagecoach money he stole earlier in the day. Before he even gets out of town, though, he learns something about the bad guys. First, Yak spots two hombres entering town and identifies them as the stage robbers. Duke follows them and figures out that the Shadow gives his instructions via a disembodied voice in the back room of the saloon. The Shadow gives instructions to his henchmen to kill the new sheriff.

When Duke rides out of town to get the express money, the robbers follow, hoping to get a chance to shoot him. But Yak follows them, tells Duke what's going on, and our heroes safely elude them. After Duke suggests that he and Yak swap horses, he takes the money out of the bags and gives it to Yak to be sure it reaches town safely. Then he mounts Yak's horse and the bad guys take off in pursuit.

Why do they switch horses? It has nothing to do with the plot. But the reason quickly becomes apparent. It allowed Yak to ride his own horse for a couple of neat stunts. First, the bad guys shoot at our hero and he pretends to fall from his horse, dropping the money bags in the process. The bad guys quickly locate the bags, but they are empty. And they can't find the new sheriff. They do see the horse he was riding running full speed off to one side, but apparently without a rider. But a new shot from a different angle shows that our hero is clinging to the side of the horse, out of sight of the bad guys. He rides into town to meet his faithful Indian companion at the express office.

Meanwhile, the two villains return to the back room of the saloon to report to the Shadow that they missed Wayne and that he brought the express money back to town. The Shadow orders them to return to the hideout. Duke and Yak see them depart and follow the men to their hideout, which is only two miles from the Matlock ranch.

Gabby Hayes does credible work as Matt Matlock, a person thought to be a decent man who turns out to be the Shadow. Actually, he never was a decent man; the Shadow had killed the real Matt Matlock and assumed his identity as a cover for his evil doings. He is also pretending to be Hillie's uncle. She came to town to inherit her half of a ranch left to her by her father. The Shadow killed her father and uncle, and then took the identity of Matt Matlock so he could claim the other half. If he can get rid of that pesky young girl, he can have the entire ranch.

He starts by trying to scare her away. His ploys include a man in a bear costume and a ghostly face in the ranch house window. Nice tries, but the young lady doesn't scare easily. In fact, she shoots at the pranksters, thus ending that round of tricks. The inept henchmen make another attempt to kill Duke, but Yak intervenes. The men are taken to jail, but they vow to be out by noon the next day.

That night, Duke and Yak explore the mysterious room and find a series of tunnels under the town. Duke eventually figures out that the villains receive their instructions via a fake wall safe. Using that information, he sets out to trap the gang and its leader. First, he takes one of his jailbirds to the room for more instructions. The Shadow tells him to get Duke into the street, where he can be shot by a sniper in a hollow tree stump. Duke switches hats and vests with his charge and goes outside. Yak gathers the honest townspeople to help him spoil the plot.

When a gun points out of a hole in the stump, Yak and the town folks take charge of the shooter. They ask him to identify the Shadow, but he is shot before he can give them the name. The Shadow slips out of town.

Duke shares his real identity with the townspeople and tells them that the Shadow will return to destroy the town. He rounds up a posse and goes after the gang. While this is happening, Anita learns that Matlock is not her real uncle. The news comes from a cook at the ranch who tells her and then rides off for help. The cook is captured, but the posse appears. The villains are either killed or captured, and the good guys have won again. The Shadow faces ultimate humiliation, being lassoed by both Duke and Yak, who drag the water-drenched villain out of the river.

Canutt's role as the Indian companion is interesting, though politically incorrect by today's standards. ("Ugh. Two men follow. Look through glass.") But the stunts are excellent and the plot is more imaginative than usual, with plenty of secret tunnels, hidden chambers and a hollow tree stump. In one scene, Wayne exchanges his hat for a white bandana, using the bandanas so that all of the posse members can distinguish themselves from the villains. The bandana later disappears when he dives into the river to save Verna. Wayne also loses his gun in the dive, and his holster is empty when he pulls Verna from the river. When he turns to mount his horse, his gun has mysteriously reappeared.

Overall, this one gets mixed reviews from fans of B Western. Smith liked it: "As 'B' Westerns go for this period, this one isn't bad. In fact, in my opinion, it's one of the best of John Wayne's early B Westerns. It has all of the right ingredients to make this an enjoyable hour."[41] Doepke agreed, writing, "Mystery, excitement, big shootouts, and a hard-riding hero. So what else could a grown-up kid ask for?"[42]

According to Doyle, "The whole plot is so rushed that there's little time to digest any of the backstory that leads up to the main storyline."[43] Ostrem wrote, "The landscapes are particularly beautiful. It's the sound that's bad. They dub in new voices that are terrible. And the music, it's some kind of spaghetti Western–sounding stuff that has nothing with the charm of the era. View at your peril."[44]

Eyles saw a stronger performance by Wayne than in *Randy Rides Alone*, perhaps because Bradbury had returned as director. Still, even he noted that Wayne "finds it difficult when he has to pause to think out a point" in the movie.[45]

Fenin and Everson may have given the most objective evaluation. As they wrote regarding a poster promoting the film, "There are no catch lines, and the appeal rests only on the type of film and the star's name."[46]

The movie ends with Duke and Anita married. Faithful Indian Yak joins them on the ranch, playing with their child. I'm just not sure Tonto would be happy with such a role.

Did the Old West have cowboys with college degrees? There were a pair of them in *The Trail Beyond*. In one of his most different B Westerns, Duke plays Rod Drew, a college grad called upon by an old friend of his father's to find out what happened to a friend and his daughter. On the train to the remote mining country where the couple were last reported, our hero runs into his best friend from college. Together they start the search while avoiding arrest on a phony murder charge.

Verna Hillie, Wayne's *Star Packer* co-star, appears again as the female lead. A young Noah Beery, Jr., best known as the father of Jim Rockford on TV's *The Rockford Files,* plays the college buddy and sidekick role, as well as Duke's rival for the hand of the girl. Noticeably absent are Yakima Canutt and George "Gabby" Hayes, both of whom appeared in many of Duke's early films. Canutt does make an appearance in some uncredited stunts. Years later he remembered the film as "the one where John, Eddie Parker [another stuntman] and I stayed wet more than we were dry."[47] This Lone Star production was directed by Robert Bradbury. It was a remake of a 1926 film, *The Wolf Hunters* with Robert McKim. The script is by Lindsley Parsons, based on James Oliver Curwood's short story "The Wolf Hunters." Miller noted that the movie was somewhat historic in that, by basing it on an outside source, "it was the first time a Monogram Wayne went outside the studio gates for a plot basis."[48] The 55-minute movie was released on October 22, 1934.

Shooting locations included some of the most scenic spots in California: Devil's Postpile National Monument, Mammoth Lakes, Big Bear Lake and Valley, King's Canyon National Park and June Lake. Two other spots were the Trem Carr Ranch near Newhall and the Railroad Station at Chatworth.

As Smith wrote, "The best thing about this film is the spectacular outdoor scenery."[49] Phillips also commented on the scenery: "For me, a lifelong lover of Mammoth Lakes, it was fun to see Crystal Crag, and a shot down at Twin Lakes from below Lake Mamie described as 'a bend in the river.'"[50] Similarly, Chance wrote, "The story is merely a trifle to fill in the lulls before, between and after the fantastic outdoor sequences."[51]

The opening scene has Duke on a dark horse approaching a ranch house. He has been summoned by a letter from his father's friend (James Marcus), asking for help. The man tells Duke about his missing friend and the man's daughter, and asks for help in locating them. As a final note, he mentions that he wants the daughter to one day inherit his ranch. Duke promises to leave on the morning train to begin the search.

Cut to Duke, in suit and tie, sitting on a train, dressed as if he's every inch the college graduate and modern businessman. His compartment is visited by Wabi, the old college friend played by Beery Jr. Duke invites him to join him, but Wabi begs off because he's in the middle of a poker game elsewhere on the train. During the game, Wabi quickly catches a gambler drawing a card from the bottom of the deck. The gambler draws his gun, a struggle ensues and a shot is fired.

Duke hears the gunshot, races to the room and finds the gambler on the floor. The others are holding Wabi for murder. Wabi says he was framed. Duke starts knocking guys around and the duo escape by jumping from the train, and into a river, as the train crosses a bridge. The duo swim to shore and shake some of the water off their clothes. Duke summarizes their situation by saying, "Nice day for a duck."

Our heroes believe a fort is nearby, so they start walking with the idea of buying a change of clothes. They make their purchases and get a couple of horses. As they mount, the local sheriff receives a telegram about two men wanted for murder. The sheriff goes to talk to the strangers, but they spur their horses and race off. "That's them all right," the sheriff shouts. He and two others mount up and give chase.

Duke and Wabi elude the small posse by jumping their horses off a cliff into a river below. If the two scenes showing the leaps look familiar, it's because Lone Star used footage from previous films. Those leaps were too dangerous to repeat every time they made a new movie.

The Royal Canadian Mounted Police have also received a message to be on the lookout for two men. One is described as a half-breed (Wabi), but there is no description of the other.

Duke and Wabi, still on their horses, are looking for a place to camp when they spot what appears to be a deserted cabin. They push through the creaky front door and are surprised to find a man's skeleton draped over a table. On the table are bags of gold dust and a map to a mine. The map is signed by John Ball, the man Duke is seeking. Now the best he can do is find the missing daughter.

The next day, they approach the Wabinosh House, a trading post for the Hudson Bay Company. Wabi enters first and hugs the attractive blonde woman inside. Her name is Felice Newsome (Hillie), and he introduces her and her father (Noah Beery, Sr.) to Duke. Duke says that they are there to hunt wolves, and they'd like to leave some things in the store's safe. The "things" are the map and gold dust. The father gives the items to a French worker named Benoit (Earl Dwire) to put in the safe, and the worker looks over the map. Duke sees him doing it. Benoit quickly finishes his chores, grabs his saddle bags, mounts his horse and departs.

At a cabin, Benoit meets with renegade trader Jules LaRocque (Robert Frazer). Benoit brings with him pocketfuls of ammunition, taken from the trading store. He tells Larocque about the bags of gold dust in the safe. The men plan to go to the trading later that night and steal it.

The two men and an Indian sneak into the trading post, but can't open the safe. They decide to find someone who they can force to open it for them. Before they get any further, though, Felice hears them in the store and gets up. The three men attack her. She knocks the Indian to the floor, but the other two overpower her. Duke and Wabi are awake by then, and they try to come to her rescue.

When they enter her room, all they find is the Indian on the floor. Felice is gone. Mr. Newsome arrives and keeps a gun on the Indian while Duke and Wabi take a canoe and go after Felice and the villains. At LaRocque's cabin, he and three other villains are discussing their situation. They believe Felice knows the combination to the safe, but she refuses to give it to them.

Duke and Wabi arrived at the cabin. Wabi takes a rifle from the saddle of a nearby horse and starts shooting into the air, while Duke circles to the back of the cabin. The gunfire brings two of the villains out the front, while Duke enters through the back door. He starts fighting with the two remaining bad guys, while Felice runs out and finds Wabi.

Duke eventually knocks out both of the villains, runs out of the cabin and leaps on a horse. All four bad guys chase him, and he leads them away from Wabi and Felice. That couple return to the canoe and start rowing back toward the trading post. While Duke is racing away from the villains, he spots the canoe passing below. That prompts him to jump off a cliff into the water and swim to the canoe. The villains realize that the heroes have escaped and they return to their cabin.

Safely back at the trading post, Duke asks Felice for help because "I didn't come up here just to hunt wolves." Felice isn't impressed. "Man-hunters aren't exactly welcomed by most people around here," she responds. Duke then explains that he's not looking for a man, but a young girl.

At their cabin, the villains talk to a brunette named Maria LaFleur (Iris Lancaster). They decide to send her to the trading post, hoping she can get the combination to the safe. She arrives at the post carrying a small suitcase and says she's looking for a job. Newsome hires her to keep the store's books.

Duke introduces himself to Marie. Felice, standing beside Wabi, is upset that Duke is interested in "that girl." Her remark makes Wabi realize that she's interested in his partner. Wabi turns to Felice and says he won't let Duke come between him and her. Felice is surprised at his response and says that she didn't realize he felt that way about her.

The next day, Duke and Wabi return to the canoe and embark on their hunting expedition. Maria tells LaRocque that she has learned nothing. LaRocque says the two men are wanted by the law; he has a plan for getting help from the law.

At Duke and Wabi's camp near the lake, a Mountie arrests them and leads them back to LaRocque's cabin. Both of our heroes are tied up and taken into another room where they find another captive: the real Mountie (Eddie Parker). The villains look at a map they found when they searched Duke. They smile when they recognize the features on the hand-drawn map, and they head out in search of treasure.

Wabi realizes why they've left, but Duke isn't upset. He hid the real map in his boot. He then knocks a bottle off a nearby table, breaks it and uses a broken piece to cut the ropes on his hands. The Mountie tells Duke not to cut him loose or he will be forced to arrest both of them. Duke cuts him loose anyway, saying he won't leave the man there to die. But he insists that the Mountie will have to go with them while they follow the real map.

In a canoe, the three men head toward the spot the map calls White Peak. The entrance to the mine is just below it. They enter it and quickly find a rich vein of gold. More importantly, they find a photo of Felice, meaning she's the young girl that Duke was sent to find. Wabi, it turns out, knew who she was all along. "I knew that if you found out, you'd take her away with you," Wabi explains. But, he adds, he knows now that Felice isn't interested in him. Duke changes the conversation, saying that LaRocque will soon realize he's been sent on a fool's errand. They leave to return to the trading post.

LaRocque and his gang, heading back to their cabin, spot the three heroes in their canoe. They grab a canoe of their own and start chasing, while firing at the trio. The Mountie returns fire, but he's quickly hit. This leads to a continuity mistake. When he's shot, the Mountie falls backwards, but in the next scene he's stretched out in the opposite direction. Duke jumps into the lake, telling Wabi to keep going. He swims underneath the villains' canoe and capsizes it. Duke swims to one side of the lake and the villains to the other.

Wabi maneuvers his canoe to the bank and gets out to check on Duke. However, he forgets to tie down the canoe. The current catches it, and— with the wounded Mountie still aboard—it drifts toward a waterfall. Duke gives chase, jumps into the water and stops the canoe just before it goes over.

Duke and Wabi take the rescued Mountie back to the Wabinosh trading post. The villains return to their cabin to plan an attack on the post. The Indian is outside their cabin and overhears their plans. He reports to the heroes that an attack is coming. The wounded Mountie deputizes Duke so he can go get more Mounties. The others start loading their guns to prepare for the attack. Wabi discovers that many of the ammunition boxes are empty.

Duke tells the Mounties what's happening and they quickly put together a team. Meanwhile, the villains are headed for the Wabinosh House. Who will get there first? The villains do. They leave their horses in the forest, find some cover and begin shooting. The heroes inside return their fire, with Felice loading their guns. Maria uses the distraction of the fight to open the safe and grabs the gold dust. She takes it outside and gives it to LaRocque.

When the Mounties arrive, Maria goes back to the safe to get more gold. The wounded Mountie catches her. She's left alone as the rest of the villains run away. LaRocque puts the gold on the back of a buckboard and drives off in it. Most of the Mounties chase the gang, but Duke goes after LaRocque.

The film cuts back and forth between the two chases. Two of the gang members are shot off their horses, using stock footage from previous films. Two others, riding double, also go down. The gang finally stops to shoot it out, but they're overrun by the posse. Meanwhile, Duke is gaining on the buggy. He tries one time to jump onto the back of the buggy, but misses and falls to the dirt. He gets back on his horse and chases it again. This time he makes the leap and grabs LaRocque.

Fenin and Everson cite this scene as a fine example of how B Westerns worked with the footage and action that they had, i.e., in the first attempt, stuntman Yakima Canutt missed the wagon.[52] (Roberts and Olson argued that this was a stunt that Wayne performed himself, thus explaining the miss on the jump.[53]) Fenin and Everson wrote:

> For a moment, he clings there, being dragged along almost under the front wheels. Obviously he realizes that there is no way to salvage the stunt, so he lets go, rolls in the dust, gets to his feet, leaps on his horse, resumes the chase, and does the stunt again—correctly. The photographer had the presence of mind to keep the camera going the whole time, and the exciting sequence was used *in toto*.[54]

The wagon crashes and Duke and LaRocque roll down a hill, still fighting. They slug it out dangerously close to a cliff, as a Mountie approaches on his horse. Duke turns to meet the lawman, and LaRocque draws a knife. Before he can throw it, the Mountie shoots him and he falls off the cliff.

The trading post is the setting for the final scene. Duke is ready to surrender to the Mounties, but he learns that they're not wanted for anything. The guy that Wabi supposedly shot in the card game didn't die, so there are no charges against them. Duke and Felice row away in a canoe, as Wabi waves goodbye to them.

Overall, *The Trail Beyond* generally gets good reviews from Duke's fans. Davis described it "one of Lone Star's better efforts."[55] Doepke wrote, "The only advantage most A Westerns have over this lowly programmer is script quality. Sure, that's a biggie, but otherwise this little VW can hold its own against the sleeker Cadillacs of the day."[56]

Hitchcock liked the film, but carped: "Dubious acting skills. Even Wayne does little to suggest a major star in the making."[57] Similarly, Eyles wrote that the movie "is too underdeveloped in characterisation and too weakly plotted to rise more than marginally above the general standard of the series."[58]

Still, it is not a typical 1930s-era Western. Its plot is more complex than most. Not surprisingly, the plot was good enough that it was remade in 1949 under the title of the original story, *The Wolf Hunters*. Kirby "Sky King" Grant had the title role, and the film was directed by a top-notch Western director in Budd Boetticher (under the name Oscar Boetticher).

The inclusion of both Noah Beerys (father and son) in the *Trail Beyond* cast adds to its appeal, but it may not have added to the working conditions for actress Verna Hillie. The senior Beery challenged her to a drinking contest on the set during filming.

Duke got to expand his craft in different locations. He was getting better with each film.

After completing eight Westerns for Monogram–Lone Star, Duke renegotiated his contract with the company.[59] He got a raise in pay, but not much improvement in the quality of the movies. Miller noted, "[Wayne's movies] slid into a routine trench. Accustomed to working with one another, the gears meshed smoothly enough, but the action became more commonplace."[60]

The first one after his new deal was *The Lawless Frontier*. The cast also includes sidekick Gabby Hayes, Sheila Terry as the female lead Ruby, Yakima Canutt as a villain and Buffalo Bill, Jr., in a small role as a gang member.

Robert Bradbury was again writer and director. His original film was 59 minutes long, but it has been subsequently cut to 52 minutes for television. It was shot on location in Kernville and Red Rock Station and on the Trem Carr Ranch. The release date was November 22, 1934.

The action takes place around Polk City in an unnamed state (presumably Arizona, given a couple of references to Apaches). It opens with a bandit attack on a ranch. Their victims are Duke's parents, and he vows revenge. His search for the killer, bandit Pandro Zanti, takes him to a ranch owned by Gabby and his daughter. Zanti, it seems, has his eyes set on Gabby's land while lusting after the beautiful Sheila.

What follows is a confusing plot, but one filled with action:

• Gabby tries to sneak Ruby away from the ranch by disguising her as a sack of supplies.
• Duke has to save her from drowning when the pack mule throws his sack of Ruby into the river.
• Duke helps Ruby and Gabby escape to town with a series of stunts that include a running mount on a horse, a leap from a tree to the back of a bandit's horse, and leaping his horse off a cliff into a river.
• Duke and Gabby try to enlist the help of the Polk City sheriff in their efforts to capture Zanti. The sheriff refuses; he's already looking for the outlaw and thinks that Duke might be part of the gang.

John Wayne (middle) with George "Gabby" Hayes (left) and Lloyd Whitlock in
***The Lawless Frontier* (1934).**

- Zanti is captured, but continues his rampage while apparently chained to a bed (sorry, but I don't understand how this happened).
- Duke is arrested for the murder of Gabby, even though Gabby was only wounded by a knife (bearing Duke's initials) thrown by an unknown assailant.
- When Zanti escapes, Gabby helps Duke escape too, so that he can follow the outlaw.
- Duke follows the outlaw to a pool of poison water, where Zanti dies without Duke having to fire a shot.
- Unaware that Zanti is dead, his gang tries to kidnap Ruby, hoping to exchange her for their boss.

Not to fear, Duke steps in and saves the day.

It's not as bad as it sounds, but not much better either. A few mistakes cropped up. In one chase scene, Ruby's horse falls down. In the distance, visible between the trees, is a modern bridge. Wayne, at one point, becomes an authorized agent of the law, but he wears his badge on the right side, not the left which is correct.

Such mistakes were one reason Tatum gave it a bad review: "This film is so sloppily edited and written, it is a dud. The first ten minutes alone show Wayne and bandits in nighttime scenes intercut with stock footage obviously shot in the day."[61]

There were some improvement in the art of stunt work, particularly in fistfights, but Wayne and Canutt still had not yet perfected it. As Miller wrote in 1976, "The Wayne-Canutt technique may have had its inception at Monogram, but full fruition definitely did not occur until Republic."[62]

As Doepke (2008a) noted, "It's Wayne at his likable peak and Hayes' Gabby is about three-quarters complete. Some great stunts, as expected from a cast that includes maestro Yakima Canutt, along with a leading lady who really can ride."[63]

In developing his acting skills, John Wayne was sometimes awkward and sometimes comfortable in front of the camera. Sometimes he was both in the same movie, as in Lone Star's 'Neath the Arizona Skies. The 52-minute film was a remake of a 1933 movie, Circle Canyon with Buddy Roosevelt. It sometimes shows up under a slightly different title, 'Neath Arizona Skies.

John Wayne (left) and two unidentified cowboys get the drop on Yakima Canutt (center) in 'Neath the Arizona Skies (1934).

Others in the cast included Sheila Terry, Shirley Jean Rickert (better known for her work in the Little Rascals shorts), Jack Rockwell. Its director, Harry Fraser (using the pseudonym Weston Edwards) plays one of the villain's henchmen. The script was provided by Burl Tuttle. The movie was shot at some of Lone Star's favorite locations: Santa Clarita, Newhall, Placerita Canyon and the Santa Clara River. It was released on December 5, 1934.

Duke is at his best when interacting with a small child. He was still a bit awkward in his love scenes. This movie has the added advantage of Gabby Hayes in the early stages of his sidekick persona, plus Buffalo Bill, Jr. (aka Jay Wilsey) in a supporting role. Davis noted that Wilsey grew up in Wyoming and was expert at riding bucking horses.[64]

Duke plays cowboy Chris Morrell, the unofficial guardian of a small Indian girl named Nina. The youngster is set to share in the profits from tribal oil rights, if Wayne can either find her real parents or establish himself as her legal guardian. Duke knows Nina's mother died two days after the little girl was born, but he suspects that her father—a cowboy who soon drifted away—may still be alive. The duo hit the trail to find him. Hard on their tracks is the Sam Black gang, outlaws intent on kidnaping the girl so they can embezzle her oil money. Yakima Canutt plays the gang leader.

Duke and Nina escape the first attack, both riding the same horse. Fearful that they will be caught, Duke sends Nina ahead to a friendly ranch while he stays back to delay the outlaws. At one point, Duke is down to just three bullets. He uses these to distract the outlaws, gets into a fistfight with Yakima, ropes another, captures one of the outlaws' horses, and runs the others off. Duke escapes, but is hit on the head in the melee. Eventually he falls from his horse, unconscious.

Nina arrives at the ranch to find its former owner has died. A new man, an unfriendly cuss, treats her rudely until cook Gabby Hayes enters the scene. He takes care of the girl and learns her family history. In town, somebody is robbing the express office. The manager unties himself and alerts the town, telling them that one robber wore a black hat and a checkered shirt. Moments later the bandit is racing from town when he comes upon the unconscious Duke. He changes shirts and hats with Duke and heads away. Along comes leading lady Clara (Sheila Terry). She assumes Duke is the missing outlaw, but helps him anyway. Duke assures her that he is innocent. And, if she will believe him, he adds, "I'll see that my little partner was safe, and then I'll find out who owns this shirt."

That doesn't take long. Clara takes him home to meet her brother, who turns out to be wearing Duke's old clothes. Duke confronts the outlaw, but promises not to hurt him or tell his sister. "Snakes like you usually die of their own poison," Duke says, giving a hint at how the movie will end.

After that, things get a bit confusing. Gabby finds Nina's real father, the two express robbers make a deal to get the girl for the outlaw gang, one thief is killed by the other, and that one is, in turn, shot by Nina's father. Gabby heads to town for help while Duke and Nina's father try to hold off Yakima and his gang. Duke runs out of ammunition again. In fact, he never reloaded after the first fight, so where his new bullets came from is a mystery.

Eventually they get out of this entanglement. Duke survives, but Nina's father does not. Still, the movie ends with Duke, Clara, Nina and Gabby as one happy family. All 'neath Arizona skies.

Generally, this film is entertaining and has excellent stunts, but is mostly just a standard B Western of its day. As one reviewer wrote, "If it wasn't John Wayne, we wouldn't even be watching it."[65] Wayne seems to be maturing as an actor. As Yeltzman wrote, "It is clear watching this film that he was growing in stature as an actor since the very early efforts where he was often a bit wooden."[66]

Roberts and Olson went further. After 'Neath the Arizona Skies, they noted, "his new image was part Western hero, part attitude, and all 'real man.'"[67]

6

1935: *Texas Terror* to *Lawless Range*

In 1935, Monogram joined Mascot, Consolidated Film and some other small production companies that merged into Republic Pictures. John Wayne made the transition to Republic also, as did producers Trem Carr and Paul Malvern. The move allowed Wayne to make more and better movies—and most were Westerns. The only problem, as Levy noted, was that the "narratives were formulaic."[1]

It also provided Republic with a cowboy star, someone comparable to Clark Gable for MGM.[2] In fact, Wayne starred in eight films in 1935 and all were Westerns: *Texas Terror, Rainbow Valley, The Desert Trail, The Dawn Rider, Paradise Canyon, Westward Ho, The New Frontier* and *Lawless Range*.

Each film played another role in Wayne's development as an actor. Goldman noted, "John Wayne really learned his craft during this period—how to dress, stage fight, handle weapons, ride a horse, and all the rest."[3]

In *Texas Terror*, Wayne plays John Higgins, a Lone Star State sheriff who resigns after he's involved in a shootout in which a friend, and the father of the leading lady, is shot to death. The sheriff is under the mistaken impression that he's responsible for the man's death. That creates a problem, since he also becomes the foreman of the ranch that the young lady inherits from her dad.

That's the basic plot of this movie, which was directed by Robert N. Bradbury from his own story. It's got enough clichés to keep it from ever becoming a classic, but the story is still a bit unusual for B Westerns of the period. (This plot was good enough that it was used again in a 1938 movie, *Guilty Trails*, starring Bob Baker in the role of Sheriff Bob Higgins.) It was shot on location on ranches near the San Bernardino National Forest and Newhall, California. The 51-minute film was released on February 1, 1935. It sometimes shows up on DVDs in a 49-minute version.

Three men rob an express office, shooting and wounding the agent. Sheriff John Higgins (Wayne) hears the shots and quickly chases after the outlaws. After Duke shoots one off his horse, the other bad guys seek refuge in a cabin along the trail, only to find that rancher Dan Matthews (Frank Ball) is already there. Matthews gets the drop on one, but the second villain shoots and kills the rancher through the window.

About that time, Duke arrives and starts shooting into the house. The villains take most of the money from the express bags, and then leave the bag and some of the money beside the rancher's body. They escape through the back, leaving Duke still shooting at the house. Our hero eventually notices that no more shots are coming his way. He cautiously approaches and finds Dan Matthews dead.

Duke returns to town and resigns. The locals give the job back to Ed Williams (Gabby Hayes), the man who held it before Higgins. The old sheriff agrees to hold the job "till you can get a better man." Duke turns into a hermit, living alone in a cabin in the forest. He grows a beard, doesn't bathe, and looks generally unkempt when he emerges to mount his horse. An Indian with a broken leg (Billy Wilkerson) spots him and calls for help. Duke loads him on the back of his horse and takes him to the local Indian camp. Chief Black Eagle is grateful that Duke provided aid to the young Indian. He gives Duke a ring as a sign of their friendship and says, "My people your friend."

Cut to a roadside scene with an overheating auto with a driver and a young lady, Bess Matthews (Lucile Browne). The driver goes to get some water from a nearby pool, using a bucket that is already conveniently placed beside the water. As he pours water into the car's radiator, Bess gets out to look at wild flowers nearby. While she's away, five villains attack and shoot the driver. The villains take an express bag from the car and race by Duke as they escape. He pursues and gets to the rider who carries the bag. After that, the tables are turned. The villains start chasing Duke in an attempt to get the express bag back.

Duke escapes by riding his horse over a steep ridge. He falls off as the horse stumbles, but regains his footing and looks to shoot any villains who peek over the ridge. Instead, he stumbles upon Bess, who first raises her hands as if captured and then faints. Duke takes her to the car, drives it away from the villains, and sends her on her way to town. As all of this occurs, Bess spots the unusual ring that Duke is wearing.

Bess describes the outlaw to Sheriff Gabby before leaving for her ranch. After she leaves, Dirty Duke walks in with the express bag and gives it to Gabby. Gabby talks Duke into cleaning up and helping Bess get her ranch going again. Duke is skeptical, but agrees to give it a try. That's how he becomes her foreman. Another employee is quickly added to the staff, a woman named Aunt Martha (Fern Emmett) who is described as the "best cook in the area."

This happy arrangement lasts for three months, during which time Duke stocks the range with horses. Bess wonders why Duke has been so standoffish, and Duke tells her, "Someday you're going to hate me. It's inevitable. When that time comes, I'm leaving this part of the country for good." But he agrees to take Bess and Aunt Martha to the Halloween dance in town. It will be the first time that any of the three have come to town since Bess' arrival. At the ranch house, Bess tells Martha that Duke has been acting strange. Martha responds, "Grown men act like jackasses when they're in love."

Soon after arriving at the dance, Duke feels something in the pocket of the pants he has rarely worn. It's his Indian ring; he quickly puts it back on his hand. The express office man is in charge of taking money at the door of the dance. He tells Duke and Gabby that the Martin boys paid for their tickets with marked money from the robbery. Duke asks both of them to keep the information quiet.

While Bess is dancing with businessman Joe Dickson (LeRoy Mason), he tells her that Duke killed her father. She thanks him for telling her the truth, noting that everyone else in town "all made a fool of me." Meanwhile, Duke follows the Martin brothers and overhears them plotting another robbery while those at the dance are busy with the cow-milking contest. He returns to the express man, suggests a plan and gets the combination to the safe in the express office.

Bess approaches Duke and spots the ring he now wears. When he leaves the dance, she follows and sees him opening the express safe to get its money. Duke plans to let the Martins rob the office and follow them to the third person involved in the first robbery. When Bess returns to the dance, the cow-milking contest between Aunt Martha and an bearded elderly man is underway. She asks Dickson to take her back to her ranch.

When Duke and Aunt Martha return, she speaks to Duke alone, saying he was "not only a bandit and a robber, but a murderer as well." She sends him packing with a final message: "I never want to see you again."

The next morning, Duke spots the Martins entering Dickson's office through the back door. When Dickson leaves, Duke follows him to the robbers' hideout where Dickson hatches a plan to rob Bess of the 1000 horses Duke has brought to her ranch. Duke goes to Black Eagle for help and they plan a trap for the villains. They spring it the next day and rout most of the villains. Dickson and the Martins escape. Duke chases the two brothers, knocks both from their horses, and gets one to confess to the express robbery. He also names Dickson as the person who really shot Dan Matthews.

Dickson rides to Bess's ranch, where he tells her that Duke tried to rustle her horses. Duke enters the ranch house from the rear and tells Dickson that he's under arrest for the murder of Dan Matthews. Matthews dives through a window to escape, but that only delays his capture.

The next scene has Bess and Aunt Martha working with yarn, while Bess mentions that Duke has been gone nearly two months (no real explanation as to why). Black Eagle and Bess' new foreman agree to take her to his cabin. After waiting two hours for Bess to return, the Indian chief and the foreman give up and leave. Otherwise, they might still be there.

But the duo's departure still leaves film historians with a mystery. The actor playing Chief Black Eagle has yet to be identified. According to studio records, the actor playing the chief was Jay Wilsey, aka Buffalo Bill, Jr. But Wilsey actually played a character named Blackie Martin. No other

John Wayne (right) with LeRoy Mason in *Rainbow Valley* (1935).

clues have been listed for the actor playing Chief Black Eagle, and later historians have been unsuccessful in learning who he was.

The movie gets generally good reviews from B Westerns fans. Smith wrote that it was "a cut above the average. It has a good plotline and plenty of action crammed into its 51-minute running time."[4]

Further, Duke's acting skills are still improving. This film requires him to go through a range of emotions. He doesn't always get them all right, but he's making progress. Doepke wrote, "He's actually a better actor than these [movies] required, and I wouldn't be surprised this was a feature where the great John Ford caught Wayne's potential before elevating him to the A-class in *Stagecoach*."[5]

When you get in too much of a hurry, even John Wayne can get confused. That appears to be the problem with *Rainbow Valley*, a quickly made Western for Monogram and Wayne's second movie released in 1935. Stanfield noted that the film was the beginning of a decline in quality for Wayne's Westerns: "Monogram's inferior product was not simply the result of a lack of concern for aesthetics but was symptomatic of an independent sector that was underfinanced, irregular and anarchic."[6]

Others in the cast included Lucile Browne, Gabby Hayes, LeRoy Mason, Lloyd Ingraham, Buffalo Bill, Jr. (Jay Wilsey), Frank Ball, Bert Dillard and an antique car named "Nellie." None are particularly effective, including Nellie, but the problem is a confusing script, not the acting. Robert Bradbury was the director, using a Lindsley Parsons story. The 52-minute film was released on March 15, 1935.

It starts with an irrelevant opening scene with Duke buying a new gun, outfit and horse. The scene only lengthens the movie and plays no role in the plot. That is an odd problem, given that the story was by Lindsley Parsons, a veteran B Western writer who usually provided a better storyline. His scripts usually had an intriguing opening scene that pulled the audience in. He misses on this one, but later provides a few good scenes. One comes early when Gabby stops Duke on the road, seeking water for Nellie. Wayne surrenders his entire canteen, only to discover that Nellie is an automobile.

Soon afterwards, Wayne meets the local postal worker (Lucile Browne), who refuses to have anything to do with him because he got into a fight soon after arriving in town. "Whadda you think about that?" Gabby says. "She's fallen for you already."

Duke takes a job as foreman of a road-building crew, where he occasionally flashes bits of philosophical wisdom such as, "Some men are like books written in a strange language, and that makes it awfully hard to read them." More frequently, he fights off attacks while looking for a way to blast a route through a canyon wall. In the first attack, Wayne and his crew fight off most of the bad guys while Gabby (driving Nellie) chases the rest, tossing sticks of dynamite. We never do see how he lights the fuses and drives at the same time.

Without supplies, the crew breaks up and the road remains unfinished. The bad guys bring in a gunman (Butch Galt) who was Duke's cellmate in prison. Wayne joins the outlaws and agrees to destroy the road, but double crosses the crooks by using their dynamite to finish blasting out the road.

When the locals discover that Duke is an ex-con, they taking off on foot to kill him. Fortunately, every citizen in town forget to ride their horses, and Duke has time to set all of his dynamite charges before they reach him.

One chase scene has an improbable bit of movie history, with two actors doubling for each other. The switcheroo occurs when Chris Morrell (Wayne) jumps from his horse to a railroad cart to catch Sam Black (Canutt). In that jump, Canutt doubles for Wayne and performs the leap. Meanwhile, Wayne plays bad guy Black and doubles for Canutt.

Anyway, Gabby discovers a long-lost letter from the governor which clears Duke. He comes to the rescue in Nellie, pulled by a team of horses because the car ran out of gas.

If all of this sounds a bit episodic, it was. By the end of the film, everything seems to be a patchwork of ideas, with the plot seemingly created as the film was shot. As Waltz wrote, the whole thing "is presented humorously, making the predictable story and obvious conclusion easier to watch."[7]

Still, Duke was working hard. As Goldenberg wrote, the movie featured "a committed performance from John Wayne, ... meaning that while the movies themselves were by no means works of art, John Wayne was always good, as he always seemed to be committed to the movie even if he knew that it wasn't supposed to be an A-level movie."[8] This one added to Wayne's résumé and experience. Otherwise, he didn't get much out of it.

One thing seemed consistent about Duke's early films: Our hero constantly stumbled into trouble and needed a little luck to clear his name. That's the basic premise behind the 1935 film *The Desert Trail.*

Mary Kornman was the female lead. She got her start in acting at the age of five, working in "Our Gang" comedies. Others in the cast included Paul Fix, Eddy Chandler, Carmen Laroux, Lafe McKee, Al Ferguson and Henry Hall. Lindsley Parsons provided the story and the screenplay. The

John Wayne with Mary Kornman in *The Desert Trail* **(1935).**

title is a puzzler, since this film has nothing to do with the desert. It is a Lone Star Production directed by Lewis D. Collins, using the pseudonym of Cullen Lewis.

Shooting for the 54-minute film took place at some of Lone Star's favorite locations: Santa Clarita, Kernville, the Trem Carr Ranch and the Walker Ranch near Newhall. The movie was released on April 22, 1935. It's a remake of the 1931 film *The Ridin' Fool*, starring Bob Steele.[9] Aboard a stagecoach, poker player John Scott (Wayne) catches the somewhat rotund dealer (Eddy Chandler) cheating. Instead of wanting restitution, he merely warns him that he'll get caught in town if he continues to deal like that. It quickly becomes apparent that the two men are partners headed for a rodeo in Rattlesnake Gulch. Duke is the rodeo rider, hoping to win some money at the cowboy event.

The two continue their conversation, revealing a little more about both personalities. They were run out of the last town because of some shenanigans involving a young lady. The inept card dealer, Kansas Charlie, accepts part of the blame. "Ever since I've been able to tip my hat, women have had a weakness for me," he explains. Duke suggests that Kansas could avoid much trouble by simply not talking to women. Kansas agrees. "It's talk that always gets you in trouble with a woman," he says. "They always think you mean more than you say."

On the outskirts of town, the stagecoach stops at a house, and a pretty woman comes out the front door. She stops briefly, pulls up her skirt to show a shapely leg, and makes some adjustments to her clothing. Then she joins them as a passenger. Wayne immediately starts talking with her passenger, while Kansas Charlie sits tight-lipped on the seat across from them. When the woman becomes curious about Kansas' behavior, Duke explains that his partner was scalped as a child and lost his ability to speak. He then adds that the scalping left the man bald.

The latest comment brings Kansas out of his self-imposed silence.

He explains to the young lady, Juanita (Carmen Laroux), that he's not bald but merely has a "high forehead." He tips his hat to prove his point. Now he tries to impress Juanita. He mentions that he has a great deal of money, but doesn't carry his cash with him. Most of it, he explains, is waiting for him at the Rattlesnake Gulch Casino. The stage reaches Juanita's house and she gets off. As she leaves, both men believe that they have a date with her later in the day. Juanita's house is familiar to fans of Duke's early films: It was seen as the Matlock ranch house in *The Star Packer* (1934). It was also used as Malgrove's house in *Blue Steel* (1934).

Duke plans to win the rodeo to impress Juanita, adding, "You won't stand a chance." Kansas believes he has a good chance to win some money in a poker game. At a poker table, he hears disturbing talk from the other cowboys in the room. According to these rodeo rider, the rodeo's promoter was only paying 25 cents on the dollar for those who won a purse.

Kansas leaves to pass the news on to Duke. The news disturbs Duke, who has had a successful day by tallying $900 in winnings so far. Rather than trying to keep riding, the duo head to the rodeo office to check on his money. They don't seem to notice the two guys lounging outside of the office.

Duke goes inside and asks the manager, Farnsworth (Henry Hall), for his $900. Farnsworth first offers 25 cents on the dollar, but eventually increases his offer to $250. Duke refuses to accept the partial settlement. Instead, Kansas goes behind the bar separating the men and gets the money out of the open safe. Both men then go outside, get on horses and race away.

Their departure opens the way for the two men lounging outside to go inside. They pull their guns and ask for all the money. Farnsworth pretends to comply, but reaches inside the safe for a gun. The robbers shoot him, take the rest of the money and escape.

The gunshot draws a crowd who find the dead manager. Somebody remembers seeing Duke and Kansas ride off, and the entire crowd thinks our heroes are the villains. The Rattlesnake Gulch sheriff quickly organizes a posse and they take off in pursuit.

The boys, unaware that they're being chased, ride up to a cabin where they've apparently been staying. Kansas starts cleaning up to keep his date with Juanita, but Duke insists that he's going to go see her. The debate is settled when Kansas takes a swing at Duke and misses. Duke overpowers him and ties him to a chair.

Duke leaves and heads to meet Juanita. Soon after his departure, the sheriff and his posse arrive to find Kansas tied up. On the trail, Duke realizes he's forgotten something. He turns around and returns to the shack. As he approaches, he sees the horses of the posse. He sneaks to the back of the building and overhears Kansas, inside, denying involvement in the robbery. The sheriff doesn't believe poor Kansas, and suggests trying and hanging him quickly. "Maybe we can try him this afternoon and hang him right away and save the county the expense of feeding him," the sheriff says.

Kansas gives up trying to persuade them and asks that they give his bankroll and watch to Juanita. When the posse members lead him outside, Duke gets the drop on them and orders them to throw down the watch and money. The sheriff complies and the posse leaves.

Cut to a scene with the real bad guys dividing their money. One villain, Pete (Al Ferguson), leaves to visit Juanita. Realizing he has money, Juanita proceeds to snuggle up to him on her couch until she and Pete hear someone (Duke) riding up. Juanita quickly hides Pete in her closet and she invites Duke inside. Duke is curious about the extra horse outside, but Juanita assures him that it's hers.

In his first move to woo the young lady, Duke offers her Kansas' watch. She modestly says that she can't accept it, so Duke quickly adds that he'll just keep it then. She proceeds to lavish her affections on Duke, just as she had Pete, until Duke offers to take her out.

Before she can answer, Kansas rides up with his hands tied behind his back. He and Duke start fighting over the girl, but the only damage is that they break Kansas' watch in Duke's pocket. They stop fighting when they realize what's happened. That's a signal for villain Pete to come out of the closet with his gun drawn. Pete robs both of them and locks both heroes in the closet.

Once in the closet, our heroic duo overhears Pete and Juanita talking and realize Pete is one of the real bandits. They start arguing, Kansas takes a swing at Duke, and that leads to more fighting. Pete leaves, refusing to take Juanita with him.

Once Pete's gone, Juanita opens the closet door and finds them fighting. The only major damage from their actions is that they are messing up her clothes. She stops the fight and throws both of them out of the house.

Outside, the duo sees the sheriff and his posse approaching. They quickly leave as the posse starts shooting at them. One of the gunshots hits Kansas' horse, and it falls to the ground. Duke, riding beside his partner, grabs Kansas and pulls him to his own horse. Then Duke quickly reins his mount to behind some bushes to hide from the posse. The posse realizes they've lost the duo and return to Juanita house. Duke and Kansas turn their attention to corralling the real thieves while recovering Duke's $900 and Kansas' watch. But they figure it's best that they not travel together. Duke plans to go to Poker City to get his money back. Kansas changes the shape of his hat, reverses his collar, and prepares to go to town as a minister.

In town, Kansas introduces himself to the sheriff (Lafe McKee) as the Reverend Harry Smith. Kansas quickly spots one of the real thieves, Jim (Paul Fix), in the crowd with the sheriff, but tells the sheriff that the gentleman was a member of his "congregation" in Rattlesnake Gulch. Kansas and Jim enter a store run by Jim's sister Anne (Mary Kornman). Blooper: Jim introduces Kansas to Anne, but Anne greets him as "Mr. Smith"—even though she has never seen him before.

Outside, a man runs up to tell the sheriff the stage was robbed. That announcement causes the sheriff to increase his suspicions of strangers in town. His concern increases when Duke rides in and introduces himself as John Jones. The sheriff complains that the town is getting too many strangers named Smith or Jones.

Still, the sheriff has no reason to arrest Mr. Jones, who now just happens to enter the store visited by Kansas. He approaches the counter just in time for Jim to say that he has to leave. Anne says that's fine, because Mr. Smith will see that she gets home safely. Duke responds that his name is Jones, not Smith. Anne quickly reaffirms her previous statement that Mr. Smith will see her home and asks if he needs something from the store.

Duke spots something on a high shelf behind her and asks for a bottle of nerve tonic. Anne uses a ladder to reach the top shelf, while Duke admires her attractive back side. She comes down, hands Duke the bottle and asks if there will be anything else. Duke says he thinks he might need a second bottle. She repeats the process, climbing the ladder to reach the top shelf. This time, though, Duke goes behind the counter and kicks the ladder out from under her. She falls but he catches her, and asks, "Shall we dance?" Duke puts her down and bends down behind the counter to retrieve something. He's still there when Kansas comes in. Duke hears Kansas speaking, stands up and greets him. When he learns that Kansas is there to escort Anne home, Duke insists that he do the honors. "I wish I had your nerve, Mr. Jones," Kansas says. "That's easy," Duke replies, and hands him a bottle of nerve tonic. They almost start to fight again, but Anne intervenes and says that both may take her home.

Outside, Pete and Jim are talking about the two new strangers in town. Jim is concerned but Pete discounts the problem, and they shift the conversation to the next gold shipment schedule for the local stagecoach.

Cut back to the store, with Duke entering again. The script lets us know that at least a day has passed since Duke and Kansas escorted her home. Mary greets Duke by asking if he's there more for more nerve tonic, noting that he purchased five bottles the previous day and "almost cleaned me out." No, Duke replies. He's there looking for Parson Smith. As Duke speaks, Kansas enters the store.

The duo go outside where Duke tells Kansas he saw the two thieves ride out of town. They mount their own horses and go after the villains. They end up being a little late. They arrive in time to see the two villains robbing the stage of its gold and taking valuables (including a watch) from the passengers. Our heroes race toward the robbery, forcing the villains to leave in a hurry. Their quick departure startles the horses pulling the stage to break into a run. The driver is shot, so nobody is in control of the stage. The duo split, with Kansas chasing the bad guys and Duke chasing the runaway stage. The villains split, creating a problem for Kansas, but he chooses to go after Jim and catches him.

Jim says Pete was the mastermind. He asks Kansas not to tell his sister. Kansas agrees, noting that Jim helped in town by not telling the sheriff they were wanted for robbery and murder. Kansas recovers their money and the watch and lets Jim go.

Duke is chasing the coach. He rides alongside it, jumps from his horse onto the team, and grabs the reins to stop it. The passengers get out to thank him for saving their lives, and they mention that they were robbed of a watch and money.

Duke drives the stage into town, creating two continuity errors in the process. First, he mounts the left side of the stage (remember, the driver is slumped over on the right side) and drives off, leaving his horse behind. However, when the stage arrives in town, Duke's horse is tied on behind the stage. Second, when the stage arrives, Duke is driving it from the right side of the coach. The driver is now slumped over on the left side.

Either way, Duke gets the stage into town and stops in front of the sheriff. The passengers get off and tell the lawman that Duke is a hero, prompting the sheriff to say his earlier suspicions regarding Duke must have been wrong. Kansas joins the crowd gathered around the passengers, as does Pete the villain. Pete tells the sheriff that our heroes are wanted for murder. Anne, also in the crowd, says she doesn't believe it. But one passenger recognizes his watch in Kansas' possession. Duke and Kansas are thrown in jail. Behind bars, the two men return to their bickering, arguing over who's to blame for their predicament. Kansas tries to strike the first blow, but misses. This time he hurts his own hand.

Jim enters the family store and hears that the two men are in jail. He tells his sister that they didn't do it, Anne agrees, and Jim pauses to write a note to tell them how to escape from jail and hide from the law. A package is thrown through the window of the jail. Duke and Kansas open it to find a gun and Jim's letter. They take the gun and successfully get out of the jail. The sheriff enters his office and quickly realizes his prisoners are gone. He goes outside, sees them on the street and starts shooting. Again, we have a minor continuity problem. When our heroes first escape from jail, Duke was wearing a gunbelt, but had no gun. In the second scene, where the sheriff spots the duo, our hero has a gun in his holster.

He needs it too. When the sheriff starts shooting at them, Duke and Kansas take refuge in Anne's store. Elsewhere, Pete and Jim are talking about their crimes. Jim wants to confess, and turns to walk toward the sheriff to surrender. Pete shoots Jim in the back. Anne sees Jim fall and rushes to his side. Pete heads to the town's bank.

Kansas and Duke use the diversion to escape into the attic of the store. With the sheriff and his deputies providing a diversion, Pete robs the bank. Kansas and Duke emerge from a second-floor window above the store and see Pete mounting his horse and racing out of town. Our heroes jump to the ground, grab horses and take off in pursuit. About the same time, the banker finds the sheriff and tells him about the robbery. The posse heads off in pursuit too. What follows is a triple-chase scene: the posse chasing Duke and Kansas while our faithful heroes chase Pete. And continuity is simply discarded in the process.

Pete fires his six gun 13 times over the next few minutes—nine while running from Duke and Kansas, once after Duke hits his horse, and three more times after he runs inside the house serving as his hideout. Kansas finds a good spot to shoot and fires his gun often enough to keep Pete busy. Duke rides to the back of the house and leaps from his horse and through a window. He knocks Pete out. But the posse chasing all three men is getting closer. Duke moves to a window and starts firing his gun to hold them off.

At Anne's store, Jim is stretched out on a sofa while a doctor and Anne tend to his wound. He gets them to stop long enough to confess that he shot and killed the rodeo promoter. Anne and another nearby man go outside, climb into a buggy and head for the outlaw's hideout.

Meanwhile, Duke is still shooting out the window while Kansas tries to wake up Pete. "Why'd you have to hit him so hard for?" Kansas asks. Anne arrives and tells the sheriff that Jim has confessed. The sheriff orders his deputies to stop firing.

In the house, Duke notices that the gunfire has stopped, but there's not much he can do to take advantage of the ceasefire. He's out of ammunition. He sees the sheriff, Anne and two others approach the cabin. Duke and Kansas raise their hands to surrender, but the sheriff says he's made a mistake. Pete is arrested.

In the final scene. Kansas, still in his Reverend Smith persona, pretends to be marrying Duke and Anne. Before he gets deep into the ceremony, Duke interrupts him: "Get out of here. I want this thing to be legal."

I suppose it was. But by then, the duo had been bickering so much, and gotten into so much trouble, that the finale was just a bit too easy. They got out of trouble due more to luck than to anything that they actually did.

The movie generally gets bad reviews. One fan wrote, "Sadly, the exciting action elements we find in many other Lone Stars are sorely missing here. No Yakima Canutt. Cheap and bad uses of stock footage of riders falling off horses. No George Hayes."[10] Another agreed, writing, "It just doesn't gel enough, or go anywhere interesting beyond the occasional funniness."[11] Ricci, Zmijewsky and Zmijewsky noted, "There are some good rodeo sequences."[12] They didn't mention that it was stock footage from the rodeo scenes of *The Man from Utah* (1934).

Doepke noted, "This one gave me a lot more chuckles than I ever expected, and I may be wrong, but I don't think Wayne ever again reached quite this level of relaxed comedic acting."[13] Indeed, Wayne seemed to be getting better, and there was a reason for it: Paul Fix. The actor, who was also a former playwright and director, stood behind the camera for each of Duke's scenes and offered suggestions between takes.[14] As Davis noted, "Duke learned how to deliver lines from Fix and under his guidance developed the halting cadence that became a trademark."[15]

The Lone Star production *The Dawn Rider* was Duke's fourth 1935 Western. It was directed by Robert N. Bradbury from a story by Lloyd Nosler. Marion Burns was the female lead. It was shot on location in Santa Clarita, the Iverson Ranch near Chatsworth and the Trem Carr Ranch. The 53-minute film was released on June 20, 1935. Today it sometimes shows up on DVD under the title *Cold Vengeance*. It was a remake of a 1931 Tom Tyler movie, *Galloping Thru*, directed by Nosler. It was later remade again as *Western Trails* (1938) with Bob Baker—and again in 2012 as *Dawn Rider* in a 94-minute version that starred Christian Slater and Jill Hennessy (from TV's *Crossing Jordan* and *Law & Order*). The modern version retains the title of Duke's film, even though the title has nothing to do with the movie itself.

It opens with an undertaker (Nelson McDowell) complaining to a townsman named Ben (Reed Howes) about a lack of business. His spirits pick up when he hears shots coming from the saloon. The two men arrive at the swinging doors just as one man runs and hides in a wagon. Another comes out, looking to shoot the runaway.

Ben disarms the gunman and makes him dance in the street by peppering shots into the ground. Duke rides up, dismounts and watches it all with a smile. When the dancing gunman falls to the ground, Ben orders him out of town and throws him into a mud puddle in the street. Duke saunters over and says to Ben, "You must be the joker in the deck."

"Well, I ain't the queen," Ben replies.

"Well, I'm not so sure," Duke says. "You're acting like an old woman."

Ben goes for his gun, apparently forgetting that he emptied it while making his victim dance. That doesn't matter, because Duke beats him to draw—pointing his gun at Ben before the other man can clear leather. Both men then toss their guns to the side and start fighting. Eventually, Duke stops the fight, saying, "You got me licked, fellow."

"That's not what my jaw tells me," Ben replies.

Laughing, the two men go inside and have a drink together. Duke introduces himself as John Mason. Ben, it turns out, works for John's father Ben Mason, who runs the local freight company. The duo head for the freight office, but stop to talk briefly with a young lady, Alice (Marion Burns).

They enter to find a robbery in process. Their

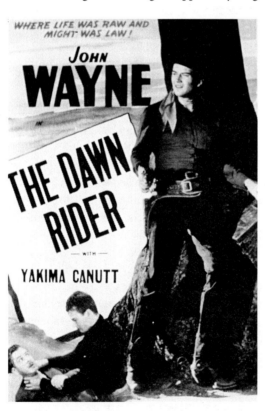

Poster for *The Dawn Rider* (1935).

arrival gives Dad a chance to get his gun from the safe. He gets the drop on one thief, but is shot by another. The robbers run off, while John and Ben rush to Dad's side. Dying, Dad tells Duke that he was shot by a man wearing a polka dot handkerchief. Duke's fans will recognize the "polka dot handkerchief" as an element from his 1934 film *Blue Steel.*

Duke races outside and shoots one escaping outlaw. Then, doubling for Duke, Yakima Canutt does a neat leaping rear mount of his horse and chases after the others. The outlaws shoot Duke off his horse; he manages to shoot one more outlaw before he passes out.

Ben finds the wounded Duke and takes him to Alice's ranch. There the local sawbones bandages him up. Back at the saloon, the man who shot Duke's dad is talking to the saloon owner, the real leader of the gang. They decide Duke should be killed so that he can't identify them.

Cut back to Alice's house, where Duke is still recovering. Ben is there too, and not just because Duke is wounded. Ben really wants Alice to marry him; he awkwardly kisses her before leaving, catching her by surprise.

One of the villains sees Ben depart, draws his gun and enters the house. He holsters the gun when he sees Alice. Alice takes a moment to introduce him to Duke as her brother Rudd (Denny Meadows). Soon afterwards, Ben is driving freight into town when four villains rob him. He drives on to town and tells folks he's been robbed, losing the engagement ring he bought for Alice. One of his listeners, Rudd, has the ring in his pocket.

Alice scans a catalogue and sees an engagement ring circled. Duke tells her not to throw the catalogue away; he's been looking for a gift for someone, something that they can wear for a long time. Alice smiles hopefully, but as Duke continues it becomes apparent that he's talking about buying a new pair of boots for Ben.

Rudd rides with Ben to see Alice and Duke. When they arrive, Duke spots Rudd wearing a polka dot handkerchief. Later, at the saloon, Duke is talking to the owner and Rudd. He tells the two villains that he will start the day's freight run earlier than usual to throw off the bandits. When he leaves, two of the bandits climb into the back of the wagon and hide. In the freight office, Duke and his driver Pete (Earl Dwire) are rigging up a "surprise" in the strongbox they will be carrying. When they climb on the wagon, Duke spots movement in the back and knows the men are there.

Outside of town, Duke and Pete stop the wagon and force the two villains in the back to take over the duties as driver and guard. Sure enough, they soon round a bend in the road and a group of robbers start shooting. Duke returns fire and hits one of the villains. One of the other villains on the wagon is shot by his own gang. Duke ends up in a fistfight with the other. Duke wins that fight and shoots another thief off his horse. As the wagon passes beneath a tree, he grabs a limb and climbs into the branches. When two more villains pass below, still chasing the wagon, he drops down and knocks one off his horse. By then, Pete has been shot. Duke chases the runaway wagon and stops the horses, but the wagon—complete with strongbox and driver—crashes off a cliff. One of the villains races away. Duke gets on another horse, chases after him and trails him to Alice's ranch, where the bandit swaps horses.

When Duke tells Alice that he's looking for Rudd. When she realizes that Rudd is in trouble, she grabs Duke by both arms and begs him to tell her what the problem is. That's when Ben rides up and sees the two in a semi-embrace. He misreads what's going on and rides away.

Duke follows Rudd to the saloon and faces the thief. Ben arrives soon afterwards and Rudd changes the topic—telling Duke to stay away from his sister. Further, he gives Duke one hour—until four—to leave town or be shot on sight. Duke turns to leave and stops in front of Ben, but Ben refuses to talk and Duke leaves. Rudd goes up to Ben and further incites him about Duke and Alice.

Duke goes to his room, reloads his gun and gets ready for the show-down. Ben arrives and throws a punch at Duke. Duke refuses to fight back, saying, "You've got me licked." Alice enters the room and pleads for Rob's life, saying she doesn't want anything to happen to either of them. Duke leaves to saddle his horse, while Ben tells Alice that he won't let Duke harm her brother. When she leaves, he unloads Duke's guns.

Duke returns and tells Ben about the scene at the ranch and that Rudd killed his father. He says goodbye and rides toward town. Ben paces about the room and finally decides to follow Duke.

In town, the two remaining villains prepare to ambush Duke, with Rudd hiding behind a barrel in an alley and Yak prepared to shoot from a second floor window. They wait while Duke walks down the center of the street. Ben arrives, sees Rudd ready to shoot, and shoots the thief himself. Yakima shoots Ben. Duke tries to shoot the saloon owner, but quickly realizes his gun isn't loaded.

Instead he climbs to the second floor and disarms the gang leader. After an extended fight, Duke knocks the saloon owner over the second floor railing, with the villain apparently dying as a result of the fall. Duke rushes to Ben's side, where the man apologizes and dies. The only one cheerful about the turn of events is the undertaker, who is seen measuring the saloonkeeper's body.

In the final scene, John Mason and Alice leave the office of the justice of the peace. The board a buggy with a sign that reads **JUST HITCHED UP** and leave town.

That's the end of the movie, but the plot leaves a lot hanging. What was the "surprise" in the strongbox that Duke rigged for the robbers? What happened to Pete, who was shot and went over the cliff with the wagon? As Slocum noted, the movie "doesn't expect you to care any more than they did, and it shows."[16] But the film was wittier than most B Westerns, and Duke seems to be improving as an actor. He delivers most of his lines with a sense of nuance that fits the scene. As Haynie wrote of Duke, "He was genuinely the John Wayne of legend by that time. It took another four or five years for Hollywood to notice, though."[17]

Paradise Canyon is one of the Duke's better pre–*Stagecoach* entries and his last film under the Monogram–Lone Star banner. Others in the cast included Marion Burns, Reed Howes, Earle Hodgins, Gino Corrado, Yakima Canutt and Perry Murdock. The story was written by Robert Emmett Tansey, a veteran B Western writer, using a story provided by Lindsley Parsons. As reviewer Les Adams noted, Tansey "never wrote a plot he didn't get at least five versions out of." Tansey did get a least three versions of this script on the screen: Its plot appeared again in *Arizona Days* (1937, starring Tex Ritter, with Lindsley Parsons as the writer), *The Rangers Round-Up* (1938, starring Fred Scott, and with George Plympton as the writer) and *Harmony Trail* (1944, starring Ken Maynard and Eddie Dean). Tansey is listed as the writer of the latter entry, but under the name Robert Emmett.

The movie was directed by Carl L. Pierson, the first film he did with Wayne. After *Paradise Canyon*, Wayne went on to Republic and better production values.

Filming under the working title of *Paradise Ranch* was done at Santa Clarita, Kernville and the Trem Carr Ranch. It was released on July 20, 1935. It has also been released on DVD under the title *Guns Along the Trail*.

Counterfeiters operate out of Paradise Canyon, Arizona, a small town on the Mexican border. The authorities suspect that the medicine show operator, recently released after a ten-year prison term, is part of the gang.

Duke gains the confidence of the crooks after helping the medicine show escape from a New Mexico town amidst some unpaid bills. He quickly falls for the leader's daughter (Marion Burns) and uses his sharp-shooting skills to become part of the show.

Once they arrive in Paradise Canyon, Duke quickly figures out that the real villain is Curly Joe, a saloon owner who operates his counterfeit operation from a cavern beneath his saloon on the Mexican side of the border. Duke teams up with the Mexican authorities to clean out the nest of thieves.

The movie features two musical numbers, "When We Were Young and Foolish" and "Snap Those Old Suspenders Once Again," both performed by the duet of Perry Murdock and Gordon Clifford. The two also handled the guitar-playing for the tunes.

It did have one more thing going for it in terms on modern audiences. A poster featuring the film appeared in a 1987 episode of the television show *Wiseguy*; that series focused on an FBI agent who infiltrated organized crime. Perhaps its inclusion was an inside joke, since Wayne goes undercover in this film to identify the villains.

This movie has its moments. As Waltz wrote, "Wayne is at his low-budget best," adding that, of these early 1930s movies by Wayne, "This is one of the better ones."[18] What sets the film apart from the run-of-the-mill quickies are Yakima Canutt's excellent stunt work and the characterizations of the medicine show owner.

During a fight scene between Wayne and Yakima, Yakima doubled for Wayne while another stuntman took over Yak's role. Things went well until Yak was knocked down, with his back to the camera, and his hat flew off. The audience gets a brief look at Canutt's balding head in that moment. Yakima later received a letter from a young viewer which read, "Why don't the producers get smart and give you a break, because Wayne must be getting old. He's getting bald."[19] Yak showed the letter to Wayne. After that, Duke insisted that Canutt's bald spot be covered with dark makeup.

Medicine show owner Doc Carter (Earle Hodgins) hawks his 180-proof Indian remedy for a dollar per bottle, while spouting nonsensical rhetoric on a variety of issues and themes. He talks about his own brush with fame by telling others, "Shake the hand that shook the hand of Buffalo Bill." He has sold medicine all his life, he adds, except for a ten-year period: "I took the opportunity to be connected with a government institution for a time." His keen insight on Western expansion included the comment, "Long before man set foot in this canyon, it was uninhabited." His sales pitch includes the value of combining determination and his wonder medicine: "I once knew a man who didn't have a tooth in his head, but he learned to play a bass drum."

Lines like that are too good to resist. Chance noted that actor Earle

Hodgins continued the same type of performances in other films, turning "his carnival barker style of acting schtick into most of his over 300 movie and TV appearances!"[20]

B Western fan Micklon also gave it a good review. "The acting in this movie is very decent, and pretty believable all around. Not one performance was weak in fact. You had good chemistry between the main players, and none of them looked as if they were just there to get paid."[21]

Duke probably learned the value of humor in some Western plots. More importantly, though, he was about to move to Republic Pictures and better production values. That meant he was on the verge of taking a major step toward becoming the John Wayne that today's film audiences remember. As Waltz wrote, "There's plenty to enjoy in this very short Western comedy, and Wayne is at his low-budget best."[22]

Westward Ho is one of the first musical Westerns, the first movie released by Republic, and the first of eight that Wayne did under contract with Republic—at least technically. As Miller noted, the movie "bore the Republic trademark, but in all other aspects it was Monogram, a leftover from the old company before the deluge."[23]

John Wayne cradles Frank McGlynn, Jr., in *Westward Ho* (1935).

It was also one of its most expensive B Westerns of the era, costing around $35,000 to make and taking three weeks of filming.[24] The film turned a tidy profit when it grossed about half a million dollars.[25]

Released in August, it grossed that half-million $500,000 by the end of the year and established Republic as "a power with which to reckon."[26] Republic expected most of Wayne's films to make only a 3-to-1 profit. As Hurst noted, "Republic had hoped for major status from the very beginning but it took a few years to lay the firm foundation of pre-eminence in the B market."[27] Still, by this time, John Wayne was Republic's "leading contract player."[28]

Wayne played John Wyatt, the same character he played in *Paradise Canyon*. Perhaps the studio was trying to established an identifiable character for a series of films, but Duke never used that character name again. The cast also included Frank McGlynn Jr.; Miller noted that McGlynn, "not seen often in Westerns, was a welcome villain."[29] Yakima Canutt and Glenn Strange also had small roles. Roberts and Olson described the cast as "a Monogram family reunion."[30]

Robert Bradbury served as director, using a story provided by Robert Emmett Tansey and Lindsley Parsons. Filming was done on location in the Alabama Hills near Lone Pine and in Owens Valley. It was released on August 19, 1935.

By the mid–1930s, the Hollywood musical was in full swing, but nobody had made much of an effort at blending the genre with a Western plot. That changed with *Westward Ho*, as Duke led a band of singing vigilantes who cleaned up the countryside of outlaws. Duke did none of the singing himself; that was left to the band of riders who joined him. They would pass time around the campfire by harmonizing on a few tunes.

Duke's character is a young man who, as a child, saw his parents killed and his brother kidnaped by outlaws. As an adult, he has sworn "to get the man who killed my parents and stole my younger brother." His younger brother Jim is played by Dickie Jones, who would grow up to play in a number of B Westerns. In most cases, he showed up as the sidekick of the hero. But he was also a talented horseman and did a lot of stunt riding for those same movies.

Unable to get the local government to help him, Wayne forms a group of vigilantes. To identify themselves in battle, they all ride white horses and wear black shirts and white masks. The riders are so successful as the enemies of Buckhorn Trail outlaws that the thieves adopt a more subtle approach to their banditry" They have one of their members join wagon trains heading through the valley.

Wayne goes undercover, joining one of the groups himself. Unknown to him, another newcomer is his brother (Frank McGlynn Jr.), the bandits' spy. Eventually they reunite and fight the outlaws together. The showdown comes in a dramatic fight scene which ends when the bad guys' wagon goes off a cliff.

This was all popular at the time and made a lot of money for the studio. The riding scenes are exciting, and the coordinated outfits of the singing bandits were appealing. But the script was sometimes inconsistent. One bad guy, for example, reports to the head villain that the Duke is hunting him before Duke has even identified who he is.

The singing is pretty bad, sounding more like a Tin Pan Alley chorus than yodeling cowboys. And Duke pretends to serenade Sheila at one point, but the singing is obviously dubbed. Jack Kirk and Bill Bradbury (son of the director) did some uncredited singing for the film, but it's hard to know who did what. But none of that bothered the movie fans of the day. O'Keefe wrote that the film featured "a strong performance from John Wayne."[31]

Wayne continued to make movies for Republic up through 1951, although the relationship between him and the studio was not always pleasant. Still, it was a productive association.

Duke, though. realized that the singing cowboy phenomenon was not for him. That became even more obvious when he made personal appearances and kids would ask him to sing "The Desert Song."[32]

Goldman reported that the problem was twofold, i.e., Wayne was "embarrassed when his horse relieved himself while the audience yelled for Wayne to sing."[33] After that, Wayne angrily went to Herbert J. Yates, president of Republic, and insisted that he do no more singing. As a result, Wayne "did his last lip-synching in *Westward Ho.*"[34] Instead, Republic started looking for a real singing cowboy. They settled on a young man named Gene Autry, and movie history was made.[35] Roy Rogers was another popular singing cowboy at Republic.[36]

In 1936, the animated character Porky Pig starred in a spoof of this film, *Westward Whoa.* Edgar Kennedy followed with a parody of his own, the 1941 short *Westward Ho-Hum.* Both of those were barely a blip in the history of movie Westerns. John Wayne was becoming a star and would last a lot longer.

Miller noted that *The New Frontier* "represented the transition period from Monogram to Republic" for Wayne.[37] Eyman described it as one of the few anti–New Deal films released during the Great Depression, because it featured a group of homesteaders fighting against the building of a dam in their area.[38] The movie took a look at the lawlessness that developed around new towns that sprang up after Oklahoma's Cherokee Strip was opened to settlement. The plot is similar to *The Red Raiders*, a 1927 Ken Maynard Western.

The New Frontier is not one of the Duke's better films, but it still provides a look at the man who was on the verge of becoming a star. It was later remade into another John Wayne entry, 1939's *New Frontier*, one of his Three Mesquiteers Westerns.

Wayne has the lead role of John Dawson. The movie was directed by Carl Pierson, with a script provided by Robert Emmett Tansey. Eyman described the script as "overly ambitious for the short shooting schedule that [the director] had to deal with."[39] Filming was done in the Alabama Hills, Kernville and the Trem Carr Ranch. The movie was released on October 24, 1935. The original movie ran 60 minutes, but it was been edited to 54 minutes for television audiences.

The film is set in 1889 and has an interesting opening sequence. The camera focuses on a book on a library shelf until its title *The New Frontier*, becomes clear. A hand lifts it from the shelf and turns the first few pages, showing the credits for the film. When it cuts to the movie, it repeats the acting credits by showing the actors in their roles. Then it switches to on-screen superimposures to summarize the historical setting, ending with the hand of President Benjamin Harrison signing the Cherokee Strip proclamation.

The original proclamation opening the Cherokee Strip up to homesteaders was actually signed in 1893 by President Grover Cleveland. However, Benjamin Harrison did make a major addition to Cleveland's original decree when he signed a proclamation that prohibited herding or grazing on the land. The addition essentially meant that the land could only by used for farming homesteads, not ranches.[40]

Duke and his dad Milt Dawson settle in one of the new towns, a growing community complete with a new church and a saloon. The saloon and its owner soon become the center of illegal activities, and Duke's dad is called on to help.

Wayne returns from a job as a trail herder to discover that his father has been shot in the back while trying to clean up the town. Duke takes on the job of marshal and orders the saloon closed by six in the evening. The crooks counter by luring him out of town and into a trap, but Wayne turns the tables on the bad guys. Returning to town, he enlists a friend, a feller on the wrong side of the law, to help him battle the bad guys. "He's a great friend, and I'd hate to have him for an enemy," Duke's friend Kit tells the rest of his gang. Besides, Kit has an old score to settle with the local bad guy himself.

Kit's entire gang agrees to be deputized. "Now we can do anything we want," one eager gang member gloats. "Anything he tells us," Kit corrects. A big gun battle erupts, the bad guys are killed, and the saloon burns down while most of the town waits safely in the church. The entire scene is one of a heaven-and-hell comparison that is hard to overlook.

As Eaves noted, the cutting from one scene to the other created "the juxtaposition of the prayer meeting led by the parson with the gunfight between the lawless element and the town's menfolk led by Wayne. A lot of movies, even today, shy away from religious themes that involve actual religious characters but this one shows the irony of prayerful words against a backdrop of killing and the burning of the town."[41]

One thing that distinguishes the film is the lack of Wayne's usual cadre of supporting B Western actors. Neither Yakima Canutt nor Gabby Hayes make an appearance. In their absence, Duke displays flashes of the charisma that would later make him famous, and his acting style is starting to rise above the supporting cast around him. Only leading lady Muriel Evans approaches his level of work. During her career, she frequently appeared in Hal Roach comedies.

The film also tries to take advantage of the popularity of singing cowboy films. Two songs, "The New Frontier" and "Outlaw Range" (both written by Glenn Strange), are in the film, but Duke does not sing in either of them.

The movie has a few minor mistakes. For example, it is set in Kansas, a state with no mountains. Yet snow-capped peaks can be seen at times. A bigger problem is that Duke's "Singing Sandy" character never was much of a success as a singing cowboy. Fortunately, this movie seems to recognize that. If nothing else, *The New Frontier* captured the formula that would make John Wayne famous—a tough cowboy who chased the bad guys.

Let somebody else do the singing.

Although *Lawless Range* was a Republic release, Miller described it as "Monogram through and through."[42] Republic had obtained the movie when it took over the Monogram properties, and the new studio simply withheld it from release for a while.

Directed by Robert N. Bradbury and produced by Paul Malvern, *Lawless Range* features Wayne in the lead role of John Middleton. Yakima Canutt is in the cast and handled much of the stuntwork. It was filmed on location in Santa Clarita, the Alabama Hills, Lone Pine and Vasquez Rocks Natural Area Park and released on November 4, 1935.

The movie opens with Wayne practicing for the Cheyenne rodeo, a project that he abandons when a friend of his father's calls for help. The

John Wayne is held up by Tex Palmer as Charles Brinley (right) and others look on in *Lawless Range* (1935).

rodeo is never mentioned again. The family friend is one of several ranchers in an isolated area known as Pequeno Valley. He and the other ranchers are being forced off their land by a local banker who wants to mine it for gold.

These villains are known as the Butch Martin gang, although we never see Butch Martin. He is a straw man to hide the identity of the real boss. Canutt plays the official leader of the gang, but the plot has him occasionally reporting to an unknown higher-up.

Eventually the movie reveals that the town banker (Frank McGlynn, Jr.) is the real boss of the bad guys. He's out to get the rights to all of the land in the area because he knows that gold lies beneath the surface of all that grassland.

Regardless, these villains are really mean. Not only do they rustle cattle, but they set up a blockade of the town in an effort to starve the citizens into submission. Any wagon trains attempting to take supplies into the town are robbed. Wayne becomes a deputy marshal with an undercover identity of an outlaw named John Allen to help ferret out the evildoers. He tries to get enough information to help the local marshal (Jack Curtis) arrest them.

The Duke makes a friend when he jumps off a cliff into a river to avoid the villains, and then saves Ann from a murderous crossfire. He later gets arrested, under the mistaken impression that he's a member of the gang, and almost lynched, but Ann steps in to speak for him.

Wayne gets supplies through to the town. He also tries to lead a roundup that collects the cattle of all the ranchers and herd them to market in a coordinated cattle drive. The villainous banker gets the ranchers to start the drive early so that his gang can rustle the cattle.

Our hero is captured by the gang and tossed into a cave that's already occupied by Emmett (Earl Dwire), a local rancher who mysteriously disappeared earlier in the movie. The two men are able to escape, although how they recovered their guns remains a mystery. Duke manages to learn the villains' plans and reports them to the marshal. The lawman has a posse just waiting to take advantage of the information. Justice prevails and John and Ann are together in the final scene. Look for Glenn Strange in a small, uncredited role as one of the crooks, but he is not listed in the credits.

There are occasional mistakes. Singing Wayne strums on a guitar as he approaches the town. The guitar disappears when he arrives in town, but shows up again in a later scene. In another instance, he loses two guns from one scene to the next. His hat changes color from white to black in consecutive scenes.

This movie started out as a Monogram–Lone Star release. Most of the crew were the same people who had worked on previous Lone Star productions. By the time it was finished, Republic Pictures got the credit because of Republic's temporary takeover of Monogram in 1935.

The movie includes three songs. "On the Banks of the Sunny San Juan" is supposedly sung by Wayne as he serenades Ann Mason. Jack Kirk actually provided the dubbed singing voice. "Down the Old Dusty Road" is a tune sung by the ranch hands as they herd cattle during a roundup; it is officially credited to a group called "The Wranglers." "The Girl I Loved Long Ago," was written by director Robert Bradbury.

As for John Wayne, his acting was getting better in this one. His singing wasn't.

7

1936: *The Oregon Trail* to *Winds of the Wasteland*

By 1936, Duke Morrison was still a long way from becoming John Wayne. Back at home, he was still Duke Morrison. John Wayne was just a stage name used for making movies. Further, that's the way wife Josephine wanted it. Duke married Josephine Saenz on June 24, 1933, at the home of his close friend Loretta Young and attended by Henry Fonda.[1] It was the start of a rocky marriage.

On the positive side, he was making enough money—more than most people during the Depression—that he could buy a two-story mansion. Josephine liked that, and she became a fixture of local society. But she was ashamed of what Duke was doing to pay the bills. Being an actor, she seemed to think, was not something for people in high society. And as long as John Wayne was just a stage name, maybe most of their neighbors wouldn't know about his profession.

There wasn't much Duke could do about it either. His film career was moving, but he was not moving up. He was still stuck in B movies.

After Wayne's contract with Republic expired in 1935, he was tired of making Westerns and didn't renew with the studio. He actually worked outside of the film industry. He tried his hand at a brokerage firm, as a real estate agent and as a professional boxer, but none of those worked out. He was lured back to films by an offer from a bigger studio, Universal, to appear in non-Westerns. He made seven films in 1936, two of them non–Westerns (*Sea Spoilers* and *Conflict*). Both of the non-Westerns were a chance for Wayne to broaden his acting experiences outside of Westerns.

They may have succeeded somewhat in doing that, but they didn't separate him from the Western genre. Wayne still did five Westerns in 1936: *The Oregon Trail, The Lawless Nineties, King of the Pecos, The Lonely Trail* and *Winds of the Wasteland.*

Sea Spoilers is a naval whodunit about a Coast Guard commander who checks on a yacht that his girlfriend, an actress (Nan Grey), was visiting. Instead of his girlfriend, he finds the body of the yacht's owner and a cache of smuggled seal skins. His girlfriend is missing. Wayne played the lead role of Bob Randall. The movie was directed by Frank Strayer.

Conflict, based on a Jack London story, is about a boxer, Pat Glendon (Wayne), in a local logging and mining camp who is viewed as the camp's champion. He gets a chance to make some extra money by facing a professional named Gus "Knockout" Carrigan (Ward Bond) and throwing the fight to the champion. He goes along with the plan but changes his mind after he meets pretty reporter Maude Sangster (Jean Rogers). The movie was directed by David Howard. Ward Bond went on to appear in a number of Duke's Westerns, many of them directed by John Ford.[2]

In the end, neither of these non-Western films made him a true star. If John Wayne were to become John Wayne, he would have to return to the Western genre. As a result, five Westerns filled out the year.

The authors would love to provide a detailed summary of the plot for *The Oregon Trail*, but we've never had a chance to see this movie. Of course, neither have many other movie fans who are currently alive. No copy is known to exist. Not even an old poster is available, although 40 still photos were discovered in 2013 by a collector.

Wayne starred as Army Captain John Delmont, who takes a leave of absence from his military duties so he can track down the villains who killed his father. To complete that task, he leads a wagon train out west. His father and his troops had been abandoned and left to starve to death in snowy mountains by an evil officer (Ben Hendricks). Wayne gets help from some friends (Yakima Canutt, Frank Rice) and joins with some Mexicans to fight off an attack. Now he attacks the fort which houses the villains.

Scott Pembroke was the director, and the script came from a story provided by the inventive Lindsley Parsons. The 59-minute movie was shot in the Alabama Hills, near Lone Pine, under the working title *Trail's End*. It was released on January 18, 1936.

Duke's co-star was an A-level actress, Ann Rutherford. It was her first film with Wayne; she was his leading lady in two other 1936 Westerns, *The Lawless Nineties* and *The Lonely Trail*. Rutherford later described Wayne as a good man who brought his children to the set. "It didn't surprise me that he became such a big star," she once said. "John had an aura about him—a presence. The only other man I knew who had that was Clark Gable."[3]

The only other major Wayne regular in the film was Yakima Canutt, who had a major supporting role.

The basic premise of the plot is known. A villain ambushes Wayne's father and forces his troopers to die of starvation in the snowy mountains. Wayne goes after the evil man, "falls in love with Ann Rutherford en route, and with the help of Spanish soldiers, defeats and captures the renegades."[4]

Perhaps a copy of *The Oregon Trail* will eventually be discovered in a forgotten Hollywood film vault. Or maybe one is residing in the closet of some shuttered movie house that went under during the Great Depression.

Ann Rutherford was next in Wayne's *The Lawless Nineties*. She later became famous for playing opposite Mickey Rooney in the Andy Hardy series and for playing Scarlett O'Hara's younger sister in *Gone with the Wind*.[5] Rutherford was only 19 at the time the movie was released. She later spoke of the pairing with Duke by saying, "What did I know. I was a kid. I just stuffed a lot of Kleenex in my bra and said, 'I'm a leading lady.'"[6]

Gabby Hayes played her father Major Carter, a transplanted Southern aristocrat. He and daughter Janet are settlers from Virginia who owned

George "Gabby" Hayes, Fred "Snowflake" Toones and Ann Rutherford in *The Lawless Nineties* (1936).

one of those big Wyoming ranches. Comic relief was provided by black servants Moses (Fred "Snowflake" Toones) and Mary Lou Schaefer (Etta McDaniel). They rely mainly on black stereotypes in their efforts to be funny. Toones appeared in hundreds of movies, often as a shoeshine boy or servant. McDaniel was often typecast as a maid or servant. She was the sister of Hattie McDaniel, who became the first African-American to win an Academy Award for her performance in *Gone with the Wind* (1939).

Joseph Kane was the director of this Republic production, the first of three films in which he directed Wayne. Kane was a former film editor who had been working as a director for only a year.[7] The Joseph F. Poland screenplay was based on an original story developed by Poland and Scott Pembroke. The 55-minute film was shot on location at the Trem Carr Ranch and released on February 15, 1936.

The entire story is pure fiction, but it is based on a historical event. Wyoming became the 44th state to join the union on July 10, 1890. The territory had granted women the right to vote in 1869, only one year after it had officially become a territory. Thus Wyoming entered the union as the only state in which women were allowed to vote.[8]

Wyoming was one of six states, all Republican-leaning in their political ideology, that entered the Union during the presidency of Rutherford B. Hayes. Hayes, a Republican, then had the support of GOP majorities in both the House of Representatives and the Senate. Adding six Republican states to the nation increased that partisan support even more.

Duke plays federal agent John Tipton. He and fellow agent Bridger (Lane Chandler) are sent to Wyoming to supervise the statehood vote and ensure that it's done properly. That sounds like an easy enough job, but things quickly get complicated. Somebody believes its to their financial advantage for the area to remain a territory. They will even resort to violence to see that the referendum goes their way. They use dynamite to throw a scare into the locals and kill a local newspaper editor.

The villain is businessman Charles Plummer (Harry Woods), whose henchmen target the federal agents. They know everything that the government is planning because they've tapped into the local telegraph signal. They read the latest communications even faster than they can get to Duke. The villains use that information to kill his partner, but our hero is not scared off. Instead, he starts cutting down the odds.

First. he figures out that the bad guys are monitoring the telegraph lines. He uses that information and sends out some fake telegrams that lure some of the henchmen into a trap. Then he organizes the ranchers and leads them into town on election day. They find the town barricaded by Plummer's men, who have no intention of letting them in to vote. Duke and his group of ranchers and sodbusters win the encounter and—just as in the history books—Wyoming becomes a state.

The plot is better than most B Westerns. After all, not many use the idea of bugging a telegraph wire as part of their story. Fenin and Everson consider *The Lawless Nineties* one of Wayne's "historical Westerns" that he made for Republic, adding, "Republic never made a *really bad* Western in this period, and even the weakest had elements to recommend it."[9]

And Duke's acting skills continue to show improvement. He's gaining both the experience and the skills that will eventually turn him into a Western icon.

Revenge is a dish best served cold. At least that's the theme of *King of the Pecos*, a John Wayne Western set in Texas. And another proverb might also apply: If at first you don't succeed, try again. That's what Wayne has to do in this oater.

Muriel Evans is the female lead, playing Belle Jackson; she more frequently appeared as the female lead in Buck Jones Westerns of the time. Yakima Canutt has a small role as one of the villains and Earl Dwire has an uncredited role as a rancher.

Joseph Kane directed this Republic production, using a screenplay written by Bernard McConville, Dorrell McGowan and Stuart McGowan (based on an original story by McConville). Nevins described the movie as "by far the best of Kane's work with Wayne."[10] Miller agreed, adding, "The Republic stamp of Western quality was now becoming assertive."[11]

Trem Carr was the producer, while Jack Marta handled the camerawork. The stunt team was led by Joe Yrigoyen. The film was shot on location in the Alabama Hills under the working title *West of God's Country*. It was released on March 9, 1936.

The setting is in the Pecos River region of Western Texas. The source of the river is in Eastern New Mexico; it flows along the Texas border before emptying into the Rio Grande. The movie opens with text on screen to establish the situation: "In the seventies, Texas and New Mexico constituted a vast, open cattle range. Land laws and water rights were indefinite and millions of acres of range were often claimed thru a so-called 'right of discovery.'" That pretty much summed up the land and water laws of the area at the time. The ambiguous nature of the law plus the ability to back what one claimed often determined who won and who lost.

Cattle baron Alexander Stiles (Cy Kendall) decides to have Clayborn (John Beck) killed because he refuses to sell his land and water rights for $1000. Stiles turns the dirty deed over to his chief henchman Ash (Jack

John Wayne (right) with Muriel Evans and two unidentified cowboys in *King of the Pecos* **(1936).**

Clifford) and his gang. They kill Clayborn and his wife (Mary MacLaren), but ten-year-old John Clayborn escapes.

The youngster spends the next ten years living with his grandfather in Austin, working on his shooting skills, and becoming a lawyer. Now played by Wayne, he returns to the Pecos and opens a law practice in the town of Cottonwood under the name John Clay. There he tries to use his legal knowledge to stop Stiles' illegal activities. That's not an easy task. By this time, Stiles has a monopoly on the water in the area, giving him control of more than a million acres of range land. And he runs a highly successful rustling enterprise.

Anyway, this is a Western film. That means that Wayne's legal plans don't work, and gunplay and fisticuffs became necessary for the good guys to win. Duke quickly adapts to the town and soon meets two other victims of Stiles' evil deeds, Hank Matthews (Arthur Aylesworth) and Josh Billings (Herbert Heywood). They become victims to a new Stiles tactic, i.e., giving them cattle to stock their ranches and then buying them back at low prices, using worthless notes, when they can't pay to get their herds to water.

By the time Duke figures all of this out, Stiles is wealthy and intimidates most residents of the area. Some of his henchmen even call him "Salamander," an apparent reference to a safe that he bought for his office. That safe is called a "Salamander" because it was made to survive intense heat.

Duke quickly tries his first legal maneuver, serving a summons on Stiles to bring him into court. But that doesn't work. The local judge, it seems, is too scared of Stiles to actually enforce the law against him. That leads to legal move #2: Hank helps Duke by rounding up other cattlemen who have also been victimized by Stiles. To increase the chances of success, Duke also arranges for the judge to have an armed escort for protection. The judge eventually rules against Stiles, returning most of the water rights into the public domain, while Stiles dies in the end.

Roberts and Olson noted that Cy Kendall, who played Stiles, was "a sinister character actor destined in every picture to be done in by his own greed. Indeed, in *King of the Pecos,* (his character) is crushed by his own safe."[12] Duke gets help from a couple of guys who also provide comic relief. One is a bit hard of hearing, and that serves as the premise of the little humor in the film.

Yakima Canutt was underused in this film. His role was a small one, and there were no major stunts. There was a scene in which a horse trips and throws its rider, but it was stock footage used in a number of Duke's early Westerns.

One other stunt looked dangerous. Stiles tries to escape from a shootout by driving a wagon pulled by a team of horses. His ploy fails when the wagon breaks away and crashes off a cliff, while the horses suffer a major spill. The stunt looked more dangerous for the horses than for the actors.

Duke gets to ride an impressive white horse that looks like "Duke," his equine partner in those early Ken Maynard remakes. But the horse gets no billing here.

Republic's budget for Westerns was considerably bigger than those of his early films for Monogram and Mascot. That meant better production and better writing in *King of the Pecos* than in his pre–1936 films. Wayne's acting skills also showed improvement. He was getting closer to becoming the John Wayne who became a Western icon, but he's not there yet. As Pollar wrote, "He seems to just be doing the lines without putting any feeling into them."[13]

Perhaps the biggest impact of this movie for John Wayne was that it laid the foundation for a future role in a more memorable film. Denver argued that Wayne's role in *King of the Pecos* was essentially the classic role he reprised 25 years later in *The Man Who Shot Liberty Valance,*[14] one of John Ford's classics.

The plot, Nevins noted, was "constructed around the conflict between law that exploits the people and law that serves the people, but broke new ground in placing two lawyer characters at the heart of the conflict."[15]

With no reason to waste a good plot, this one was remade four years later as *Texas Terror* starring Don "Red" Barry.

The Lonely Trail (1936) could have been called "When Johnny Comes Marching Home." It's the story of Capt. John Ashley, a Union veteran returning from the Civil War to find his Texas hometown under the dictatorial command of a Yankee carpetbagger. And Duke makes this return to the beat of some good music. The movie co-starred Ann Rutherford, her third appearance with Wayne in a Republic Western. The fine African-American performer billed as Snowflake (Fred Toones) also appeared.

Others in the cast included Bob Kortman, Sam Flint (as the governor of Texas), Dennis Moore (aka Denny Meadows), Jim Toney (aka Jim Tony), Etta McDaniel and Lloyd Ingraham. Jack Kirk and Lafe McKee have small, uncredited roles.

Joseph Kane directed from a script by Bernard McConville and Jack Natteford that was based on a story by McConville. It was released on May 26, 1936.

The carpetbaggers are in full control of the area when Duke returns to his ranch. Because of his Union alliance, he gets a cool reception from the other ranchers, including his former fiancée (Rutherford). He gets an offer to join the local troopers by the head carpetbagger, Gen. Benedict Holden (Kendall). At first, the naive Duke turns down the offer. But

John Wayne with Jim Toney in *The Lonely Trail* (1936).

when he sees the Yankee troops shoot a man in the back (the troops have orders to bring in no prisoners without giving them a chance to escape), he joins the army as a spy.

Over the next few days, he warns the ranchers of impending attacks so successfully that the bad guys get suspicious. They set a trap, which reveals his true allegiance. Arrested and sentenced to death, Duke and a partner plot to escape. Meanwhile, the carpetbaggers plan to shoot him in the escape attempt, while the local ranchers try to rouse support to release him.

Fortunately, all three plots come together at about the same time that the governor arrives to investigate the fort. The bad guys get shot by their own men, Duke is freed and the governor gets rid of the carpetbaggers.

The plot is a notch above the average B Westerns of the day, but nothing great. Still, it was good enough to trigger a remake. In 1941, the plot was reworked into the Three Musketeers' *West of Cimarron*, starring Bob Steele, Tom Tyler and Rufe Davis.

Regardless, this is still one of Duke's more entertaining early efforts. That's partly because of the humor provided by the supporting cast, including one cowboy with a brandy-tasting cough medicine who complains, "Shucks, me without no cough."

One fan gave it a positive review: "This B Western, despite its budget, had a really intelligent script and a talented director and, most of all, some of the best actors available."[16] Another wrote that the movie "is involving and action-packed and loaded with classic early Western character actors of the era, such as Cy Kendall, Sam Flint and the legendary Canutt." He added that the film demonstrated how Wayne and Yakima Canutt "developed the drawback punch that's become the standard in film fights ever since."[17]

Waltz noted that the movie "mixes both comedy and drama with political intrigue, and ranks as one of John Wayne's best Republic films before he went on to superstardom with *Stagecoach*."[18]

The real highlights, though, are some excellent musical numbers. This movie doesn't qualify as a singing cowboy film, because all of the music is provided by the black cast members portraying ex-slaves. Etta McDaniel provided the lead voice. The ex-slaves used a musical code to warn their former masters of approaching Yankees, singing and performing "Suwannee River" and other Stephen Foster songs. To help one rebel leader escape, they fake a funeral while singing "Swing Low, Sweet Chariot."

Duke doesn't sing, and neither do other cowboys. But it may be Wayne's best musical.

In *Winds of the Wasteland* (1936), the Pony Express has folded, driven to bankruptcy by the gelegraph. The riders for the historic mail service have been released, given their pay and two horses each from the company's huge herd. So what can an ex–Express rider do?

If you're John Wayne, you partner with another rider (Yakima Canutt) and use your four horses to form a stage line. That's the opening of Republic's *Winds of the Wasteland*. The Duke runs into a problem, though, when he sinks all of his cash into a stage line running to a ghost town, Crescent City.

Phyllis Fraser plays the female lead, Barbara Forsythe. Fraser was a cousin to a Hollywood legend, Ginger Rogers, and was maid of honor at her wedding.[19] Mack V. Wright was the director. The screenplay was by Joseph F. Poland, who based it on his own original story. The movie was shot on location on the Agoura Ranch, Brandeis Ranch and in the Sacramento River Valley. Some stock footage featuring California's Sierra Madre Mountains was used. The film was released on July 6, 1936. It was later released as a DVD under the title *Stagecoach Run*. The movie was Wayne's last for Republic for a couple of years. He moved over to Universal Studios after this one was completed.

Crescent City, the broken-down site of Duke's new investment, is not a real ghost town. When Duke and his partner arrive, there are still two residents, a doctor and a politician (i.e., sheriff, mayor, treasurer, president of the Board of Health, and porter at the local hotel). By moving into town, the new owners of the stage line double its population. It reaches a grand total of five when Phyllis Fraser arrives. She's an Easterner lured west by the glowing letters from her father, the doctor.

Duke prevents a telegraph crew from drinking poison water. He then talks them into running the magic wire through the town. That's still not enough to keep Duke's stage line afloat, so he goes after a $25,000 contract to carry mail to Sacramento. His only competition is the corrupt stage owner who sold him the worthless route. That becomes the setup for a plot that Roberts and Olson described as "The moneyed interests versus the people."[20]

Naturally, the evil villain takes a number of steps to make sure Wayne cannot enter the decisive race—first attempting to ambush him, then setting fire to his coach, and finally having him arrested for killing one of the arsonists. Wayne's coach makes it to the starting line anyway, and Duke gets out of jail in time to board it after the race begins.

That causes the villains to try more nefarious means of winning the race. First, they dynamite a tree in an attempt to block Duke's path. Then they try roping his lead horse. But Duke has a secret weapon: those four Pony Express horses. At the halfway point, he changes teams and hitches the Pony Express horses to his stage. He uses them to drive around the downed tree. When his lead horse gets roped, he simply veers to one side, pulling his opponent off the opposing stage. Not surprisingly, Duke wins the race. The ghost town becomes a thriving metropolis. And Duke gets the girl.

There are some occasional mistakes. The most obvious is that Duke's vest changes color (shades, really, since this is black-and-white movie) during the final stagecoach race. Wayne fan Smith noted, "The highlight of the film, and a sequence that sets it apart, is the climactic and very well staged race.... Veteran director Mack V. Wright gives us plenty of action and a realistic race to boot."[21] Skinner called it "a 54-minute movie that will keep you interested all through the movie!"[22]

Overall, this is one of Wayne's better efforts, even if the movie itself isn't that good. The plot is stretched a bit thin, and only the Crescent City mayor-sheriff-treasurer gets any good lines ("As Sheriff, I could arrest you for that, but as mayor, I welcome you to Crescent City"). He's also the only one who gets to play with the movie's animal star, a skunk.

Fenin and Everson noted that *Winds of the Wasteland* was one of several "historical Westerns" that Wayne made with Republic, adding that it "provided much stock footage for later Westerns."[23] Wayne's ability as an actor is starting to expand. He shows more range than in any of this earlier works.

Fenin and Everson described *Winds of the Wasteland* as one film in "a good series of historical Westerns" that Wayne did for Republic. And, they added, "Republic never made a *really bad* Western in this period, and even the weakest had elements to recommend it."[24] Waltz agreed, writing that the movie is "an entertaining programmer that Duke fans will want to watch again and again."[25]

However, the plot needed fine tuning. As Micklon noted, "One of those subplots that was completely missed was the romantic subplot between Barbara Forsythe (Fraser) and both of the lead actors. There is no story that describes how she appears to go after one of them, but ends up with the other."[26]

The stagecoach race provides a setup for a number of excellent stunts, all the work of Yakima Canutt. That alone makes it worth watching. As for Duke, this movie shows him moving up from just an actor to an on-screen entertainer. He's getting even closer to the on-screen persona of John Wayne.

But there was a problem. As Roberts and Olson noted, "Wayne wanted to break the cycle [of B Westerns] and he was willing to give up steady work to do so."[27]

8

1937: *Born to the West*

In 1937, the Duke moved to Universal, lured there by his old boss Trem Carr of Monogram. Wayne was still under contract to Republic, but Republic loaned Wayne to the competing studio.[1]

The problem, as Miller noted, is that Carr "enticed Wayne over to star in an action series, [but] none of them officially Westerns."[2] As a result, Wayne faced something of an identity crisis when it came to his films. He made only five, and four of those were not Westerns: *I Cover the War, Idol of the Crowds, Adventure's End* and *California Straight Ahead!*, all directed by Arthur Lubin. As Wayne later said of the move, "I had lost my stature as a Western star—and got nothing in return."[3]

In *I Cover the War*, newsreel cameraman Bob Adams (Wayne) travels to North Africa to cover an Arab uprising against the British. Problems arise when his younger brother Don (James Bush) wants to get into the profession and Bob refuses. As a result, Donsoon finds himself manipulated by others in the field who have questionable ethics.

Idol of the Crowds features Wayne as Johnny Hanson, a hockey player who wants to make enough money in the game to expand his chicken farm. Gangsters try to use his desire for money to force him to throw the championship game. To ensure that he blows the game, the gamblers enlist the help of a pretty girl, played by Sheila Bromley.

Adventure's End features Duke as pearl diver Duke Slade, who angers natives of a Pacific island by diving in their waters. To escape the natives, he boards a whaling ship and soon becomes friends with the captain (Montagu Love). As the captain is dying, he talks Duke into promising to marry his daughter (Diana Gibson). But the ship's first mate (Moroni Olsen) desires the girl. The 67-minute *California Straight Ahead!* was an action-adventure in which Wayne leads a caravan of trucks in a race with a train to the West Coast.

That left only one more Western to add to his résumé, *Born to the West*.

In *Born to the West*, Western hero Johnny Mack Brown is a key cast member, although in a supporting role.[4] That's a bit surprising, since Brown was then an established B Western star in his own right. He was a former start for the Alabama Crimson Tide football team who played his final game in the 1926 Rose Bowl for the Tide. He scored two touchdowns in the 20–19 win over the Washington Huskies as Alabama claimed the NCAA national championship for the year.

John Wayne was unmistakably the star, playing the lead role of Dare Rudd. His co-star Marsha Hunt was a talented actress and model, known for her sense of style, whose career might have gone further had she not been blacklisted in the McCarthy era.[5] Hunt said of Wayne, "His screen self drawled his sparse lines almost hesitantly, seeming to grope for what he wanted to say. He was big, he moved and rode well and handled guns with great ease."[6]

Brown played Tom Fillmore, Dare's cousin. Even Olympic hero Jim Thorpe had a small but uncredited role in a barroom scene. And Alan Ladd is sometimes listed as part of the cast. For example, Ricci, Zmijewsky

John Wayne with Marsha Hunt in *Born to the West* (1937).

and Zmijewsky include Ladd in their list of the cast members,[7] even though he never appears in the film.[8]

Syd Saylor had a small, uncredited role. Saylor later became more famous as a sidekick to Western stars like Buck Jones and Bob Steele.[9] Others in the cast included Monte Blue, John Patterson and Lucien Littlefield. The Stuart Anthony-Robert Yost-Jack Natteford. script was based on a Zane Grey novel.

Paramount had the rights to a continuing series of movies based on the Grey novels and they had used a number of actors in the leads, including Randolph Scott, Buster Crabbe and Gilbert Roland. Each film did well at the box office because "the Grey name was a selling help and the studio offered good productions for each entry."[10]

Directed by Charles Barton, the 51-minute movie was shot on location near Kernville and Lone Pine and released on December 10, 1937.

After Wayne became more famous, another distributor purchased the rights to the movie from Paramount and renamed it *Hell Town*. They then added several additional minutes of stock footage of cattle drives and outlaws attacking. As Miller noted, most of the padding "was spliced to the beginning, making it seem an interminable length of time before the story proper got underway."[11]

The music in the film was also interesting. The opening theme song was also included in a 1936 Harold Lloyd comedy, *The Milky Way*. Another song, "You're the One That I Crave," is background music during a poker game; it had previously been heard in the 1932 Marx Brothers comedy *Horse Feathers*.

The film is a remake of a 1926 Jack Holt Western of the same name. It opens with Dare (Wayne) and his friend Dinkey Hooley (Saylor) riding from Wyoming to Montana to visit Dare's cousin, banker-rancher Tom Fillmore (Brown). Tom offers both men a job, but they decline. Neither of them believes they need honest work. Duke mistakenly believes that he's a great poker player. Dinkey prefers to make money from selling lightning rods and provides the movie with comic relief in his sales pitch to innocent customers.

Duke changes his mind when he sees Tom's girlfriend, Judy Worstall (Hunt). Before he gets much of a chance to impress the young lady, our hero is put to work leading a cattle drive. He replaces the previous foreman, Lynn Hardy (John Patterson), who has been helping local rustler Bart Hammond (Monte Blue) help himself to Fillmore's cattle. Hardy, now just a hand on the drive, conspires with Hammond to steal the cattle along the trail, but Duke keeps foiling them. Along the way, he also saves the girl when her horse becomes a runaway.

The good news: Duke gets the cattle through to the railroad and sells them. The bad news: Before returning to the ranch, he gets into a crooked poker game. Duke, still suffering from self-delusion about his poker skills, loses most of the money.

When Duke doesn't show back up at the ranch, Fillmore goes to see what happened. He arrives in time and discovers that the gambler, Buck Brady (James Craig), is switching decks. The good guys recover their money and head back to the ranch before the villains have a chance to regroup.

Fillmore gets the money from his cattle, but he loses the girl to Duke. Still, why she would prefer a rascally hero and poor poker player to a wealthy rancher is a bit hard to see.

Born to the West has more complex characterizations, at least for the hero, than most B Westerns. Duke is still a macho hero, but he also has a gambling problem and views himself as a ladies' man. As Morrison noted, "This film is a milestone in the Duke's career, giving him an opportunity to show his innate talent, and giving audiences an opportunity to appreciate that talent."[12] The film has several good lines. At one point, Wayne is asked about the location of Wyoming. He responds, "Right over yonder beyond that hill … unless somebody's moved it." At another point, Wayne is asked about why he's not married. His response is, "I don't like branding. It hurts in the wrong place."

There are a few continuity problems. In the poker scene, the cards used in the game have twentieth-century numerals that are unlike the cards used in the old West. A portrait of George Washington on a wall disappears in the middle of the scene, and then appears again. One character throws the same pen on the same desk twice in the same scene. Another lifts his knife and fork twice in the same scene.

Fan Eyles noted, "The action sequences of the cattle drive, the midnight raid by rustlers, and an episode with a runaway horse attracted the most attention at the time and were almost certainly stock footage from earlier films."[13] Chance gave it a lukewarm review: "The villains are all too easily dispatched in group horseback shootouts; and the only time John Wayne chases after anyone is to catch Judy on her runaway horse."[14] Pratt really liked it: "John Wayne was 30 years of age when he made this picture and Marsha Hunt was 20…. They both gave outstanding performances and Marsha looked very beautiful."[15]

But that's all minor. The important factor here is that this movie marked a major advancement in Duke Morrison becoming John Wayne. Prior to this, Wayne was still not much more than a stage name, and the

John Wayne persona had not yet developed. That persona still had a way to go before reaching full status in *Stagecoach*, but it's definitely there in this film.

Perhaps it's because Duke returned to the Western genre after appearing in a number of consecutive, rather routine non-Westerns. When he got a chance to star in this one, he took advantage and enjoyed the role. And he did it without either Gabby Hayes or Yakima Canutt.

Further, this film marks the last time that Wayne plays a supporting role in a Western. In *Born to the West*, his is a secondary character with a gambling problem. He has to be saved from his own actions by the star of the film. That scenario never shows up in another John Wayne movie. After this, Wayne was a hero, a screen hero and a hero to his audiences.

John Wayne would soon become his own man.

9

1938: *Pals of the Saddle* to *Red River Range*

Wayne was fast growing tired of the direction in his career, but his negativity didn't show up on screen. There were just four movies in 1938, because he was finding himself cast in an increasing number of quality films. And all four were Westerns: *Pals of the Saddle, Overland Stage Raiders, Santa Fe Stampede* and *Red River Range*. Still, as Miller wrote, "It was a comedown for Wayne, after his action series at Universal and the Paramount effort."[1]

All four films were in the popular "Three Mesquiteers" series, with Duke playing the main man Stony Brooke. One source describe the Three Mesquiteers series as "the best series of Westerns ever produced."[2] Fenin and Everson considered the series "one of the best Western series any studio has ever made."[3] The series started in 1936 and continued through 1943. These Westerns paid no attention to the year in which they were set. Still, as Miller noted, "the series was liked, in spite of no particular cohesion to it as a whole."[4]

As Fenin and Everson noted, "The films strangely contradicted each other with regard to the period in which they were set."[5] Some were set in the old West, some appeared to be in the 1930s, and some seemed to have elements of both periods. That didn't matter to movie fans, who generally sought them out for Saturday afternoon entertainment.

As for Wayne, he got a prestigious role, even if it was in a B Western, but little else. As Eyles wrote, "It required rather less of Wayne than his earlier work for there were three leading players instead of one in each adventure sharing screen time and requiring their own individual moments."[6]

In 1936, three years before finding stardom in *Stagecoach*, John Wayne signed with Universal Studios to make a string of cheap, non-Western action films. By 1938, though, Duke was concerned that his action flicks were costing him his Western fans.

As a result, Wayne returned to Republic to replace Bob Livingston in the Three Mesquiteers series. The series was so popular in England that some theater owners installed rows of rocking horses near the screen so that kids "could ride and shoot (if they brought their toy guns) right along with the characters on screen."[7] As Miller noted, the Wayne entries in the Mesquiteers series "rate among the best in that long and distinguished series."[8]

The strength of the series, Fenin and Everson added. was that they were "dedicated to action first, last, and always, but with pleasant comic moments" provided by Max Terhune, a ventriloquist, with an "easygoing country cousin appeal" who appeared in 21 of the Three Mesquiteers entries.[9] Further, they carefully "avoided the 'streamlined' plots and musical elements of the Autry and Rogers films."[10]

Livingston was removed from the series because of ongoing tensions between him and co-star Ray Corrigan.[11] Duke played Stony Brooke in the films, Corrigan was Tucson Smith[12] and Max Terhune was Lullaby Joslin.

Corrigan and Terhune left the series and Republic in the 1940s. Both landed at Monogram where they made two movies in a new series called "The Range Busters." The films involved a team of three heroes and were an obvious attempt to attain the same type of success that the Three Mesquiteers had provided for Republic.[13]

The first four Mesquiteers films featuring Wayne were directed by George Sherman, who later directed Wayne in the big-budget Batjac film *Big Jake.* Sherman remembered that the Three Mesquiteers films "were awful, and it certainly wasn't Duke's fault. ...Wayne was the romantic hero whose love life was generally the cause of the trouble.... Terhune was the so-called comedian, and Corrigan was the cowboy who never fell in love!"[14]

Duke didn't like the films because he believed that Republic planned to keep him in obscurity while they had greater plans for Corrigan. Those grand plans for Corrigan never worked out, and he retired in the 1950s.

Characters developed by William Colt MacDonald, the Three Mesquiteers were an obvious attempt to transfer the Three Musketeers concept to the Old West.[15] It worked remarkably well with a variety of actors in the three roles, all using the same format: two heroes to do the fighting and one comic sidekick.

The three heroes shared ownership of the 3M Ranch, a spread that Kehr described as one "that seems to magically tend itself" since the heroes are rarely around to do the ranch work.[16] Kehr added that the movies occurred in both the Old West and in the modern era. Out in the countryside, it's still the Old West of the 1880s; but when the action moves to town, it looks more like the 1930s and "the America of Franklin D. Roosevelt, complete with cars, radios, airplanes and a full New Deal complement of greedy businessmen and crooked bankers to provide villainy."[17]

In *Pals of the Saddle*, cast members included Doreen McKay, George Douglas and Ted Adams. McKay's career only lasted for three credited roles, but two were with Wayne (she appeared with him again in his 1939 Three Mesquiteers entry *The Night Riders*). The brother of Melvyn Douglas, George Douglas had roles in a number of other movies, including 1958's *Attack of the 50 Foot Woman*. Adams had a career of 20-plus years in which he appeared in Westerns, usually playing a villain.

This 55-minute movie was shot on location at Ray Corrigan's ranch Corriganville and in Red Rock Canyon State Park.[18] Corriganville became a popular place for shooting Western movies. Corrigan paid $10,000 for the 17,000-acre spread that was mostly a dumping ground for trash when he purchased it; he cleaned it up and turned it into an outdoor movie studio.[19]

Pals of the Saddle was released on August 28, 1938. (It was remade in 1944 as *Song of the Range* starring Jimmy Wakely.[20]) It's distinctively more modern than some of the others in the series, since the plot deals with enemy agents who illegally mine tungsten and sell an important chemical to a foreign power in violation of the Neutrality Act. As Fenin and Everson wrote, the plot brings "gangster methods into the villainy."[21] Nevins called it one of "the best Hitler-inspired" Westerns of the era.[22]

Thus the boys get involved with the U.S. Secret Service in a fight against Nazi agents trying to smuggle the chemicals out of the U.S. Never mind that the duties of the Secret Service were limited to protecting the president and chasing people who counterfeited money. The Secret Service label sounded impressive and spy-like.

It starts with Stony saving a girl on a runaway horse. Unfortunately, she didn't want to be saved, but pretends to be grateful when the other two cowboys arrive.

Finding a gun which the pretty brunette lost in the excitement, the boys head to Sherwood Dude Ranch to return her property and to flirt. Instead of romance, though, Stony finds himself accused of murdering the girl's boyfriend. Wayne often played a hero who ended up getting arrested.

Tucson and Lullaby help Stony escape, and he goes after the real killer. He nabs the guy, but that doesn't help much. It turns out that the shooter was a Secret Service agent and the victim a foreign spy.

When the Secret Service agent dies, Stony is recruited to take his place in an undercover plan to capture the spies. At first he balks, but then agrees to the arrangement to clear his name. By this time, Stony has a $1,000 dead-or-alive price on his head for the murder charge. Stony handles that by trading identities with the dead agent and collecting the reward on himself.

Afterwards, he infiltrates the gang and uncovers their plan for shipping poisonous chemicals out of the States. At the same time, Tucson and Lullaby seek the man who killed their friend. When they finally catch up with the bounty hunter, they recognize Duke and get caught up in the intrigue. Eventually they get some help and the trio stop the shipment of wartime materials. The final scene is an exciting shootout, with the good guys prevailing.

The film includes the obligatory humor from ventriloquist Max Terhune and his friend Elmer. The best comedy line comes from Duke, who hears Max imitating a bird and says, "Between you and that canary, give me the bird." Helpful dummy Elmer tries to oblige. And Duke has an engaging scene where he tells a young admirer how he killed himself. He is thoroughly caught up in the story, providing a glimpse of the talent that would make him a star the following year.

As for the series as a whole, this was one of its solid entries. As Fenin and Everson wrote, "The films were consistent ... in delivering first-class Western action. The photography was sharp and clean, the musical scores effectively animated, and the action fast and furious."[23] Modern fans typically liked the movie. Elliott called it "one of the better films in the series."[24] O'Keefe described it thus: "Fast horses and stray bullets travel with the familiar generic background music."[25] As Smith noted, the film demonstrates "how far Wayne had developed his on-screen presence. He appeared much more confident and more at ease."[26]

Still, as Miller noted, "Wayne didn't fit in. He was too much like Corrigan in build, and missed Livingston's debonair charm, too stolid for banter at this stage in his career."[27]

The movie had one major implication for Wayne's long-term career. It was his first Western where he was fighting for the nation as a patriotic duty. In his previous oaters, the hero worked to protect a rancher, a business person beset by problems, and even an entire town. *Pals in the Saddle* was the first Western in which John Wayne displayed his nationalistic patriotism.

The movie was not unique in expressing that tone in 1938. The tensions preceding World War II were affecting the attitudes of the nation.

Fenin and Everson noted: "With the war in Europe brewing, standard plots were topically revamped" to express patriotic ideals.[28]

Still, it was a first for Wayne. Other such roles would follow, most notably his Batjac production *The Alamo* (1960) when he portrayed Davy Crockett. And there were other, non–Western films in which the Duke displayed his patriotic side, including *Flying Tigers* (1942), *The Fighting Seabees* (1944), *Back to Bataan* (1945), *Sands of Iwo Jima* (1949) and *Operation Pacific* (1951)—a total of 18 patriotic war movies in all. As Goldman wrote, "He played, at one time or another, a member of virtually every branch of the military."[29]

In 1968, he starred in and directed the only pro-war film to be released during and about the Vietnam War when he was the lead in *The Green Berets*.

Overland Stage Raiders, the next in the Three Mesquiteers series, again starred Wayne. This film features the three heroes looking for an airplane (okay, that's an odd item for a Western) in one of those modern Westerns where it's hard to tell the difference between the old West and the new one. Louise Brooks played the sister of the pilot of the airplane in what turned out to be her final film appearance. Yakima Canutt had a small uncredited role as a bus driver. The film was directed by George Sherman from a script provided by Bernard McConville, Edmund Kelso and Luci Ward. It was shot on location at the Iverson Ranch in Chatsworth and released on September 20, 1938.

Louise Brooks was perhaps best known for popularizing the bob haircut, or pageboy in today's style.[30] She was one of the most famous actresses of the silent era, starring as Lulu in the 1929 German Expressionist classic *Pandora's Box*, but didn't have much of a career once the talkies came around. She appeared in one other early Western, *Empty Saddles* (1936) with Buck Jones. She appeared in *Overland Stage Raiders* for $300. Brooks noted that she really needed the money but the salary "did little to cheer me up at the prospect of working in a typical Hollywood Western whose unreality disgusted me."[31]

As Kehr wrote, "The fire in her eyes has dimmed. But there she is, providing the perfunctory love interest in a low-budget feature meant for Saturday morning children's matinees."[32] Soon afterwards, she was reportedly working as a sales clerk at Saks Fifth Avenue, making $40 per week.

Regardless, she left the movie with a high opinion of John Wayne. She later wrote that he was "a Duke born to reign" in Hollywood, adding that when she first met him she thought, "This is no actor but the hero of all mythology miraculously brought to life."[33]

John Wayne (right) with Anthony Marsh and Louise Brooks in *Overland Stage Raiders* (1938).

Tritten described the plot as "both far-fetched and intriguing for its ingenuity."[34] That pretty much sums it up. It opens with someone parachuting out of an airplane. He turns out to be Wayne, who joins this two pals to break up a robbery attempt: Villains have stopped a bus, gotten the passengers outside, and are ready to rob them when the heroes ride up to save the day.

The boys take the thousand dollars reward money they get for foiling the robbery and look around for an investment. They choose that newfangled invention, the airplane, to solve their problems. They even try to convince the other locals to sell their cattle and invest in their new idea. They get enough money together to launch the idea, but their plan doesn't work out well. Instead, the owner of the bus line hires some bad guys from the east to hijack the plane and steal the gold shipment that it carried. Where else but in a Three Mesquiteers film would you feature an airplane holdup?

After that, things get complicated and the plot looks nothing like a Western. Instead, the script uses aerial tactics, gas hand grenades, parachuting cowboys and the hijacking of a cattle train.

If all that sounds a bit strange, it is. One critic called the plot "a preposterous hodgepodge," but added that it was worth viewing because the Mesquiteers series was "probably the best series of the 1930s 'Poverty Row' films, and it is a pure joy to see the workmanlike love put into these programmers. ...[These movies] aren't auteur classics, but for many viewers in the period, they were what movies were all about."[35]

Similarly, another described it as racing "onward, heedless to logic, but gifted in ineptitude."[36] And there were numerous continuity errors, the most obvious of which was the use of an airplane door as the shield from bullets. The door survives the gunfight without a crease or dent in its structure.

Another called it "a disappointment in every way," adding: "Only a Western-John Wayne-Louise Brooks completist should own this film."[37] Jeffrey Anderson wrote, "It appears that dialogue was cheaper than action sequences, and the movie spends a great deal of time with characters telling the plot to each other."[38]

One Western fan wrote that it was "one of the best of the Three Mesquiteer series with a very novel setting for a story."[39] Tritten described it as "a real solid class B Western with a pre–John Ford John Wayne at his shooting and roping best."[40] Galbraith wrote that the films in the series "were modest program pictures tailored for undemanding audiences. But they're fast-paced and in their own way quite amusing, fun for those able to suspend a mountain of disbelief."[41]

I tend to agree with the critics who panned the film. What is supposed to be a stagecoach is really a passenger bus, and the villains actually get it to stop while riding their horses. Now why would the driver allow that to happen when all he has to do is step on the accelerator?

Further, the hijacking of the plane seems contrived, with the passengers ordered to jump out with parachutes and limited instructions ("Count to three and pull the cord, lady!"). That idea seems totally at odds with the film's title regarding "overland" stage raiders. Those factors are why one reviewer wrote that it was "a filmic hodgepodge bordering on insanity."[42] And even Tritten, who otherwise liked the movie, agreed that it had "a very lackluster ending."[43]

Finally, it was a weak vehicle for Louise Brooks' final film, with her role having little to do with the plot. Brooks does not wear her trademark bob hairstyle and is barely recognizable. Further, he voice is not what her fans expected. No wonder it was her last film.

On the plus side, Duke's talent was starting to shine through. He was in the final stages of becoming John Wayne. As one reviewer noted, "The presence, the charisma, and the physicality that would make him a colossus are all here."[44] Another wrote, "Wayne was *not* a happy actor at the time, having tried to get out of Poverty Row Westerns, but now he was back at Republic and making less money than before. Yet, his performance is not affected: he appears cheery throughout this film."[45]

The bottom line on *Overland Stage Raiders* is its role in history and the intersection of two famous actors. As one critic wrote, it was the unique pairing of the "greatest Western actor opposite the greatest actress in the history of German Expressionism while he was on his way up and she was on her way out. They met in obscurity and went on to immortality."[46]

It was a memorable film for both actors, but for totally different reasons.

Santa Fe Stampede has nothing to do with Santa Fe and there's not really a stampede in the film. The "Santa Fe" in the title comes from a fictional town called Santa Fe Junction, not the New Mexico city. And there's not even any cattle in the film, so the only "stampede" is a crowd of unruly humans.

Still, it's a historic movie for film buffs, for a rather grisly reason. It is the first known movie out of Hollywood in which the villain kills a child. The victim was a young girl who is killed when her buckboard crashes over the side of a mountain pass. As Galbraith wrote, "How all this passed unnoticed by the Production Code is a mystery."[47]

Some video versions omit the scene, apparently believing it still to be too graphic for young audiences. Regardless, until *Santa Fe Stampede*, that was a violent episode that had been taboo. Further, the idea that the unofficial prohibition was broken by a B Western is somewhat ironic. After all, the primary audience for B Westerns were young kids.

John Wayne in *Santa Fe Stampede* (1938).

The entire purpose of the B Westerns was to provide those kids with a safe way to spend a Saturday afternoon. Having a villain kill a child on-screen would make that audience uneasy, giving them no reason to return the following week.

The plot is simple, based around the idea of crooks in politics. The Three Mesquiteers capture a horse thief, only to see the bad guy go free because of a crooked judge. They try to get the judge removed from office by circulating a petition to send to the governor. Then a friend of the three cowboys is murdered and evidence points toward Stony Brooke (Wayne), in his third appearance on the Three Mesquiteers series.

Ray Corrigan and Max Terhune return as the other two members of the trio. June Martel plays Nancy Carson, who attracts romantic interest from both Wayne and Corrigan (neither manages to get her). Former silent star William Farnum appears as oldtimer Dave Carson.

George Sherman served as director, using a script provided by Luci Ward and Betty Burbridge. Ward also provided the original story. A longtime friend of Wayne's, Sherman directed a number of his movies.

Thomas Flood served as the uncredited second unit director. He worked with Yakima Canutt, George Montgomery and Bob Woodward, who handled the stunt work. Montgomery was still in the early stages of his career, years before he would become a household name as a Western star himself. It was partly shot at the Brandeis Ranch outside of Los Angeles and Ray Corrigan's Simi Valley ranch. The film was released on November 28, 1938, making its premiere at the Rialto Theater in Manhatten.[48]

The movie opens with the three heroes riding up to a sign that reads, "Trespassers will be shot." Lullaby says, "Looks like folks ain't exactly welcome around here." "Well, I don't believe in signs," Stony says as they ride past the warning.

The boys aren't worried because the person who posted the sign, Dave Carson (William Farnum), sent for them. Carson needed help enforcing the "no trespassing" sign and registering his mining claim (some unscrupulous townspeople are trying to get ahold of it). The Mesquiteers had given the old man a grubstake, so that makes them partners in the rich mine.

Mayor Gil Byron (LeRoy Mason, Republic's favorite villain) learns of the strike and wants the gold. He's the Boss Hogg of Santa Fe Junction, and controls everybody of importance in the town, including the sheriff (Dick Rush) and the judge (Ferris Taylor).

The three heroes get a sample of the mayor's power when a pair of horse thieves try to run off with a couple of Carson's horses. The three heroes manage to chase down and capture one of the thieves. They take him to town where he goes to trial in front of an drunk judge controlled by the mayor, and is set free. After a fight breaks out in the courtroom, the trio get charged with contempt of court. "Words fail to express my contempt for this court!" our hero says. The other thief brings the mayor a sample of the gold from Carson's mine. The mayor starts plotting to get the mine.

The Mesquiteers try to take a petition to the governor for help. Carson and his young daughter agree to drive their buckboard, with the petition, to the governor, while Wayne rides to another town to register the claim. The two horse thieves attack the buckboard and it crashes, killing father and daughter. Byron frames Duke for the murders, leading the townspeople who were supporting the petition to turn on Duke.

A U.S. marshal (Tom London) brings Duke back to town. He is arrested, ends up in jail and needs help from his two partners to prove his innocence. The duo leave town to look for witnesses who can clear Duke's name. Meanwhile, the mayor stirs up a lynch mob to string up our hero. After all, if Wayne is around for a trial, some of the mayor's nefarious actions may come to light. Astute fans might notice that the scene is similar to one in the 1931 film *Range Feud*, starring Buck Jones. Duke was merely a supporting player in that movie, and Buck had to ride to the rescue at the last minute.

The angry locals don't succeed in lynching Stony, but they do set the jail on fire while he's being visited by Nancy Carson. She plans to unlock the jail and let Wayne out the back, but she's knocked unconscious by a thrown rock before she can do either. Looks like both are going to die, but the remaining two members of the duo ride to the rescue.

Does the Duke escape? Well, certainly. But how he does it is an ending that would befit any of the classic cliffhanger serials of the 1930s. In keeping with the approach of other reviewers of the film, I won't reveal how that occurs.

Santa Fe Stampede is one of the better Three Mesquiteers entries, well above average for a B Western. As one modern fan wrote, it is a "fast-paced and enjoyable Western, even if the other Two Mesquiteers (Corrigan and Terhune) were underutilized compared with Wayne."[49] Smith noted, "Wayne, Corrigan and Terhune look comfortable in their hero roles."[50]

Some people consider *Santa Fe Stampede* to be Duke's final B Western before John Ford signed him for *Stagecoach*. There is little doubt that his skills had been well honed by this time, and he was ready for the big time. As Elliott noted, "You can tell Wayne is having a lot of fun here…. Wayne has all the vibrant energy to carry the film."[51]

Indeed, John Wayne had become a star. He just needed a really good film to display his talents. That would soon come.

Red River Range is Duke's most alliterative B Western title from the 1930s. Unlike *Santa Fe Stampede*, which is a true Western, this 56-minute entry places the Three Mesquiteers in the modern era. They face a gang of cattle rustlers (I know, that sounds like an Old West plot), but these rustlers use refrigerated vans and portable slaughterhouses. That plot element makes it similar to the 1937 Gene Autry movie *Public Cowboy No. 1*. Reviewer Dave Kehr described *Red River Range* as "engagingly implau-

John Wayne (white hat) grapples with William Royle (left) as unidentified henchman look on in *Red River Range* (1938).

sible."[52] That pretty much sums it up. But it can be fun to watch, despite
that major problem.

John Wayne returns as Stony Brooke, with Ray Corrigan playing
Tucson Smith and Max Terhune as Lullaby Smith. However, perhaps
for the only time in the Three Mesquiteers series, they are joined by a
fourth partner: Kirby Grant plays Tex Reilly, who joins the trio by pretending to be Stony Brooke. (Is that confusing enough?). Grant later
played the lead in a few Westerns, during the early 1950s but he went
on to bigger fame as television's *Sky King*, a modern-day cowboy who
flew an airplane.

Former vaudevillian Polly Moran provides some humor as a tourist
at a local dude ranch who would like to capture Duke for herself and tries
to do so by giving him riding lessons.

Stony drifts into town pretending to be a wanted outlaw. The idea is
that Stony can infiltrate the rustlers' gang and let the other three know
about future raids. This plot element is the most obvious situation in
which Wayne demonstrates his separation from the other Mesquiteers.
As Levy wrote, Wayne's character in the Mesquiteers series was "usually

acting independently of the other two."[53] Yakima Canutt and Tommy Coats handled the stuntwork, although neither received credit.

George Sherman again served as Wayne's director, using a script by Stanley Roberts, Betty Burbridge and Luci Ward. Ward also provided the original story. The movie was filmed on location in Agoura and released on December 22, 1938. The film cost $40,000 to produce, with Wayne getting his usual fee of $3000.

The plot centers around those pesky cattle rustlers. The Cattlemen's Association ask the governor to send in a special investigator. He does better than that: He sends four. First, he turns to the Three Mesquiteers for help. And why not? He's checked out their dossier on file with the Civilian Volunteer Reserve and he likes what he sees. The file reads: "Lullaby Joslin / Stony Brooke / Tucson Smith Alias: The Three Mesquiteers. Address: Three M Ranch, Mesquite County. Qualifications: Top Hands–Expert Gunmen–Closed Mouthed–Dependable–Absolutely Honest."

The boys take the assignment, but they need help from another investigator. The Retail Butchers Association, alarmed at the steep decrease in meat prices caused by the rustling, has hired Tex Reilly (Grant) for the same job. On the way back to town, the four investigators bump into each other. Reilly already had a run-in with the rustlers, and those outlaws may already know his face. If so, they will know he's a lawman.

The solution? Reilly joins the trio to pose as Stony Brooke. Meanwhile, Stony (Wayne) will pose as an escaped murderer named Killer Madigan in an effort to infiltrate the rustling gang. He plans to hide out by pretending to be an easterner at a local dude ranch. The other three continue to town and find lodging at the Mason ranch where they can all keep an eye on the beautiful Jane Mason (Lorna Gray).

On their first day, outlaws attack the ranch and shoot up their meal. The three heroes take off in pursuit, but Tex is shot and wounded. They return to the ranch where Jane starts nursing Tex back to health. Soon afterwards, the outlaws steal the herd from the Jones ranch, killing the father and making young Tommy an orphan. He has to move in with the Masons too.

How are the outlaws so efficient? The Mesquiteers focus their investigation on a local dude ranch, the Payne Health Hacienda. Turns out that they use guests at the ranch to help them round up the steers. That cuts down on the number of bad guys who have to work in the gang. The naive dudes are clueless, convinced by their hosts that robbing from other ranches is "all part of their carefully planned Western experience."[54]

Wayne, staying at the ranch as a dude, figures most of it out. He even convinces most of the other guests that he doesn't know much about the West, although he can ride a horse "if the horse is gentle." When Polly tries to teach him how to mount a horse, he tries to get on from the wrong side and falls down.

Duke soon runs into Jane and Tommy moving things from the Jones ranch. He volunteers to help, taking them back to the Mason ranch. There he meets his old partners and tells him his suspicions about the dude ranch. With another "rustling" experience set for later, the Mesquiteers decided to tag along and see what happens.

The villains pull off the robbery with no problem, but two things happen. First, Tucson and Lullaby spot some buried cowhides and figure out how the rustlers are escaping. Second, Wayne gets pulled into the gang by the rustlers, who still think he's an escaped convict. To test his loyalty, they insist that he kill the Mesquiteers. Two of the bad guys go with him to make sure he does the job.

The three men go to the Mason ranch. Duke goes inside while the two villains remain outside. A couple of shots come from inside the house, Duke comes running out, and the three men make their getaway. The next morning, the local paper reports that the Mesquiteers have been killed. Wayne appears to be accepted by the gang. The gang plans one last rustling job to coincide with the funerals of the heroes.

When Wayne goes to town with the bad guys, Jane spots him and he updates her on what is happening. She hurries to the Cattlemen's Association and reveals the heroes' plot. They band together to break up the robbery planned for Box Canyon. Unfortunately, one of the cattlemen is part of the rustlers' gang; he calls his cohorts and they change their plans.

The four heroes intercept one of the trucks headed toward the herd. They get the correct location from the driver by freezing the information out of him, i.e., they lock him in the refrigerated truck and turn the thermostat down to minus 15. With the new information, they first contact the posse and then load some of the horses in the back of the truck. Their plan is to ride up to the rustlers and surprise them with part of the posse in the truck, like a Trojan Horse on wheels.

The plan is in danger, though, because the evil cattleman is riding up front while Tucson drives. Duke, in the back with the others, figures out that he must be the inside man. He responds by climbing up to the cab. Tucson knocks the villain out of the truck while Duke takes over driving.

The truck and the posse arrive at the rustling site at the same time, and they subdue the villains. Those that aren't shot are loaded into the back of a truck to be transported to town. In the process, Tex Reilly, aka Stony Brooke, wins the girl and gets married. That provides another source of humor. It starts with the justice of the peace (Robert McKenzie) complaining that the marriage is occurring on the opening day of fishing season. "Why didn't you come in yesterday?" he asks. "'Cause the lady didn't say 'Yes' until today," Tex replies.

During the ceremony, the justice gets confused and starts by saying, "Do you swear to tell the truth and nothing but the truth, so help…. Pardon me." Then he corrects himself and says, "Do you, Tex Reilly, take this woman to be your lawfully wedded wife, so help you?" Elmer, Lullaby's dummy, summarizes the scene by saying, "'So help him' is right!"

The film suffers from continuity problems. There is one scene in which Tex refers to "the kid," talking about Tommy Jones, played by Sammy McKim, who is the kid in the movie. However, there's been no mention nor appearance by Tommy when Tex makes his remark. Tex doesn't meet Tommy until he and Tucson run into the child in the next scene. Was a scene edited out, or was the plot changed?

Problems such as that prompted one modern fan wrote that *Red River Range* "is not as polished as some of the other movies … in the series."[55] Galbraith described it as "outlandish and amusing, if juvenile."[56] Elliott gave it a lukewarm reception: "This is really no better or worse than the thousands of B films made during this period," he wrote, "but you do have Wayne here, which puts it a notch above other films that did this very storyline. There's some nice action but the story is oh so predictable."[57] Davis wrote that *Red River Range* "did nothing to relieve Wayne's depressed state of mind. At 31 years of age, he felt burned out."[58] But things were about to change.

The bottom line is that a lot of the criticism of the film didn't really matter. The Saturday matinee fans enjoyed what they saw, and Wayne was about to become a household name. This was the last film that Duke made before taking a leave of absence to work in *Stagecoach*.

Actually, in many ways, he already *was* a household name. As Roberts and Olson wrote, "By the time his Republic contract expired, he was America's leading B Western star."[59]

10

1939: *Stagecoach*

Finally there was the breakout year of 1939. Duke started with a bang, playing the Ringo Kid in John Ford's epic *Stagecoach*. The movie would alter Wayne's career, making him an A-list star who would go on to set box office records.

Appropriately, it was a Western, and a classic one. The film was based on a short story by Western novelist Ernest Haycox called "Stagecoach to Lordsville." Ford acquired the rights to the story himself.[1] The plot is the simple story of a stagecoach traveling from the town of Tonto to Lordsburg. Bosworth noted that the two towns "prove to be moral mirrors of each other."[2]

Two subplots dominate the tale. First, the journey requires the stage to go through Indian territory, and those pesky Native Americans are rumored to be on the warpath. Second, another rumor tells of an outlaw nearby, a bad guy by the name of the Ringo Kid.

Haycox and Dudley Nichols worked together to turn the short story into a screenplay. In doing so, they came up with something special. As Munn wrote, they took a basic Western tale "and filled it with fully rounded, three-dimensional characters."[3]

Anderson noted that the plot borrowed heavily from a French short story, Guy de Maupassant's "Boule de Suif," about a prostitute who shares a carriage with some snobbish passengers trying to get away from the Franco-Prusian War. As in *Stagecoach*, the prostitute "proves herself their moral superior."[4]

If Duke had his way, he might have missed the opportunity to star in *Stagecoach*. Director John Ford invited the actor to his yacht and showed him the script. Duke liked it and suggested that Lloyd Nolan should play Ringo without realizing that Ford had him in mind for the role.

Goldman, who had access to Wayne's unpublished autobiography, noted that Duke suggested Nolan because he had enjoyed the actor's performance in the 1936 movie *The Texas Rangers*.[5] According to Wayne, when Ford asked if *he* could handle the role, "I said yes and spent the next two weeks making sure that [Ford] would see Lloyd Nolan in [*The Texas Rangers*]."[6]

Duke's clueless response was understandable. After all, Ford had shown no interest in Wayne's acting career after hiring him to herd geese for his 1928 movie *Mother Machree*.[7] Ford later used him as a laborer and prop man for some other films, and gave him an uncredited role in *Salute* in 1929. As Munn wrote, "It didn't even occur to Wayne that Ford would have wanted him for a leading role in such a prestigious picture."[8]

One theory for Ford's dismissal of Wayne was mentioned earlier, i.e., the fact that Raoul Walsh beat Ford to the punch by casting Duke in *The Big Trail*. If so, it took nine years for Ford to get over that slight and get his revenge. That's one reason director Peter Bogdanovich described *Stagecoach* as "Ford's thumbing of his nose at Walsh."[9]

There is another possibility. Duke may have believed he wasn't ready for such an important role. He had already turned down the lead role of Texas Ranger Dusty Rivers in Cecil B. DeMille's *North West Mounted Police*, a film scheduled for release in 1940.[10] Instead, the part went to Gary Cooper.

Even when Ford made it clear that he wanted Duke for the movie, the decision still wasn't final. Producer David Selznick wasn't interested in doing a Western with Wayne, afraid that it would be viewed as another B entry in the genre.[11] Ford formed a production company, Argosy Pictures, to get around that problem.

Producer Walter Wanger stepped in but he was also leery of the casting and insisted on a screen test for the young actor with Claire Trevor. It didn't go well. The John Wayne who would later appear so comfortable on camera was nervous and wooden with Trevor. Still, for whatever reason, Wanger approved him for the role.

Trevor believed that Ford convinced Wanger to use Wayne, and she thought she knew why. "I think Ford knew exactly what kind of performance he would get from Duke, and how he would get it," she told Munn, "which was basically to bully him and humiliate him."[12]

Wayne himself later acknowledged that his first three weeks in Monument Valley "were the most difficult of his career" and that he seriously considered quitting as the pressure mounted.[13] Fortunately, he stayed on the set. Ricci, Zmijewsky and Zmijewsky argued that Ford had two reasons for bullying Wayne in the film.[14] First, he felt he would trigger Duke's emotions and that would lead to a better performance. Second, Ford did it for the benefit of the other actors (all well-known) who might resent him using this young man for such a major role.

Frankel thought it was more a feature of Ford's personality.[15] He described Ford as drunk and a bully, but also acknowledge that he was a genius who "shoots a picture in his mind before he ever turns on a camera."

And Ford's bullying of Wayne did not stop with *Stagecoach*. Maureen O'Hara, who worked with Wayne and Ford in 1950's *Rio Grande*, noted that Ford constantly bullied Wayne on the set of that film. "It made me sick to my stomach," she recalled, "and more than once I had to excuse myself from the set so I could go to the bathroom and vomit."[16]

It took years for Wayne to feel comfortable working with Ford again, even though he did it in several later movies. As Duke later recalled, talking about Ford, "I don't think he really had any respect for me as an actor until I made *Red River* for Howard Hawks, ten years later. Even then, I was never quite sure."[17]

Ford may not have respected John Wayne, but he had a lot of respect for the Western genre. As Johnson and Bone wrote, "John Ford's films come largely from his personal vision of American history expressed in the genre of the Western film."[18] They added, "In his Westerns, Ford uses universal patterns of human experiences—dances, weddings, births, funerals, honor, and above all, sacrifice. We respond to these rituals with emotion."[19]

Shooting started with four days on location in October 1938. Ford chose Monument Valley, the scenic region on the Utah-Arizona state line, for the location. Rosebrook and Rosebrook argued that Ford was talked into using the valley by Harry and Leone Goulding, owners of a trading post in the area.[20] That seems to be a minority opinion. There is more support for the idea that Wayne should get the credit. Duke had previously visited the area, and later said that he suggested the location to Ford.[21] When Ford later said that it was his idea, Wayne didn't argue about it. "So far as I'm concerned," he wrote, "John Ford discovered Monument Valley. I guess you might say I found it for him to discover."[22]

Akitt wrote that Ford "turned Monument Valley into an allegory of the mythical Western landscape, whilst rewriting the history of the conquest of the West."[23] *Stagecoach* was among the earliest movies ever shot there. Its majestic views would become a staple of Western movies, especially those directed by Ford. Ford used the setting so often that Anderson described it as "Ford's personal movie set."[24]

Using the region required the permission of the Navajo Indians whose reservation covered the area. An added advantage was that the Navajos provided a source of extras for the movie. That feature turned out to be a financial boost to the Navajos.

In 1971, Wayne returned to the reservation for the filming of a CBS-TV salute to John Ford. He and Ford attended a barbeque that was hosted by the Navajos, with the two men both giving short speeches in the native language of their hosts.[25]

The story opens in the town of Tonto as passengers prepare for the trip. Two undesirables—a dance hall girl named Dallas (Trevor) and alcoholic Doc Boone (Thomas Mitchell)—are being kicked out of town by the Women's Law and Order League, a collection of women that Taylor described as "a group of crones without a whisper of compassion among them." Taylor added, "The faces of these meddling biddies become windows into their sour, gnarled souls. They seem to have existed before you even see them."[26]

John Wayne seated with Claire Trevor, Louise Platt, an unidentified actor, Francis Ford and Thomas Mitchell around the table in *Stagecoach* (1939). Standing from left to right are Donald Meek, Andy Devine, George Bancroft, Tim Holt and John Carradine.

Doc Boone and Dallas are joined in the passenger compartment by Lucy Mallory (Louise Pratt), a pregnant woman hoping to meet up with her husband, an army officer. The final passenger is a last-minute addition, a banker skipping town after embezzling his customers' money.

Charity noted that this cast "presents us with a social microcosm of the kind we meet more regularly these days in disaster movies."[27] And that microcosm has some surprises. By the end of the story, as Anderson noted, "In typical Ford fashion, the least reputable members of this ragtag group perform most heroically."[28] Bosworth noted that the characters' social order "is indicted for its intolerance as well as its corruption."[29]

The stage is driven by the lovable, rotund Buck, played by the affable Andy Devine. Devine was an unusual yet inspired bit of casting as the driver. He was known for playing mostly comic relief as a sidekick to cowboy heroes in B Westerns. However, as screenwriter Oliver Drake noted, "In *Stagecoach*, ... he was very comic and also serious. That's because he was an actor first."[30]

Because of the outlaw threat from the Ringo Kid, the local lawman Curly is riding shotgun. Curly was portrayed by George Bancroft in one of his rare roles as a good guy. Bancroft was better known for his tough-guy rogues in most other movies.

Each of these characters is identified quickly in the film. Munn wrote that *Stagecoach* was "a movie made by filmmakers at the top of their game—precise, emphatic compositions, perfect editing that never leaves a shot on-screen for less time than it needs to be understood, unforced exposition that expertly delineates seven major characters inside of 12 minutes."[31]

The movie is 18 minutes old when Ringo appears, standing in the middle of the road. Davis wrote that the scene "immediately commands the audience's attention" and that Wayne "emits an aura of bedrock strength."[32] Didion wrote that "he had a sexual authority so strong that even a child could perceive it."[33]

Bosworth saw the introduction as a metaphor. "The Ringo Kid arrives on the scene in a manner that silently evokes the traditional frontier hero," he wrote, "that natural man appears to emerge from the moral perfection of the wilderness itself."[34]

The script originally called for Ringo to greet the stage with his horse, a saddle and a rifle in his hands. That idea didn't work, because Wayne had to deal with two large props and handle the horse too. Ford got rid of the horse, making the scene easier.

Instead, what is seen on screen is Ringo as he holds a saddle over his left shoulder, a rifle in his right hand, and doesn't look anything like the movie stereotype of an outlaw. As Munn wrote, "What we see is not a dangerous outlaw but a boyish young man in bold relief—a gentle but resolute character.... This is an actor you have probably seen before, in one movie or another, but never like this, never showcased with such elemental force."[35]

Ford wanted Duke to make a dramatic entrance on film, and he used two techniques to accomplish that. The first: have his young star do something dramatic with his rifle, although Ford wasn't exactly sure what that should be. As Munn wrote, "Ford wanted him to do something flashy, but it couldn't happen too quickly for the audience to take it in."[36]

Wayne didn't come up with an answer, but Yakima Canutt did. Canutt, whom Duke had convinced Ford to hire for the film, had seen Buffalo Bill's Wild West show when he was a teenager. He remembered one of Buffalo Bill's cowboys cocking a rifle by spinning it in one hand. He suggested that Duke try that.

Wayne needed help to do the trick. The 1892 Winchester he was using was too long to spin under his arm, and there was no way to hold the gun while it spun. The prop department stepped in, shortening the length of the barrel and adding a ring to the handle so the trick could work. It worked so well that Wayne used the same trick in *True Grit*, this time on the back of a horse.

The second point of emphasis came from Ford's use of the camera as Wayne stands "in front of what appears to be a projected background."[37] After Duke spins and cocks his rifle, the camera quickly dollies in from a full-length shot of Ringo to an extreme close-up of his face. It was a dramatic camera movement, and, as Munn wrote, "an extremely unusual one for Ford, who had grown to prefer a stable camera."[38] Further, as Kehr noted, "The shot briefly goes out of focus as Ford's cinematographer, Bert Glennon, struggles to keep up with the change in scale—an effect that may have been accidental, but which grants Wayne an almost supernatural aura, as his face emerges from the blur to fill the screen in a dominating close-up."[39]

The only flaw in the scene was the way Ringo was dressed. Instead of a belt, he wore suspenders. The suspenders were Ford's idea. He had patterned Ringo "after a Western hero he had devised with Harry Carey during the silent era."[40] That character, Cheyenne Harry, wore suspenders instead of a belt. Ford wanted Ringo to do the same. Wayne did not object. After all, as Davis added, "Wayne had seen the Carey pictures as a boy and had chosen him as a role model when he first became an actor in Westerns."[41]

Still, that costume may have been the only thing in the movie that didn't work. As Fenin and Everson wrote, "Juvenile audiences in particular found this most distressing; they thought he looked half-dressed and not very glamorous. The costume has not been worn since."[42]

Still, in one scene, Ford had introduced a future star to movie audiences. "The audience sees, truly sees, John Wayne for the first time," Munn wrote. "[T]his is less an expertly choreographed entrance for an actor than it is the annunciation of a star. John Ford is telling us that this man warrants our attention in a way that transcends the immediate narrative of the movie."[43]

His persona was already apparent on the screen. As Eliot wrote, Ringo "comes off as a character with the exterior charm of Roy Rogers and inner darkness of Harry Carey."[44] Taylor had a similar reaction, noting, "We never doubt the Kid's goodness, just as we never doubt the rottenness of the banker Gatewood (Berton Churchill) … [or that] the pregnant young mother Mrs. Mallory (Louise Platt) is a cold snob to Claire Trevor's Dallas,

George Bancroft, John Wayne and Claire Trevor in *Stagecoach* **(1939).**

the hooker who tries to comfort her during their journey."[45] Mist argued that the characters reflected "Ford's preference for good-hearted, simple people—good-hearted despite their human fallibilities—over the evil-hearted rich."[46]

After that, it was merely a matter of how Ford presented Wayne on screen. Eyman noted Wayne was not the star of the movie, but he was its major focus.[47] Despite Wayne having little dialogue, Ford usually cut to him for his reaction to whatever else was said or done. In essence, Ford presented the film as if it were told from Ringo's viewpoint. Eliot noted the same technique and wrote, "From Wayne's entrance, Ford is consciously creating a star."[48]

The major scene is an Indian attack on the stagecoach as it races through the desert around Monument Valley.[49] Taylor wrote, "[I]t remains one of the most thrilling sequences ever put on film."[50] Mist noted that "the key dramatic conflict is between the humanness of the coach society and the savagery of he Apaches."[51] Richard Schickel wrote that the scene "is about as well staged as any such movie encounter—equaled, but not exceeded, in the future."[52] Bosworth argued that the confrontation reflected a common theme from Ford, i.e., the victory comes from "linking the heroism of the exceptional individual to the cooperative heroics of the group."[53]

The raid includes a classic stunt by Yakima Canutt, who portrays an Indian trying to stop the racing stage by jumping onto the back of one of its horses. The character is shot and falls to the ground between the hooves of the galloping horses. He remains there as the horses and the stage go past him. The stunt was so dangerous that Ford refused Canutt's offer to repeat it for another take.

The rest of the journey includes Mrs. Malloy searching for her Army officer husband, the birth of her child, more bickering between the passengers, and decisions about whether to continue the journey to Lordsburg or to return to Tonto.

The stage finally reaches Lordsburg, where Ringo gets his showdown with the real villain, Luke Plummer, who rises to face Ringo and tosses his last hand of poker on the table—a pair of aces and a pair of eights, i.e., the Dead Man's Hand that Wild Bill Hickok held when he was shot in the back of the head by Jack McCall. Never one to waste a good idea, Ford later used the same poker hand for Liberty Valance (Lee Marvin) just before he left the saloon for his fateful shootout with Ransom Stoddard (James Stewart) in *The Man Who Shot Liberty Valance* (1962).

The gunfight itself, Kehr noted, was "played so perfunctorily by Ford that it seems like an anticlimax (though a brilliant one, I think)."[54] The final shootout is so anticlimactic that Ford doesn't even show it on screen. Instead, there is a brief shot of the three villains walking down the street and then Duke firing one shot as he dives to the ground.

The rest of the gunfight is audio only, as the audience joins Dallas as she fearfully listens to the exchange of gunfire. The audience doesn't learn that Ringo won the fight until he shows up to hug Dallas. Eyles wrote, "There is far more artistry, more delicacy of mood and staging in this ... sequence than in the attack."[55]

Ringo and Dallas ride off together, headed for a remote country where Ringo has a ranch. Doc Boone bids them goodbye, along with his hope that they never have to deal with civilization. As Kehr wrote, "Ford seems to imagine them as a new Adam and Eve, whose children will populate an American Eden of freedom and democracy."[56]

Taylor also saw significance in the escape of the two lovers, noting that *Stagecoach* "has long been spoken of as a metaphor for how American civilization tamed the wilderness. But as Ford and his screenwriter, Dudley Nichols, portray it, civilization is something to escape. This is, after all, a movie where the hero, the young and charming John Wayne as the Ringo Kid, is an outlaw who has just busted out of prison."[57]

That doesn't mean that the entire film was full of happy themes. *Stagecoach* is consistent with a theme that frequently appears in Ford's Westerns, the idea that "the American West as the place in the modern world where traditional virtues go to die."[58]

Mist similarly argued that the film used the West to represent an uncivilized society. "For a film that masquerades as an action-packed Western, *Stagecoach* is an intimate film of human interaction rather than exciting events. ... [N]inety minutes of its length is a film of faces and personalities. The coach itself becomes Ford's metaphor for civilized society.... The stagecoach is a machine built by civilized hands that sets out to tame the vast uncivilized Western wastes."[59]

As Kehr wrote, the film was important because, through it, "the Western achieves self-consciousness, an awareness of itself as America's official foundation myth."[60] Anderson wrote that its success "lies in the excellence of its ensemble cast, the intelligence of its script, the thrill of its action and the assurance of its director, who was setting the standard for the genre."[61] Schickel, even more impressed, wrote:

> [S]uch is the skill with which the picture is made that you can accept it as just an ordinary Western, especially if you are 15 years old when you first encounter it. (You didn't expect to find moral complexity in Westerns at that time.) You are left

wrestling with it—mildly—for the rest of your life. It doesn't exactly haunt you, but it stubbornly sits there—John Ford's not inconsequential contribution ... to the ongoing debate about how much truth we can stand when faced with the question of what lies we need to sustain or keep our ambiguous American democratic faith alive.[62]

The only negative voice among modern reviewers is Eyles, who believes the film has lost some of its appeal over time. Thus he wrote, "Its impact has been eroded by imitation, and its script is too polished and contrived to stand the test of time." Still, even Eyles noted that visually "it is still magical…, and its action scenes are as thrilling and well-staged as one could wish on seeing it today."[63]

And it made John Wayne a star. Contrary to popular belief, though, that didn't happen quickly. As Munn wrote, Wayne's performance "certainly did not make a great impression with the major studios as none of them attempted to buy his contract from Republic. And there is no evidence to suppose that Republic immediately realized that they had a potential gold mine in their hands."[64]

But it did set the stage for the rest of Duke's career because "the way Ford presented the actor, the way the actor played the part—served as the template for about half of his career: dignity, intent, competence, and, if necessary, skill in combat, all added to a foundation of innate likability."[65] Akitt wrote that Wayne's performance "set a precedent for generations of Westerns that followed."[66] As Eliot noted, Wayne "had pulled off an amazing and nearly impossible feat, coming all the way back from the failure of *The Big Trail*, and the decade-long exile from big pictures."[67]

Further, *Stagecoach* revitalized the Western as a genre that could appeal to a wide audience. According to Akitt, "The Western movie was defined by John Ford" in this film.[68] Sarris argued that the film represented "the renaissance of the Western."[69] Charity agreed, writing that the movie "rehabilitated the genre after a decade of, if not disrepute, then benign condescension."[70] Nevins went further: "[M]ost film scholars continue to believe that no talking Westerns worth a moment of their attention were made until John Ford's *Stagecoach*."[71]

As Anderson wrote, "When you think of Westerns, this is the film you have in mind—whether you know it or not."[72] Anderson added, "*Stagecoach* may be the most influential Western in movie history, so much so that it has be denigrated as 'the Western that created the clichés.' Yet it remains as fresh and exciting as [when it was released]."[73]

Duke was still married to Josephine, but the two had little in common. While filming *Stagecoach*, Wayne had a heated affair with Claire

Trevor.[74] He and Josephine did not officially divorce until 1945, but the marriage was unofficially over.

Duke Morrison was now free to become John Wayne. *Stagecoach* had become his launching pad. As McGee wrote, "John Wayne's Ringo Kid is not the 'macho' figure that Wayne would perfect in his later career, but he is such a masculine hero in formation."[75]

11

Wrapping up 1939: *The Night Riders* to *The New Frontier*

Despite the success of *Stagecoach* (or perhaps because of it), John Wayne's B Western career wasn't over. After all, Republic had merely loaned Wayne to Walter Wanger Productions to make *Stagecoach*. Republic immediately had a problem, since the movie's popularity meant that "requests to borrow Wayne became so insistent that Republic found it difficult to keep him on the home lot to complete a film."[1]

Still, Republic still had four more films in the Three Mesquiteers series for him. Duke was probably hoping the studio would not release the low-budget films.[2] Hurst noted that Wayne "felt that Republic could not deliver a true major production."[3] But the studio quickly recognized the profit potential of these films and put all four into production. After all, why waste a new star when he was still under contract?

The Night Riders was released in April 1939, a month after *Stagecoach*. Wayne again had the role of Stony Brooke opposite Ray Corrigan and Max Terhune. Terhune provided comic relief with his ventriloquism act, using a dummy who brags about coming "from a long line of blockheads." This is one of those true Westerns in the Three Mesquiteers series, not one set in modern times. As Haynie wrote, "The Three Mesquiteers were able to jump through time from one film to another."[4]

George Sherman served as director on this and Wayne's last three Mesquiteers movies. Kehr described Sherman as "a greatly talented (and still seriously underrated) filmmaker."[5] He added, "Sherman would go on to make more complex and personal films in his later years at Republic, Universal and Fox, but these early efforts (among his first outings) display great fluidity and a sense of fun."[6]

Yakima Canutt, Glenn Strange and George Montgomery have small,

John Wayne with (from left) Ray Corrigan, Jennifer Jones, an unidentified actor, George Douglas and Max Terhune in *The Night Riders* (1939).

uncredited roles. Tom Tyler played one of the villains in the movie. He would take over the role of Stony Brooke in later movies in the series. Kermit Maynard has a supporting role as a lawman. That was the beginning of a downhill slide for the actor. He had played the lead in some Western films prior to this entry. Using the working title *Lone Star Bullets,* the movie was shot on location at the Agoura Ranch.

The Night Riders places the trio in an unusual role, for them, of being outside the law while they try to unravel a land grant scam. They don masks to rob from a rich land baron and giving the money to poor settlers who are fighting to stay on their homesteads. Eyles described the plot as being in the best tradition of Robin Hood and Zorro.[7]

They start their vendetta after being evicted from their own ranch, the 3M. The villain takes over the land using a forged land grant and using a local card shark to pose as owner of the grant. When the grant is ruled legitimate by the court, the villain starts tossing people off their land.

That includes our heroes, who rebel by donning masks and white robes as they fight back. Known in the area as Los Capaqueros (the Caped

Riders), they become heroes to the locals. The disguises bear a strong resemblance to the robes of the Ku Klux Klan. However, as Kehr noted, "Once the crisis has passed, the boys dutifully turn in their robes to a local law enforcement official. Republic may have been willing to confront fascism, but was not about to endorse vigilantism as an alternative."[8]

The capes contribute to the mystique of the movie. Adding to the enjoyment is a historical tie-in. The trio's antics are unofficially endorsed by then President James A. Garfield, whom they meet while he is traveling out west, something that didn't actually occur in real history. Unfortunately, he is helpless to help the settlers without proof of illegality. The tie-in continues until Garfield is assassinated in 1881, just prior to getting the boys out of jail.[9]

Viewers hear the shots and are informed of the killing when the news is sent out by telegraph. The messenger boy is told that the president was on his way to Williams College when the shooting occurred, a fact that is historically correct. Garfield was scheduled to give a speech there that day.

That meeting with the president is as close as the Mesquiteers come to working for the government. That is a bit unusual for the series, since the Mesquiteers usually act as federal agents in most of the other films in the series.

Eventually they have are captured and sentenced to die by firing squad on July 3. Never fear, Stony eventually meets the former land grant owner and recognizes him as a card shark he's met before. The boys reveal the land baron as a crook and restore the lands of the local settlers. Turns out that there was a federal connection to the fraud in the plot too. The baron was a crooked gambler who teamed up with a former engraver with the U.S. mint to produce the phony land grants.

As Winthrop noted, the entire plot is copied from a real historic event known as the Peralta Grant, a con game led by a real thief name James Addison Reavis.[10] Reavis attempted to use forged land grants in the 19th century to gain title to much of Arizona for his wife.[11]

This Mesquiteers entry maintained its historical accuracy by being set in the Old West of the 1880s. Still, as Miller wrote, "it was somewhat disconcerting to have the trio land in the days of President Garfield's assassination."[12]

If you like the plot, you can watch it again. The film was remade in 1942 as *Arizona Terrors*, starring Don "Red" Barry, or try 1950's *The Baron of Arizona*, featuring Vincent Price and Ellen Drew.

Three Texas Steers has nothing to do with steers; instead the plot

revolves around a circus. Wayne, Ray Corrigan and Max "Lullaby" Terhune again make up the trio who come to the aid of a circus owner with
a rundown ranch and a lonely gorilla named Willie. Carole Landis plays
the female lead, Nancy Evans. Landis, 20 years old at the time, appeared
in another Three Mesquiteers adventure, *Cowboys from Texas,* later that
year. Wayne had left the series by then. Others in the cast included Ralph
Graves, Collette Lyons and Billy Curtis (playing Hercules the Midget).
Filming was done on Ray Corrigan's ranch in Simi Valley. The film was
released May 12, 1939.

Supporting player Roscoe Ates had small roles in a number of important films, including *Alice in Wonderland* (1933) and *Gone with the Wind*
(1939). He is more often remembered today for his role as Soapy Jones,
the stuttering sidekick in several of Eddie Dean's singing cowboy films.[13]
Dean later recalled that many of the comic routines in those movies were
not in the script but were improvised by him and Ates. "A lot of times we'd
end up completely away from the script," Dean once said.[14]

The film had something of an image problem. Sometimes it appears
under the title *Danger Rides the Range,* the title used when it was released
in Great Britain. In Italy, it was known as *Texas Kid.* In any version, circus
owner Nancy Evans enjoys her career under the big top until she turns
down an offer from someone who wants to buy a remote ranch she inherited. Soon afterwards, her circus is beset by a series of accidents ("We
couldn't have a show
without having an
accident," she says).

Eyles liked one
scene in particular:
"There is an impres-
sive montage of tilted
angles during a scene
of the audience pan-
icking after [the vil-
lain] has started a
fire."[15] That scene was
stock footage from an
earlier Republic, *Cir-
cus Girl* (1937). It was
used again by the stu-
dio in the 1955 serial
King of the Carnival.

**John Wayne with Carole Landis in *Three Texas Steers*
(1939).**

The villain, her business manager, hopes the financial setbacks will force her to sell the ranch to keep the show afloat. Instead, she decides to close the circus and move to her WE Ranch. The circus folks end up on the 3M ranch because a 3M sign has been turned upside down, making it look like WE. The boys, reluctant to tell the tired travelers that they are in the wrong place, go to the real WE to spend the night. They are there when the villains arrive, intending to burn the place down.

The three heroes figure out that someone wants the land to resell at a large profit based on inside information about a dam the government wants to build on the land. Unfortunately, they are suspected of being behind the plot. They go on the lam, stealing the circus show horse Rajah in the process. Then they train their new steed as a harness racer, hoping to win first prize at a local fair. That way they can pay off all mortgages on the property and save the ranch for the lovely lady.

Duke tries to outrun a posse with his horse pulling a buggy in a harness trot (a ridiculous scene, by the way) and is quickly chased down. In jail, the three cowboys plead that they are innocent. The sheriff, convinced, lets them out long enough to run in the race. But Rajah has a weakness for music. At the sound of a trumpet, he stops racing and starts dancing.

While all of this nonsense erupts, Terhune has his own problem: The lonely gorilla (played by Ray Corrigan) has taken a liking to him. One of the circus performers refers to the gorilla as an "upholstered nitwit." As Kehr noted, "If nothing else, the circus angle gives the second-billed Mesquiteer, Corrigan, a sterling opportunity to take advantage of his side-line as a gorilla impersonator—a talent he would continue to exploit … long after his career as a human had faded. On Poverty Row, it was always a good idea to have something to fall back on."[16]

Despite these rather ludicrous plot twists, there are a few entertaining lines. When the neophyte ranchers first see their new rural home, one asks, "I wonder how long it takes to learn how to milk a chicken." When a woman with the circus learns that Stony is a cowhand, she responds, "If I could only learn to moo." Terhune's ventriloquist dummy keeps him awake at night, the little fellow claiming he can't sleep because his "back heels as stiff as a board." And there's one piece of advice we all could follow: "Never stand close to a horse's mouth after he's eaten."

One interesting aspect of the film is the work of Carole Landis in the female lead. Although relatively unknown today, Landis was quite a celebrity during her prime. Rex Harrison once described her as "a liberated woman who unfortunately lived before her time." Landis ran away from home at the age of 14, was married by 15, and had her first film role at 18.

By the time she appeared with Duke in this oater, she had an off-camera reputation for instability.

Fleming wrote that, in *Three Texas Steers,* Landis was "beautiful though miscast as a circus owner, and handles her role with charm. Her athleticism is evident ... as she rides horses and throws herself around the set."[17] Landis later became a wartime pin-up girl. Despite a thriving career in which she appeared in 49 movies, Landis committed suicide on the Fourth of July in 1948 at the age of 29.[18] She had dined with Rex Harrison the night before, and he was the one who discovered her body.[19]

Despite her presence, this is a truly bad film. It lacks the action of the good Mesquiteers films, and it seems to be constantly in search of a plot. As Western fan Elliott wrote, "If you've ever wanted to see John Wayne act next to a midget and gorilla then this is the film for you."[20] But in Miller his opinion, "It was a fast, furious and very funny story ... with a wild conclusion played for laughs."[21]

Duke does a solid job, but you get the feeling that he's ready for his career to really take off. As Eyles wrote, "Wayne doesn't have much chance to stand out, though he shows himself as the brains of the outfit."[22]

John Wayne with Pamela Blake, Yakima Canutt, Leroy Mason and Katherine Kenworthy in *Wyoming Outlaw* (1939).

Wyoming Outlaw, the third Mesquiteers film Republic released after Wayne appeared in *Stagecoach,* was of better quality than *Three Texas Steers.* It's a remake of an early Mesquiteers entry, 1938's *Outlaws of Sonora* with Robert Livingston in the role of Stony Brooke.

Don "Red" Barry, better known for his later work as Red Ryder, co-stars with the boys. Pamela Blake, performing under the name Adele Pearce, is the female lead. Others in the cast included LeRoy Mason, Charles Middleton, Katherine Kenworthy, Elmo Lincoln, Jack Ingram and Yakima Canutt. Lincoln was a silent era star who came out of retirement to play the sheriff. Like many of Wayne's Mesquiteers entries, it was shot at Corriganville and in Simi Valley. It was released on June 27, 1939.

Set during the Dust Bowl era following World War I, the film examines the impact of local government corruption on farmers. Mesquiteers Wayne and Corrigan are joined by Raymond Hatton as Rusty Joslin. This was Hatton's first appearance in the Mesquiteers series. As Miller noted, "Hatton was less the hayseed than Terhune and was inclined to treat his conquered adversaries with no tenderness whatsoever, booting them in the rear as they would be escorted to incarceration."[23] Hatton had a long career as a sidekick for a number of B Western cowboys.[24]

A hungry farmer steals one of their steers. Rather than being outraged at the theft, the three cowboys are curious about a man who can slaughter a steer and is strong enough to walk off with the entire carcass. They stop in town, mention the steer-totin' outlaw, and are soon pointed toward Will Parker (Barry), the son of a local hard-luck family.

At a dance, Duke strikes up a friendship with Parker's sister (Pearce), who promptly steals $20 from him. The boys soon discover that the Parkers have been down on their luck since they bucked the local political boss, a villain who is forcing the locals to pay him bribes to keep their jobs. Unemployment and the ravages of the weather have driven the family to the brink of starvation.

The boys experience the ravages of the weather themselves when they get caught in a dust storm. The event causes Rusty to comment on the "magnificent" view: "You can see the Rocky Mountains," he says. "That's them blowing by." The 3M team hires Will as a cowhand, but his reputation prevents him from working and eventually leads to his arrest for poaching. Will breaks out of jail, intent on killing the local political boss.

Instead, he kills a couple of the boss' henchmen (including Yakima Canutt) and becomes a wanted man. The boys try to deliver him peacefully to justice while removing the villain from power. They resolve it with an ending that is not one you typically see in B Westerns. In fact, the whole movie creates a different sense of the modern West than is typical for the genre. Much of the credit goes to Barry, who overpowers the other actors. It's understandable why he eventually became a leading man himself.

The action scenes are excellent, including a couple of leaps into a river and one superb fight scene. In the latter, Rusty handles two of the villains easily, while Ray and Duke struggle to handle one bad guy each. Duke's opponent is Yakima, and they put on one dandy display of movie fighting.

Stanfield, an academic critic, was particularly complimentary: "[It's] relatively hard-hitting in its commentary on the issues raised by the Dust Bowl and the Depression and their effects on the rural population."[25]

One fan, Phillips, wasn't impressed, writing that "the special effects were cheesy."[26] But Elliott like it, particularly one performer: "it does have a strong benefit of featuring a terrific performance by Barry who easily steals the show. He manages to be a very likable Robin Hood character."[27] Miller wrote, "Barry gave the role strength, and more than the ordinary amount of depth."[28]

Anyway, this one is worth watching. And Duke is inching one movie closer to being a star. As Miller wrote, "*Stagecoach* had been in release for a time by now, and it became increasingly obvious that Wayne was not about to continue going through the motions as Stony Brooke."[29] Republic even started letting those in the industry know that Livingston would be returning the series for movies released in 1940.

New Frontier, Wayne's last film in the Three Mesquiteers series, was released in September 1939 just as war was breaking out in Europe. Duke was familiar with the plot: It's a remake of his 1935 film *The New Frontier.* The movie was filmed under the working title of *Raiders of the Wasteland* and was later re-released in 1949, after Duke was a well-known star, under the title *Frontier Horizon.* It usually appears under the latter title when shown on TV.

To save production costs, Republic edited in scenes that were shot for Wayne's first film, *The Big Trail* (1930), and *Billy the Kid Returns,* a 1938 Roy Rogers movie. Much of the other filming was done at Ray Corrigan's ranch. The script was provided by Betty Burbridge and Luci Ward. Yakima Canutt led the stunt team, which also included Walt LaRue and George Montgomery.

The most obvious problem with the film is that of historical accuracy. It opens at the end of the Civil War, but quickly moves 50 years into the future, i.e., well after the turn of the century. The three heroes were hypo-

Clockwise, standing are Burr Caruth, Harrison Greene, John Wayne, LeRoy Mason and Dave O'Brien, and seated Hal Price, and Eddy Waller in *New Frontier* **(1939).**

thetically Pony Express riders, but that occupation had long since died. It only lasted from 1860 to 1861 before being killed off by the invention of the telegraph.[30]

Further, while much of the action is supposed to occur around 1914, the settlers continue to dress as if it were still the post–Civil War period. And they all ride horses or drive buggies—no automobiles although they were fairly common in 1914.

The film also has another famous element: It was the movie debut of Jennifer Jones.[31] She appears under the name Phylis Isley. Only four years later, as Jennifer Jones, she won an Oscar for her performance in 1943's *The Song of Bernadette*. Under the name Charles Whitaker, Slim Whitakern makes a brief appearance as Jed Turner.

The plot involves the Three Mesquiteers taking the leadership role in a land swap. Following the Civil War, a group of settlers had established their homesteads in a place they called New Hope Valley. They remain happy there for 50 years, celebrating the settlement's golden anniversary with the Mesquiteers watching the event. The celebration is short-lived, however. It turns out that the state government is planning to build a dam that will put New Hope Valley underwater.

The trio convinces the settlers to swap their land for some other property. What they don't know is that the state was planning to pay those settlers a fair price for their land. The land that they traded for turns out to be worthless. The villains, a greedy real estate promoter, arranged for the swap so that they could get the state's money for the settlers' land. Once the Mesquiteers discover that they've been duped, they try to warn the settlers and stop the trade. To do so, they have to take on both the villains and the local law officials. What with the anachronisms and the repetitive plot, this was a weak Mesquiteers entry. Amateur reviewer Miller wrote simply that it "didn't reach the standards set by preceding entries."[32]

Its release on August 10, 1939, ended the involvement of two members of the trio. Ray Corrigan left the series in search of success as a star in his own series. He was replaced as Tucson Smith by Bob Steele. For John Wayne, *New Frontier* represented the end of his career in cheap B Westerns. As Connors noted, "Wayne was obviously off to greener pastures."[33] He was replaced in the series by Robert Livingston, who had played Stony Brooke before Duke took the role.

The 1940s were approaching and Duke Morrison had completed his transformation into John Wayne.

Now it was time to be a star.

12

Looking Back, Looking Forward

As the decade of the 1930s ended, John Wayne was on the verge of superstardom. It didn't come as quickly as he might have hoped. Ironically, though, he never legally changed his name. That caused him some problems later on, e.g., when he applied for passports. For example, in 1972, the Duke made an effort to collect documentation about his birth. His letter to the County of Los Angeles asked if they could certify that the was born Marion Robert Morrison. And, he added, "I have used the name of John Wayne for the past 43 years, both in my business and professional life."[1]

Even his children were legally born as Morrison and retain that name on their birth certificates. Patrick later noted, however, "Obviously, we are Waynes."[2]

Duke himself rarely responded to the name John, only to "Duke" or "Wayne."[3] When he filmed an introduction for the first episode of TV's *Gunsmoke*, starring his friend James Arness, he addressed the camera simply by saying, "My name's Wayne."

During the decades that followed *Stagecoach*, he refined his on-screen persona, which was an ideal projection of himself. As Rafferty wrote, "The whole point of the character Wayne embodied in something like 150 pictures … was that there was no mystery to him at all: What you saw was what you got, and if you didn't like it, tough."[4]

He expanded that image in the 1940s, while successfully becoming a star. In the 1950s, it grew stronger—so much stronger that he essentially portrayed a critique of himself in *The Man Who Shot Liberty Valance*. He merely used *Liberty Valance* as a breather, though, quickly jumping back into full Wayne mode.

By the 1960s, the image was set in stone, or at least adobe. His own production of *The Alamo* is perhaps his most personable interpretation of his film persona. The Davy Crockett who fought at the Alamo, based on Wayne's portrayal, seems to express views that have a lot in common with the film persona of John Wayne.

In the 1970s, he received his only Oscar (for *True Grit*) and portrayed himself dying in *The Shootist*. After his death, the image lived on. In death, his political and personal views seems to move off stage. Newspaper and magazine articles included fewer critiques about his political ideology while offering more insight into his acting and his movies. He had become an influential figure, not necessarily from a political view, but as a person who expressed common hopes. As Didion wrote, "When John Wayne rode through my childhood…, he determined forever the shape of certain of our dreams."[5]

He also expressed common values. As Cavinder noted, "In a John Wayne Western, … pride is part of the American way, toughness is part of manhood, gentleness toward women is a mandate, fear is something one has only for God, and a hero of the Great Southwest must be true to his word and his kin and fast with his gun."[6]

And Wayne continued to place his faith in the Western genre. "Don't ever make the mistake of looking down your nose at Westerns," he once said. "They're art—the good ones, I mean. Sure, they're simple. But simplicity is art…. Westerns are folklore…. And folklore is international…. And besides that, they're fun. I like making Westerns."[7]

Through his Westerns, John Wayne was, finally, the film hero who reflected the idea that "What you saw was what you got, and it you didn't like it, tough."

Despite opposition by some to his political views, most people liked it.

Concluding Thoughts

Since the time that movies became commercially profitable, there has always been a distinction between actors and stars. Stage actors who start acting in films soon realized just how limiting the technology of film is. One of the biggest differences is in the physical performance of the actor. Stage actors must learn to project their voices and exaggerate their gestures enough to be heard in the last row of the theater (regardless of the acoustics of the room). Movies, on the other hand, exaggerate the actors' voices and gestures to the point where movie actors must learn to underplay these characteristics. A shrug on stage may be the appropriate dramatic gesture, but when amplified to a 40-foot screen will seem comical. Wayne faced that problem in his first movie *The Big Trail*. There was one account of director Raoul Walsh constantly scolding Wayne for over-acting. Almost as an act of petulance, Wayne gave the performance in what he considered to be perfect deadpan, and the director yelled, "That's it! Now you've got it!"

On the other hand, the medium of film lends itself for an actor to develop signature non-verbal characteristics to work into an overarching persona. Cary Grant's nondescript accent, Humphrey Bogart's curled lip sneer, Marilyn Monroe's breathy delivery, Kirk Douglas' gravelly punch on this lines and Jack Nicholson's wild-eyed stare are all good examples of actors who have identifiable acting quirks that made them immediately identifiable. In such cases, the audience member will say, "Oh look, there is Cary Grant acting as a cat burglar" or "I love a good Bogie movie." In all cases, the audience is reacting to the actor, not necessarily the specific performance. John Wayne had that capability too.

Oprah Winfrey recounts taking acting classes when she was preparing for *The Color Purple* and constantly struggling with her teacher. That teacher finally stopped and angrily accused her of not wanting to be an actor but rather a movie star. She smiled and said, "Of course." That response made her teacher laugh and change his approach.

Movies have always created that dialectic between acting and stardom. The movies needed actors to move the plot forward and provide a narrative for the audience. But the industry needed stars to make money. Studios learned that audiences came to the movies to watch stars. That's why they cultivated those stars so carefully. Once an actor was identified as a star, the studio carefully chose films that met their star persona. Meanwhile, those same studios saw B movies as the proving ground for future stars. And that's where John Wayne rose to stardom, in the B Westerns of the 1930s, as he waited for his chance to become a star in *Stagecoach*.

Wayne was the prototypical movie star. Over the course of his career he only received two Academy Award nominations and one Oscar. He was nominated for his performance in *Sands of Iwo Jima* and then won the Oscar for playing Rooster Cogburn in *True Grit*. Ironically it is arguable that the role of Rooster Cogburn was the character most counter to the Wayne persona. While not an out-and-out mercenary like the roles his counterpart Clint Eastwood was making famous at the time, Cogburn was a self-indulgent, alcoholic, shoot-first gunfighter with little or no moral compass. He was hardly the white-hat good guy that Wayne had become so synonymous with.

Most of Wayne's awards were for his popularity, his star quality and his patriotism.[8] All this speaks to his persona, rather than his acting ability. Wayne may have made some questionable acting choices, perhaps the worst being taking on the role of Genghis Khan in *The Conqueror*. That movie was laughably bad and likely the worst performance ever turned in by a movie star. It must be noted, however, that the role played directly into Wayne's rugged two-fisted persona. So his acting credentials may have been called into question, but his movie star persona remained intact, and continued to serve him throughout the rest of his career and life.

John Wayne the Star

Wayne's early career was spent in B movies which were used by the bigger studios to cultivate new stars. Movie studios liked the star system, because it provided them with an easy way to make money. As Fowles noted, "By allowing a large number of people to focus on a small number of performers, these technologies fashioned the crucible of extensive public attention from which issued the star role."[9] He added, "The ability to provide people across the nation with virtually simultaneous exposure to a star was an important feature of the movies."[10]

Wayne's stardom was based on his physical presence. He often claimed that his secret to acting was simply reacting to what was happening in a scene. But it was more than that. Through his work in B Westerns, he had learned the value of physical presence and movement. Eyman wrote, "Wayne's characters would always be defined as much by movement and attitude as by words."[11]

From that perspective, perhaps it is no surprise that his work in Westerns in the 1930s led to him becoming the nation's biggest Western star. But what sticks out is that he made it, while so many of his contemporaries and those who came later never did. Wayne's early movies included co-starring roles with Ray Corrigan, for example. Corrigan had the physique and good looks of a movie star, plus a memorable nickname ("Crash"), but never achieved stardom. He finished out his career in small roles, acting in his gorilla suit, and renting out his ranch to movie companies.[12] Similarly, Bob Steele had a solid career as a B Western star, but he lacked the imposing physique to become a star. In the 1940s, Allan "Rocky" Lane looked like he had star potential with his good looks and physical presence, but he never broke out of the B Western mold; he spent the latter part of his career playing supporting parts and, on TV, providing the voice of the horse Mister Ed.[13] Similarly, Audie Murphy came out of World War II and looked like he was on the verge of major stardom as a B Western actor, but he was never able to break out of that mold.[14] Only Clint Eastwood would match Wayne's achievement as a Western star, and Eastwood did it through television and spaghetti Westerns, not from B movies. The only B Western stars to reach anywhere near the level of fame as John Wayne were Gene Autry and Roy Rogers, and both of them had to stay within the B genre to achieve their stardom. The list of B movie stars who never made it to true stardom is thus lengthy, including such names as Tex Ritter, Hoot Gibson, Lash LaRue, Eddie Dean and many others. Only John Wayne escaped to the stardom of A-list films.

John Wayne's Popularity

John Wayne's popularity was unmatched for decades. He was on the list of top ten box offices stars for 25 out of 26 years, from 1949 to 1974—an achievement unmatched by any other actor. He was in the top four for 19 of those years. Even today, decades after this death, he is still listed among the favorite actors of all time. He was and still is a commercial and popular success. As Eyman wrote, "Successive generations desired John Wayne in a way shared by no other star of his generation."[15]

Perhaps one reason Wayne was so popular was that he never forgot his humble beginnings. Goldman noted that there was a "relentless normalcy to the man. As a young actor, he was quite aware that he was not a natural talent, that he came to acting from being a crew member—a 'regular guy'—and he never forgot that person."[16] Goldman added that there was a lesson in Wayne's life: "that a single individual, even one constantly spotlighted under the bright glare of fame, can privately, personally, and deeply influence those around him in a way that far outshines even his impact as a global figure."[17]

He liked being a movie cowboy and seemed more comfortable in Westerns than in any other genre. Goldman noted, "He often spoke poetically of wanting to capture the pioneering spirit of the Old West."[18] That desire likely translated itself on screen to an audience that was fascinated with the Western mythology and its influence on the nation's growth. It was an ideal match of popularity: an audience that was clinging to the memory of the Western myth and an actor who embodied it.

A look at his acting awards provides an insight into his star power. He was only nominated for two Best Actor Oscars—for *Sands of Iwo Jima, and True Grit*, with a win for *True Grit*. The lack of awards were probably an indication that he was not the most versatile of actors. It was clear he hardly shifted his on-screen persona at all. His award for *True Grit* was often satirized as his greatest stretch because he played John Wayne as an alcoholic with an eye patch.

On the other hand, Wayne won scores of awards that attested to his immense popularity as a movie star. If he rarely achieved critical acclaim, audiences loved him. He also never catered to the tastes of Hollywood or New York. As Eyman wrote, "It was in Middle America that Wayne found his audience."[19] Because of that, he was a bankable star during the studio system and tremendously popular for his Westerns and war movies.

John Wayne the Patriot

Wayne's political views were unapologetically conservative. When Jimmy Carter was elected president in 1976, Wayne sent a brief note of congratulations to him and signed it "The Loyal Opposition."[20] He and the president later became friends, although Wayne never voted for Carter. Wayne participated in Carter's inaugural concert and helped him lobby for the passage of the Panama Canal Treaty. "John Wayne was bigger than life," Carter later said.[21] He added:

> In an age of few heroes, he was the genuine article. But he was more than a hero. He was a symbol of so many of the qualities that made America great. The ruggedness, the tough independence, the sense of personal courage—on and off the screen—reflected the best of our national character.[22]

"What I learned from him," the president added, "was that patriotism, policy debates, even major disagreements about the nation's direction need not be hostile or personal or contentious."[23] That's a lesson that the nation could still learn today.

Wayne represented a world where the quintessential struggle was between good and evil. The vast majority of his Westerns skirted the Native American issue (in fact, the few times that Native Americans were portrayed, they were mostly sympathetic characters), his movies dealt with the proverbial white hat-black hat struggles. Law and order vs. evil and chaos, and America was always on the side of law and order.

His war movies never showed any ambiguity or sympathy towards the enemy. Whether the enemy were outlaws, the Germans or Japanese during World War II, the North Koreans and Chinese in the Korean War, or the North Vietnamese in *The Green Berets* (likely his most controversial role), John Wayne was on the side of America. Again, he was lauded with as many patriot awards as acting awards. As Neil Gebler wrote:

> From the time he reached stardom in the 1940s, Wayne was not just a movie star, though he was one of the biggest. Nor was he just an icon, though he was one of the most compelling—a whole generation of men imitated his bearish growl and lumbering walk. More important, Wayne presented values that many now associate with America itself.[24]

For more than half a century, John Wayne defined what it was to be an American man.

Wayne tended to view his enemies (Nazis, outlaws, Communists, etc.) as existential threats; if he were alive today he would undoubtedly be making movies about Middle Eastern terrorists. But he never viewed his political rivals in such a way. Though a staunch conservative and Republican, he maintained close friendships with outspoken liberal and Democratic actors like Henry Fonda. His relationship with Jimmy Carter clearly showed that he understood the notion of democratic loyal opposition. He likely would not approve of the growing hostility between the left and right today.

John Wayne Inventing John Wayne

The John Wayne transformation was so complete that he did not just blur the lines between the man and the movie star, he completely obliterated them. It is hard to find an actor who was so completely successful at creating an image that they would essentially become the person they created. Many actors chafe at the idea of being typecast. Sean Connery, Matt Damon, Alec Baldwin and many others have worked hard to not be typecast. Many even walked away from lucrative franchises to avoid being stuck with a specific image. Perhaps Connery leaving the James Bond series is the best example of this.

But John did not worry about typecasting. In fact, he embraced it. No matter what role you saw him in, he was John Wayne. Whether he was cast as a cowboy, soldier or even Genghis Khan, he was John Wayne. If you saw him in an interview or on the news, he was John Wayne. He was the rough, ultra-patriotic, unapologetic hero who marched through life with his indistinct drawl, loping sideways on a line as straight as an arrow. He breathed and lived the role for all to see. Officially, and legally, he remained Marion Michael Morrison, but in public and in his life he had become the person he invented: John Wayne.

A few action stars, such as Chuck Norris and Bruce Lee, tried to replicate this career strategy. And, arguably, Marilyn Monroe tried to inhabit the persona she created for herself; though some would argue that the pressure of the charade was one of the factors that drove her to suicide. But nobody else has been as successful at inventing and living their persona as was John Wayne. As Eyman wrote, "John Wayne would be the vehicle through which Duke Morrison acquired power as an actor and as a man."[25] Having created the persona of John Wayne, there was no going back for Duke Morrison. If all the world's a stage, then John Wayne proudly walked the boards as John Wayne.

His image was that of a man who never faced self-doubt.[26] Some of his latter movies were deliberately crafted to reflect his ideology and image, including his self-produced epic *The Alamo* and his version of the Billy the Kid saga, *Chisum*., French noted, "*Chisum* was carefully designed for John Wayne by his producer son Patrick, and the screenwriter Andrew J. Fenady, to express Wayne's political views."[27] French argued that *Rio Bravo* "is as much about John Wayne and the notion of heroism he represents in the cinema as it is about this particular gunfighter."[28] In some instances, Wayne took his lack of self-doubt too far. His film persona led to a psychological phenomenon called the John Wayne Syndrome. It was a condition for military veterans who experienced both guilt and shame over the normal human mixture of fear and bravery during battle.[29]

Regardless, for good or bad, the John Wayne persona had been built. It was not going to be torn down.

Chapter Notes

Introduction

1. Ethan Wayne, "The Cowboy Way," In *John Wayne* (New York: Topix Media, 2015), 21.

2. F. D. Cavinder, "John Wayne: How He Won the West," *Saturday Evening Post*, July/August, 1979, 60.

3. *Ibid.,* 58.

4. Helen Akitt, *Hollywood Westerns: The Movies, the Heroes* (East Bridgewater, MA: World Publications, 2013), 43.

5. Michael Goldman, *John Wayne: The Genuine Article* (San Rafael, CA: Insight, 2015).

6. Scott Eyman, *John Wayne: The Life and Legend* (New York: Simon & Schuster, 2014).

7. Mark Ricci, Boris Zmijewsky and Steve Zmijewsky, *The Films of John Wayne* (Secaucus, NY: Citadel Press, 1970), 11.

8. George N. Fenin and William K. Everson, *The Western: From Silents to the Seventies* (New York: Grossman, 1973).

9. Marilyn Ann Moss, *Raoul Walsh: The True Adventures of Hollywood's Legendary Director* (Lexington: University Press of Kentucky, 2011).

10. Todd McCarthy and Charles Flynn, eds. *King of the Bs: Working within the Hollywood System* (New York: E. P. Dutton, 1975).

11. Mark Ricci, Boris Zmijewsky, and Steven Zmijewsky, *The Films of John Wayne* (New York: The Citadel Press, 1970).

12. Bobby Copeland, *B Westerns Boot Hill* (Madison, NC: Empire, 1999), 7.

13. Dave Kehr, "Tall in the Saddle in 2 Eras at Once," *New York Times* (New York), Sep. 30, 2012.

14. Bobby J. Copeland and Richard B. Smith III, *Gabby Hayes: King of the Cowboy Comics* (Madison, NC: Empire, 2008).

15. David D. Rothel, *Those Great Cowboy Sidekicks* (Madison, NC: Empire, 2001).

16. Stef Donev, *The Fun of Living Dangerously: The Life of Yakima Canutt* (New York: McGraw-Hill, 2000).

17. Bobby J. Copeland and Richard B. Smith, *Gabby Hayes: King of the Cowboy Comics* (Madison, NC: Empire Publishing, 2008).

18. Ethan Wayne, "The Cowboy Way," In *John Wayne.* (New York: Topix Media, 2015), 21.

19. Lee Simmons, "The First Action Hero," *Wired*, May 2012, 96.

20. David Rothel, *The Singings Cowboys* (South Brunswick, NJ: A.S. Barnes, 1978).

21. Pete Martin, "Big John," *Saturday Evening Post*, July/August, 1979, 57c-57i, 57e.

22. George N. Fenin and William K. Everson, *The Western: From Silents to the Seventies* (New York: Grossman, 1973), 292.

23. Lee Simmons, "The First Action Hero," *Wired*, May 2012, 96.

24. James K. Crissman and Dianne R. Moran, "The Importance of Juvenile Co-Stars in B-western Movies," *Journal of the West* 50, no. 4 (2011): 17–26.

25. David Rothel, *Those Great Cowboy Sidekicks* (Madison, NC: Empire Pub, 2001), 205.

26. Michael Goldman, *John Wayne: The Genuine Article* (San Rafael, CA: Insight, 2015). 59.

27. Michael Goldman, *John Wayne: The Genuine Article* (San Rafael, CA: Insight, 2015). 62.

28. Terrence Rafferty, "Building the Duke, Film by Film," *New York Times* (New York), May 20, 2007, AR15.

29. *Ibid.*, AR15, AR17.
30. *Ibid.*, AR17.
31. Ethan Wayne, "A Timeless Western Icon," *John Wayne* (New York: Topix Media, 2015), 6.

Chapter 1

1. Marilyn Ann Moss, *Raoul Walsh: The True Adventures of Hollywood's Legendary Director* (Lexington: University Press of Kentucky, 2011).
2. Rinker Buck, *The Oregon Trail: A New American Journey* (New York: Simon & Schuster, 2015).
3. Ronald L. Davis, *Duke: The Life and Image of John Wayne* (Norman: University of Oklahoma Press, 1998).
4. *Ibid.*, 42.
5. *Ibid.*, 45.
6. Mark Ricci, Boris Zmijewsky and Steve Zmijewsky, *The Films of John Wayne* (Scausus, NJ: Citadel Press, 1970).
7. Allen Eyles, *John Wayne and the Movies* (Cranbury, NJ: A.S. Barnes, 1976).
8. Marc Eliot, *American Titan: Searching for John Wayne* (New York: Harper Collins, 2014).
9. Mark Ricci, Boris Zmijewsky and Steve Zmijewsky, *The Films of John Wayne* (Scausus, NJ: Citadel Press, 1970).
10. Michael Goldman, *John Wayne: The Genuine Article* (San Rafael, CA: Insight, 2015), 47.
11. Greg Santoro, "The Big Trail," in *100 Greatest Westerns*, ed. Greg (Leesburg, VA: Weider History Group, 2009), 57, 59.
12. Andrew Sarris, *The American Cinema: Directors and Directions, 1929–1968* (New York: Da Capo Press, 1996), 120.
13. Rinker Buck, *The Oregon Trail: A New American Journey* (New York: Simon & Schuster, 2015).
14. Mark Ricci, Boris Zmijewsky and Steve Zmijewsky, *The Films of John Wayne* (Scausus, NJ: Citadel Press, 1970).
15. Marc Eliot, *American Titan: Searching for John Wayne* (New York: Harper Collins, 2014), 51.
16. Mike Clark, "The Big Trail," *USA Today* (Mclean, VA), May 16, 2008.
17. Michael Goldman, *John Wayne: The Genuine Article* (San Rafael, CA: Insight, 2015).
18. Andrew Sarris, *The American Cinema:*

Directors and Directions: 1929–1968 (New York: Da Capo Press, 1996), 210.
19. George N. Fenin and William K. Everson, *The Western: From Silents to the Seventies* (New York: Grossman, 1973), 178.
20. Mark Ricci, Boris Zmijewsky and Steve Zmijewsky, *The Films of John Wayne* (Scausus, NJ: Citadel Press, 1970). 35–36.
21. Scott Eyman, *John Wayne: The Life and Legend* (New York: Simon & Schuster, 2014), 51.
22. Marc Eliot, *American Titan: Searching for John Wayne* (New York: Harper Collins, 2014), 51.
23. Mike Clark, "The Big Trail," *USA Today* (Mclean, VA), May 16, 2008.
24. John. M. Smith, *The Films of Raoul Walsh: A Critical Approach* (CreateSpace, 2013), 57.
25. Allen Eyles, *John Wayne and the Movies* (Cranbury, NJ: A.S. Barnes, 1976), 22.
26. Mike Clark, "The Big Trail," *USA Today* (Mclean, VA), May 16, 2008.
27. Marc Eliot, *American Titan: Searching for John Wayne* (New York: Harper Collins, 2014), 51.
28. *ibid.*
29. Allen Eyles, *John Wayne and the Movies* (Cranbury, NJ: A.S. Barnes, 1976), 22.
30. John. M. Smith, *The Films of Raoul Walsh: A Critical Approach* (CreateSpace Independent Publishing Platform, 2013), 57.
31. Michael Munn, *John Wayne: The Man behind the Myth* (New York: New American Library, 2003), 25.
32. *ibid.* 53.
33. Marc Eliot, *American Titan: Searching for John Wayne* (New York: Harper Collins, 2014), 47.
34. George N. Fenin and William K. Everson, *The Western: From Silents to the Seventies* (New York: Grossman, 1973).
35. Ronald I. Davis, *Duke: The Life and Image of John Wayne.* (Norman: University of Oklahoma Press, 1998), 46.
36. Michael Munn, *John Wayne: The Man behind the Myth* (New York: New American Library, 2003), 4.

Chapter 2

1. Ronald I. Davis, *Duke: The Life and Image of John Wayne* (Norman: University of Oklahoma Press, 1998), 48.
2. Bernard F. Dick, *Hollywood Madonna:*

Loretta Young. (Oxford: University of Mississippi Press, 2011).

3. Joan Webster Anderson, *Forever Young: The Life, Loves and Enduring Faith of a Hollywood Legend* (Allen, TX: Thomas More, 2012).

4. Gary Dickerson, "Weepy, Slight Early 1930s Melodrama," *IMDb: Internet Movie Data Base,* December 21, 2001, http://www.imdb.com/.

5. *Ibid.*

6. Mark Waltz, "He May Not Be the Duke of West Point, but He's Certainly King with the Ladies!," *IMDb: Internet Movie Database,* February 18, 2015, http://www.imdb.com/.

7. Buck Rainey, *The Life and Films of Buck Jones: The Silent Era* (Clearwater, FL: World of Yesterday, 1988).

8. Allen Eyles, *John Wayne in the Movies* (Cranbury, NJ: A.S. Barnes, 1976), 27.

9. Cristi Ciopron, "The Quiet Oldster Who Finds a Patch," *IMDb: Internet Movie Data Base,* May 24, 2015, http://www.imdb.com/.

10. George N. Fenin and William K. Everson, *The Western: From Silents to the Seventies* (New York: Grossman, 1973), 219.

11. Brian J. Smith, "Range 'Fued,'" *IMDb: Internet Movie Database,* August 9, 1999, http://www.imdb.com/.

Chapter 3

1. Richard M. Hurst, *Republic Studios: Between Poverty Row and the Majors* (Lanham, MD: Scarecrow Press, 2007).

2. Dave Kehr, "A Studio Luxuriating in Louche and Lurid," *New York Times* (New York), Sep. 15, 2013.

3. Michael Goldman, *John Wayne: The Genuine Article* (San Rafael, CA: Insight, 2015), 49–51.

4. Allen Eyles, *John Wayne and the Movies* (Cranbury, NJ: A.S. Barnes, 1976).

5. *Ibid.,* 27.

6. Tim McCoy and Ronald McCoy, *Tim McCoy Remembers the West* (New York: Doubleday, 1977).

7. Carl Rollyson, *A Real American Character: The Life of Walter Brennan* (Jackson: University Press of Mississippi, 2015).

8. John Boston, *Santa Clarita Valley* (Mount Pleasant, SC, 2009).

9. Allan Pollack, Kin Stephens, and E.J. Stephens, *Legendary Locales of the Santa Clarita Valley* (Mount Pleasant, NC: Arcadia, 2012).

10. Michael Morrison, "Excellent Cast, Generally Good Dialog, Great Directing," *IMDb: Internet Movie Database,* February 27, 2011, http://www.imdb.com/.

11. Allen Eyles, *John Wayne and the Movies* (Cranbury, NJ: A.S. Barnes, 1976), 27.

12. George N. Fenin and William K. Everson, *The Western: From Silents to the Seventies* (New York: Grossman, 1973).

13. Randy Roberts and James S. Olson, *John Wayne: American* (New York: Free Press, 1995), 143.

14. Greg Lenberg, *Classic Western Films Poster Book: 1930–1935* (CreateSpace, 2015).

15. Allen Eyles, *John Wayne and the Movies* (Cranbury, NJ: A.S. Barnes, 1976), 31.

16. George N. Fenin and William K. Everson, *The Western: From Silents to the Seventies* (New York: Grossman, 1973), 195.; see also, E. J. Stephens and Marc Wanamaker, *Early Warner Bros. Studios* (Charleston, SC: Arcadia Publishing, 2010).

17. Leonard Maltin and Jerry Beck, *Of Mice and Magic: A History of American Animated Cartoons* (New York: Penguin, 1987).

18. Marc Eliot, *American Titan: Searching for John Wayne* (New York: HarperCollins, 2014), 61.

19. *Ibid.*

20. Allen Eyles, *John Wayne and the Movies* (Cranbury, NJ: A.S. Barnes, 1976), 32.

21. Brian Smith, "Good Start to Short-Lived Series," *IMDb: Internet Movie Database,* November 27, 2006, http://www.imdb.com/.

22. Wes Connors, "Horsing Around with Maynard and the Duke," *IMDb: Internet Movie Database,* March 22, 2008, http://www.imdb.com/.

23. Neil Doyle, "Early Wayne Western Is a Good B Film," *IMDb: Internet Movie Database,* March 22, 2008, http://www.imdb.com/.

24. Ronald L. Davis, *Duke: The Life and Image of John Wayne* (Norman: University of Oklahoma Press, 1998), 53.

25. Don Miller, *Hollywood Corral* (New York: Popular Library, 1976), 63.

26. *Ibid.,* 66.

27. Gail Stephens, *Shadow of Shiloh: Major General Lew Wallace in the Civil War* (Indianapolis: Indiana Historical Society, 2010).

28. Lew Wallace, *Ben-Hur: A Tale of the Christ* (New York: Wordsworth, 1995); Ray E. Boomhower, *The Sword & the Pen: A Life of*

Lew Wallace (Indianapolis: Indiana Historical Society, 2005).

29. Mark Lee Gardner, *To Hell on a Fast Horse: The Untold Story of Billy the Kid and Pat Garrett* (New York: William Morrow, 2011).

30. Allen Eyles, *John Wayne and the Movies* (Cranbury, NJ: A.S. Barnes, 1976), 32.

31. Ronald L. Davis, *Duke: The Life and Image of John Wayne* (Norman: University of Oklahoma Press, 1998), 53.

32. Brian Smith, "Routine Early Wayne Western," *IMDb: Internet Movie Database*, December 4, 2006, http://www.imdb.com/.

33. Michael Goldman, *John Wayne: The Genuine Article* (San Rafael, CA: Insight, 2015), 52.

34. Robert G. Sherman, *Quiet on the Set!: Motion Picture History at the Iverson Movie Location Ranch* (Los Angeles: Sherway Publishing, 1984).

35. Helen Akitt, *Hollywood Westerns: The Movies, the Heroes* (East Bridgewater, MA: World Publications, 2013).

36. Ronald L. Davis, *Duke: The Life and Image of John Wayne*. (Norman: University of Oklahoma Press, 1998).

37. Allen Eyles, *John Wayne and the Movies* (Cranbury, NJ: A.S. Barnes, 1976), 32.

38. George N. Fenin and William K. Everson, *The Western: From Silents to the Seventies* (New York: Grossman, 1973), 219.

39. *Ibid.*

40. Mark Ricci, Boris Zmijewsky, and Steve Zmijewsky, *The Films of John Wayne* (Secaurus, NJ: Citadel Press, 1970), 42.

41. Neal Massey, "This Is Just a Fun Fun Western. *IMDb: Internet Movie Database*, May 29, 2004, http://www.imdb.com/.

42. Norm Vogel, "An 'Old House' Western," *IMDb: Internet Movie* Database, July 9, 1999, http://www.imdb.com/.

43. Don Miller, *Hollywood Corral* (New York: Popular Library, 1976), 66–67.

Chapter 4

1. Michael Goldman, *John Wayne: The Genuine Article* (San Rafael, CA: Insight, 2015), 50.

2. William Wellman, Jr. *Wild Bill Wellman: Hollywood Rebel* (New York: Pantheon Books, 2015).

3. *Ibid.*, 277.

4. Allen Eyles, *John Wayne and the Movies* (Cranbury, NJ: A. S. Barnes, 1976), 37.

5. A. Hausner, "Some Enjoyable Intentional and Unintentional Comedy," *IMDB: Internet Movie Data Base*, January 1, 1999, http://www.imdb.com/.

6. *Ibid.*

7. Brian Smith, "Minor John Wayne Oater," *IMDB: Internet Movie Data Base*, December 8, 2006, http://www.imdb.com/.

8. Allen Eyles, *John Wayne and the Movies* (Cranbury, NJ: A.S. Barnes, 1976), 32.

9. Yakima Canutt and Oliver Drake, *Stuntman: The Autobiography of Yakima Canutt* (Norman: University of Oklahoma Press, 1997).

10. Ronald L. Davis, *Duke: The Life and Image of John Wayne* (Norman: University of Oklahoma Press, 1998), 54.

11. Michael Goldman, *John Wayne: The Genuine Article* (San Rafael, CA: Insight, 2015), 53–54.

12. Ronald L. Davis, *Duke: The Life and Image of John Wayne* (Norman: University of Oklahoma Press, 1998), 65.

13. Michael Elliott, "Fun 'B' Western with Wayne," *IMDB: Internet Movie Data Base*, June 9, 2010, http://www.imdb.com/.

14. Wes Connors, "Wayne down South," *IMDB: Internet Movie Data Base*, January 25, 2009, http://www.imdb.com/.

15. Brian Smith, "John and Mary Ride Again," *IMDB: Internet Movie Data Base*, December 10, 2006, http://www.imdb.com/.

16. Michael Elliott, "Fun 'B' Western with Wayne," *IMDB: Internet Movie Data Base*, June 9, 2010, http://www.imdb.com/.

17. Allen Eyles, *John Wayne and the Movies* (Cranbury, NJ: A.S. Barnes, 1976), 34.

18. Ronald L. Davis, *Duke: The Life and Image of John Wayne* (Norman: University of Oklahoma Press, 1998), 54.

19. A. J. Abrams, "A Silly but Very Entertaining Early John Wayne Vehicle," *IMDB: Internet Movie Data Base*, December 23, 2010, http://www.imdb.com/.

20. Brian Smith, "John Wayne—Swashbuckler?," *IMDB: Internet Movie Data Base*, December 16, 2006, http://www.imdb.com/.

21. Chris Stone, "Don't Bother," *IMDB: Internet Movie Data Base*, September 6, 1998, http://www.imdb.com/.

22. Don Miller, *Hollywood Corral* (New York: Popular Library, 1976), 67.

23. A. J. Abrams, "A Silly but Very Entertaining Early John Wayne Vehicle," *IMDB: Internet Movie Data Base*, December 23, 2010, http://www.imdb.com/.

24. Michael Lovell, "The Man from Mon-

terey," *The video vacuum*, April 5, 2011, http://videovacuum.com.

25. Allen Eyles, *John Wayne and the Movies* (Cranbury, NJ: A.S. Barnes, 1976), 35.

26. Ronald L. Davis, *Duke: The Life and Image of John Wayne* (Norman: University of Oklahoma Press, 1998), 55.

27. Don Miller, *Hollywood Corral* (New York: Popular Library, 1976), 68.

28. Ronald L. Davis, *Duke: The Life and Image of John Wayne* (Norman: University of Oklahoma Press, 1998), 55.

29. Dave Rothel, *Those Great Cowboy Sidekicks* (Madison, NC: Empire, 2001).

30. *Ibid.*

31. *Ibid.*, 65.

32. Douglas B. Green, *Singing in the Saddle: The History of the Singing Cowboy* (Nashville: Country Music Foundation Press/Vanderbilt University Press, 2002), 100.

33. *Ibid.*, 32.

34. John W. Chance, "An Unsuccessful 'Singing Cowboy' Film, but Fun Anyway," *IMDB: Internet Movie Data Base*, February 19, 2007, http://www.imdb.com/.

35. Doug Doepke, "Hayes to Wayne: 'Tell Her You Like Her Biscuits," *IMDB: Internet Movie Data Base*, November 28, 2007, http://www.imdb.com/.

36. Randy Roberts and James S. Olson, *John Wayne: American* (New York: Free Press, 1995), 129.

37. *Ibid.*, 128–129.

38. Alan Morton, "Strangely Addictive," *IMDB: Internet Movie Data Base*, February 24, 2004, http://www.imdb.com/.

39. Wes Walker, "No Lip-Synching Gunslingers, Please!," *IMDB: Internet Movie Data Base*, August 31, 2007, http://www.imdb.com/.

40. Douglas B. Green, *Singing in the Saddle: The History of the Singing Cowboy* (Nashville: Country Music Foundation Press/Vanderbilt University Press, 2002), 100.

41. Don Miller, *Hollywood Corral* (New York: Popular Library, 1976).

42. Kenny Stier, *The First Fifty Years of Sound Western Movie Locations 1929–1979* (Corriganville, CA: Corriganville Press, 2006).

43. Randy Roberts & James S. Olson, *John Wayne: American*. (New York: Free Press, 1995), 127.

44. Eric Tippett, "Early John Wayne," *IMDB: Internet Movie Data Base*, January 18, 2007, http://www.imdb.com/.

45. Brian Smith, "Great Stuntwork!," *IMDB:*

Internet Movie Data Base, November 12, 2002, http://www.imdb.com/.

46. John W. Chance, "The Best Lone Star Western!," *IMDB: Internet Movie Data Base*, January 14, 2007, http://www.imdb.com/.

Chapter 5

1. Phillip Armour, "Reel Cowboys," *American Cowboy* 21, no. 6 (April/May, 2015): 66–71.

2. Ronald L. Davis, *Duke: The Life and Image of John Wayne* (Norman: University of Oklahoma Press, 1998), 61.

3. Michael Goldman, *John Wayne: The genuine article* (San Rafael, CA: Insight, 2015), 50.

4. Don Miller, *Hollywood Corral* (New York: Popular Library, 1976), 68.

5. J. Pritch, "One of the Best of the Lone Star Westerns," *IMDb: Internet Movie Data Base*, December 2, 1999, http://www.imdb.com/.

6. Brian Smith, "One of the Best of Wayne's Lone Star Westerns," *IMDb: Internet Movie Data Base*, June 26, 2001, http://www.imdb.com/.

7. *Ibid.*

8. Jay Raskin, "A Good Lonestar Production," *IMDb: Internet Movie Data Base*, September 24, 2007, http://www.imdb.com/.

9. Doug Doepke, "Two Stories for the Price of One," *IMDb: Internet Movie Data Base*, June 8, 2009, http://www.imdb.com/.

10. Bill Slocum, "Duke and Gabby Kick It Around," *IMDb: Internet Movie Data Base*, July 11, 2014, http://www.imdb.com/.

11. Don Miller, *Hollywood Corral* (New York: Popular Library, 1976), 68.

12. Jay Raskin, "Bad Lone Star," *IMDb: Internet Movie Data Base*, October 1, 2007, http://www.imdb.com/.

13. Allen Eyles, *John Wayne and the Movies* (Cranbury, NJ: A. S. Barnes, 1976), 38.

14. *Ibid.*, 39.

15. Robert J. Maxwell, "Masked Identities, Horses, Dust. *IMDb: Internet Movie Data Base*, March 13, 2011, http://www.imdb.com/.

16. Allen Eyles, *John Wayne and the Movies* (Cranbury, NJ: A.S. Barnes, 1976), 39.

17. Kenny Stier, *The First Fifty Years of Sound Western Movie Locations 1929–1979* (Corriganville, CA: Corriganville Press, 2006).

18. Francis N. Nevins, "Through the Great

Depression on Horseback: Legal Themes in Western Films in the 1930s," in *Legal Reelism: Movies as Legal Texts*, ed. John Denvir (Urbana: University of Illinois Press, 1996), 44–96.

19. Sue Matheson, "The West-Hardboiled: Adaptations of Film Noir Elements, Existentialism, and Ethics in John Wayne's Westerns," *Journal of Popular Culture* 38, (2005): 888–910.

20. Richard D. McGhee, *John Wayne: Actor, artist, hero* (Jefferson, NC: McFarland, 1990), 6.

21. Doug Doepke, "Head 'Em off at the Pass," *IMDb: Internet Movie Data Base*, June 1, 2007, http://www.imdb.com/.

22. Jay Raskin, "One of the Better Ones," *IMDb: Internet Movie Data Base*, October 9, 2007, http://www.imdb.com/.

23. John Howard Reid, "Duke and Gabby Team up to Knockout the Bad Guys," *IMDb: Internet Movie Data Base*, June 2, 2008, http://www.imdb.com/.

24. *Ibid.*

25. Bobby Copeland, *B Western Boot Hill* (Madison, NC: Empire, 1999).

26. Brian Smith, "Ride 'Em Duke," *IMDb: Internet Movie Data Base*, April 21, 2001, http://www.imdb.com/.

27. John W. Chance, "Too Much Stock Footage for a Short Film," *IMDb: Internet Movie Data Base*, May 25, 2007, http://www.imdb.com/.

28. Bill Slocum, "Pass This One by," *IMDb: Internet Movie Data Base*, February 26, 2015, http://www.imdb.com/.

29. Steve Haynie, "Rodeo Racketeers Run out of Luck!," *IMDb: Internet Movie Data Base*, November 19, 2007, http://www.imdb.com/.

30. David Rothel, *Those Great Cowboy Sidekicks* (Madison, NC: Empire, 2001).

31. Michael G. Ankerich, *Dangerous Curves atop Hollywood Heels: The Lives, Careers, and Misfortunes of 14 Hard-Luck Girls of the Silent Screen* (Duncan, OK: BearManor Media, 2015), 20.

32. John Howard Reid, "One for Hayes Vociferous Fans," *IMDB: International Movie Data Base*, October 24, 2014, http://www.imdb.com/.

33. Don Miller, *Hollywood Corral* (New York: Popular Library, 1976), 63.

34. Brian Smith, One of the Duke's Better Early Westerns. *IMDb: Internet Movie Data Base*, November 11, 2002, http://www.imdb.com/.

35. Allen Eyles, *John Wayne and the Movies* (Cranbury, NJ: A.S. Barnes, 1976), 35.

36. *Ibid.*

37. Doug Doepke, "And You Call Yourself a Badman." *IMDb: Internet Movie Data Base*, May 30, 2008, http://www.imdb.com/.

38. Don Miller, *Hollywood Corral* (New York: Popular Library, 1976), 63.

39. David Rothel, *Those Great Cowboy Sidekicks* (Madison, NC: Empire, 2001).

40. Allen Eyles, *John Wayne and the Movies* (Cranbury, NJ: A.S. Barnes, 1976), 40.

41. Brian J. Smith, "One of the Best of Wayne's Early 'B' Westerns," *IMDb: Internet Movie Data Base*, June 17, 1999, http://www.imdb.com/.

42. Doug Doepke, "Are Those Telephone Wires?," *IMDb: Internet Movie Data Base*, June 1, 2007, http://www.imdb.com/.

43. Neil Doyle, "Poverty Row Western Is More of a Puzzlement Than Entertaining," *IMDb: Internet Movie Data Base*, June 3, 2008, http://www.imdb.com/.

44. David Ostrem, "I Love All Thirties B Westerns," *IMDb: Internet Movie Data Base*, May 1, 2005, http://www.imdb.com/.

45. Allen Eyles, *John Wayne and the Movies* (Cranbury, NJ: A.S. Barnes, 1976), 40.

46. George N. Fenin and William K. Everson, *The Western: From Silents to the Seventies* (New York: Grossman, 1973), 223.

47. Leslie Howard Adams, "John, Yak and Eddie Get Wet... and Stay Wet," *IMDb: Internet Movie Data Base*, December 9, 2005, http://www.imdb.com/.

48. Don Miller, *Hollywood Corral* (New York: Popular Library, 1976), 68.

49. Brian Smith, "There's Those 'French-Canadian' Trappers Again," *IMDb: Internet Movie Data Base*, December 4, 2001, http://www.imdb.com/.

50. Dan Phillips, "If Seeing Young John Wayne," *IMDb: Internet Movie Data Base*, December 5, 1999, http://www.imdb.com/.

51. John W. Chance, "Not a Western—a 'Canadian' Filmed in California," *IMDb: Internet Movie Data Base*, January 20, 2007, http://www.imdb.com/.

52. George N. Fenin and William K. Everson, *The Western: From Silents to the Seventies* (New York: Grossman, 1973).

53. Randy Roberts and James S. Olson, *John Wayne: American* (New York: Free Press, 1995).

54. George N. Fenin and William K. Ever-

son, *The Western: From Silents to the Seventies* (New York: Grossman, 1973), 297.

55. Ronald L. Davis, *Duke: The Life and Image of John Wayne* (Norman: University of Oklahoma Press, 1998), 63.

56. Doug Doepke, "Just Breathe in That Mountain Air," *IMDb: Internet Movie Data Base*, June 2, 2007, http://www.imdb.com/.

57. James Hitchcock, "Surprisingly Attractive B Western," *IMDb: Internet Movie Data Base*, September 28, 2012, http://www.imdb.com/.

58. Allen Eyles, *John Wayne and the Movies* (Cranbury, NJ: A.S. Barnes, 1976), 42.

59. Ronald L. Davis, *Duke: The Life and Image of John Wayne* (Norman: University of Oklahoma Press, 1998).

60. Don Miller, *Hollywood Corral* (New York: Popular Library, 1976), 69.

61. C. T. Tatum, "One of Wayne's Weakest," *IMDb: Internet Movie Data Base*, May 21, 2000, http://www.imdb.com/.

62. Don Miller, *Hollywood Corral* (New York: Popular Library, 1976), 69.

63. Doug Doepke, "Hayes to Wayne: 'I've Got a Girl in the Sack and I Can't Swim,'" *IMDb: Internet Movie Data Base*, May 23, 2008, http://www.imdb.com/.

64. Ronald L. Davis, *Duke: The Life and Image of John Wayne* (Norman: University of Oklahoma Press, 1998), 63.

65. Tim Kidner, "Early Wayne Programmer," *IMDb: Internet Movie Data Base*, April 8. 2012, http://www.imdb.com/.

66. Matt Yeltzman, "One of the Better Early John Wayne Westerns," *IMDb: Internet Movie Data Base*, April 5, 2015, http://www.imdb.com/.

67. Randy Roberts and James S. Olson, *John Wayne: American* (New York: Free Press, 1995), 131.

Chapter 6

1. Emanuel Levy, *John Wayne: Prophet of the American Way of Life* (Metuchen, NJ: Scarecrow Press, 1998), 11.

2. Don Miller, *Hollywood Corral* (New York: Popular Library, 1976).; Scott Eyman, *John Wayne: The Life and Legend* (New York: Simon & Schuster, 2014).

3. Michael Goldman, *John Wayne: The Genuine Article* (San Rafael, CA: Insight, 2015), 50–51.

4. Brian Smith, "An Above Average Pro-grammer," *IMDB: Internet Movie Data Base*, January 21, 2001, http://www.imdb.com/.

5. Doug Doepke, "I'm Swearing off 12-Packs," *IMDb: Internet Movie Data Base*, May 30, 2009, http://www.imdb.com/.

6. Peter Stanfield, *Horse Opera: The Strange History of the 1930s Singing Cowboy* (Urbana: University of Illinois Press, 2002).

7. Mark Waltz, "Typical 'Low Budget' Oater with Fun Performance by George 'Gabby' Hayes," *IMDb: Internet Movie Data Base*, June 7, 2010, http://www.imdb.com/.

8. Edward Goldenberg, "Your Typical 1930s John Wayne B Western Fare," *IMDb: Internet Movie Data Base*, January 15, 2015, http://www.imdb.com/.

9. Bob Nareau, *The Films of Bob Steele* (Madison, NC: Empire, 1997).

10. John W. Chance, "An Edgier John Wayne with Mary Kornman," *IMDb: Internet Movie Data Base*, September 30, 2007, http://www.imdb.com/.

11. Bill Slocum, "Duke's Funny Side Buried in Weak Oater," *IMDb: Internet Movie Data Base*, September 21, 2013, http://www.imdb.com/.

12. Mark Ricci, Boris Zmijewsky, and Steve Zmijewsky, *The Films of John Wayne* (Secaurus, NJ: Citadel Press, 1970), 67.

13. Doug Doepke, "Love the View from This Angle, Miss Anne," *IMDb: Internet Movie Data Base*, June 3, 2007, http://www.imdb.com/.

14. Ronald L. Davis, *Duke: The Life and Image of John Wayne* (Norman: University of Oklahoma Press, 1998).

15. *Ibid.*, 64.

16. Bill Slocum, "Rote Poverty Row Western," *IMDB: Internet Movie Data Base*, April 17, 2014, http://www.imdb.com/.

17. Steve Haynie, "John Wayne Was Just About There," *IMDB: Internet Movie Data Base*, September 6, 2007, http://www.imdb.com/.

18. Mark Waltz, "Entertaining Oater with Laughs and Action Galore," *IMDB: Internet Movie Data Base*, July 5, 2012, http://www.imdb.com/.

19. Ronald L. Davis, *Duke: The Life and Image of John Wayne* (Norman: University of Oklahoma Press, 1998), 64.

20. John W. Chance, "The Proto Type of Formulaic Republic Westerns," *IMDb: Internet Movie Data Base*, March 16, 2008, http://www.imdb.com/.

21. Mickey Micklon, "One of the Better

Wayne Movies I've Seen Lately," *IMDB: Internet Movie Data Base,* May 14, 2010, http://www.imdb.com/.

22. Mark Waltz, "Entertaining Oater with Laughs and Action Galore," *IMDB: Internet Movie Data Base,* July 5, 2012, http://www.imdb.com/.

23. Don Miller, *Hollywood Corral* (New York: Popular Library, 1976), 69–70.

24. Richard M. Hurst, *Republic Studios: Between Poverty Row and the Majors* (Lanham, MD: Scarecrow Press, 2007).

25. Randy Roberts and James S. Olson, *John Wayne: American* (New York: Free Press, 1995).

26. Richard M. Hurst, *Republic Studios: Between Poverty Row and the Majors* (Lanham, MD: Scarecrow Press, 2007), 3.

27. *Ibid.,* 11.

28. Holly George-Warren, *Public cowboy No. 1: The Life and Times of Gene Autry* (New York: Oxford University Press, 2007).

29. Don Miller, *Hollywood Corral* (New York: Popular Library, 1976), 70.

30. Randy Roberts and James S. Olson, *John Wayne: American* (New York: Free Press, 1995). 139.

31. Michael O'Keefe, "Very Good B Western," *IMDB: Internet Movie Data Base,* November 27, 2008, http://www.imdb.com/.

32. Marc Eliot, *American Titan: Searching for John Wayne* (New York: HarperCollins, 2014).

33. Michael Goldman, *John Wayne: The Genuine Article* (San Rafael, CA: Insight, 2015), 50.

34. Douglas B. Green, *Singing in the Saddle: The History of the Singing Cowboy* (Nashville: Country Music Foundation Press/Vanderbilt University Press, 2002).

35. Holly George-Warren, *Public cowboy No. 1: The Life and Times of Gene Autry* (New York: Oxford University Press, 2007).

36. Chris Enss and Howard Kazanjian, *Cowboy and the Senorita: A Biography of Roy Rogers and Dale Evans* (Guilford, CT: Two Dot, 2005).

37. Don Miller, *Hollywood Corral* (New York: Popular Library, 1976), 70.

38. Scott Eyman, *John Wayne: The Life and Legend* (New York: Simon & Schuster, 2007), 100.

39. *Ibid.*

40. D. Earl Newsom, *The Cherokee Strip: Its History & Grand Opening* (Stillwater, OK: New Forums Press, 1992).

41. Arnold Eaves, "Not a Bad Movie As '30s B-Western Movies Go," *IMDB: Internet Movie Data Base,* February 4, 2000, http://www.imdb.com/.

42. Don Miller, *Hollywood Corral* (New York: Popular Library, 1976), 70..

Chapter 7

1. Randy Roberts and James S. Olson, *John Wayne: American* (New York: Free Press, 1995).

2. Scott Allen Nollen, *Three bad men: John Ford, John Wayne, Ward Bond* (Jefferson, NC: McFarland, 2013).

3. Phillip Done, *The Charms of Miss O'Hara: Tales of* Gone with the Wind *& the Golden Age of Hollywood from Scarlett's Little Sister* (Mountain View, CA: Gateway, 2014), 16.

4. Mark Ricci, Boris Zmijewsky, and Steve Zmijewsky, *The Films of John Wayne* (Secaurus, NJ: Citadel Press, 1970), 71.

5. Michael G. Fitzgerald and Boyd Majors, *Ladies of the Western.* (Jefferson, NC: McFarland, 2009).

6. Phillip Done, *The Charms of Miss O'Hara: Tales of* Gone with the Wind *& the Golden Age of Hollywood from Scarlett's Little Sister* (Mountain View, CA: Gateway, 2014), 15.

7. Henry Sanford, "Joseph Kane," in *Close-up: The Contract Director,* ed. Joe Tuska (Metuchen, NJ: Scarecrow Press, 1976), 143–187; John Denvir, *Legal Reelism: Movies as Legal Texts* (Urbana: University of Illinois Press, 1996).

8. T. A. Larson, *History of Wyoming* 2nd ed. (Lincoln: University of Nebraska Press, 1990).

9. George N. Fenin and William K. Everson, *The Western: From Silents to the Seventies* (New York: Grossman, 1973), 222.

10. Fred N. Nevins, "Through the Great Depression on Horseback: Legal Themes in Western Films in the 1930s," in *Legal Reelism: Movies as Legal Texts,* ed. John Denvir (Urbana: University of Illinois Press, 1996), 44–96.

11. Don Miller, *Hollywood Corral* (New York: Popular Library, 1976), 70.

12. Randy Roberts and James S. Olson, *John Wayne: American* (New York: Free Press, 1995), 113.

13. D. W. Pollar, "Uninspired Early John

Wayne Western," *IMDB: Internet Movie Data Base*, December 30, 2001, http://www.imdb.com/.

14. Fred N. Nevins, "Through the Great Depression on Horseback: Legal Themes in Western Films in the 1930s," in *Legal Reelism: Movies as Legal Texts*, ed. John Denvir (Urbana: University of Illinois Press, 1996), xiv.

15. *ibid.*, 51.

16. Michael Morrison, "Eye Opener!," *IMDB: Internet Movie Data Base*, January 6, 2015, http://www.imdb.com/.

17. Estaban Smythe, "Painful to Watch, My Eye. It's Solid Entertainment," *IMDB: Internet Movie Data Base*, April 18, 2006, http://www.imdb.com/.

18. Michael Waltz, "Enjoyable Post Civil War Drama about the Power of Intolerance," *IMDB: Internet Movie Data Base*, May 9, 2014, http://www.imdb.com/.

19. Ginger Rogers, *Ginger: My Story* (New York: Harper, 2008).

20. Randy Roberts and James S. Olson, *John Wayne: American* (New York: Free Press, 1995), 140.

21. Brian Smith, "The Great Stagecoach Race," *IMDB: Internet Movie Data Base*, November 25, 2003. http://www.imdb.com/

22. Jeffrey Skinner, "My Favorite John Wayne B-Rater," *IMDB: Internet Movie Data Base*, February 19, 2005, http://www.imdb.com/.

23. George N. Fenin and William K. Everson, *The Western: From Silents to the Seventies* (New York: Grossman, 1973), 222.

24. *Ibid.*, 122.

25. Michael Waltz, "The Duke Takes on the Stagecoach," *IMDB: Internet Movie Data Base*, July 13, 2013, http://www.imdb.com/.

26. Mickey Micklon, "A Pretty Good, but Short, Wayne Movie," *IMDB: Internet Movie Data Base*, September 19, 2010, http://www.imdb.com/.

27. Randy Roberts and James S. Olson, *John Wayne: American* (New York: Free Press, 1995), 143.

Chapter 8

1. Mark Ricci, Boris Zmijewsky, and Steve Zmijewsky, *The Films of John Wayne* (Secaurus, NJ: Citadel Press, 1970).

2. Don Miller, *Hollywood Corral* (New York: Popular Library, 1976), 70.

3. Randy Roberts and James S. Olson, *John Wayne: American* (New York: Free Press, 1995), 143.

4. John A. Rutherford, *From Pigskin to Saddle Leather: The Films of Johnny Mack Brown* (Waynesville, NC: World of Yesterday, 1987); Bobby J. Copeland, *Johnny Mack Brown: Up close and personal* (Madison, NC: Empire, 2005).

5. Marsha Hunt, *The Way We Wore: Styles of the 1930s and '40s and Our World Since* (London: Fallbrook, 1993).

6. Ronald L. Davis, *Duke: The life and image of John Wayne* (Norman: University of Oklahoma Press, 1998), 79.

7. Mark Ricci, Boris Zmijewsky, and Steve Zmijewsky, *The Films of John Wayne* (Secaurus, NJ: Citadel Press, 1970).

8. Beverly Linet, *Ladd: The Life, the Legend, the Legacy of Alan Ladd* (Gettysburg, PA: Arbor House, 1979).

9. Dave Rothel, *Those Great Cowboy Sidekicks* (Madison, NC: Empire, 2001).

10. Don Miller, *Hollywood Corral* (New York: Popular Library, 1976), 70.

11. *Ibid.*

12. Michael Morrison, "Eye-Opener! Superb Script Allows John Wayne to Demonstrate Why He Became the Biggest Star of All. *IMDB: Internet Movie Data Base*, January 6, 2015, http://www.imdb.com/.

13. Allen Eyles, *John Wayne and the Movies* (Cranbury, NJ: A.S. Barnes, 1976), 51.

14. John W. Chance, "A Well Made B Western for the Most Part." *IMDb: Internet Movie Data Base*, January 20, 2008, http://www.imdb.com/.

15. W. H. Pratt, "Great Classic Western," *IMDB: Internet Movie Data Base*, February 26, 2008, http://www.imdb.com/.

Chapter 9

1. Don Miller, *Hollywood Corral* (New York: Popular Library, 1976), 70.

2. Mark Ricci, Boris Zmijewsky, and Steve Zmijewsky, *The Films of John Wayne* (Secaurus, NJ: Citadel Press, 1970), 16.

3. George N. Fenin and William K. Everson, *The Western: From Silents to the Seventies* (New York: Grossman, 1973), 222.

4. Don Miller, *Hollywood Corral* (New York: Popular Library, 1976), 157.

5. George N. Fenin and William K. Everson, *The Western: From Silents to the Seventies* (New York: Grossman, 1973), 222–223.

6. Allen Eyles, *John Wayne and the Movies* (Cranbury, NJ: A.S. Barnes, 1976), 52.

7. *The Three Mesquiteers in Overland Stage Raiders*, directed by George Sherman (1938; Las Angeles, CA: Republic Pictures, 2012), DVD.

8. Don Miller, *Hollywood Corral* (New York: Popular Library, 1976), 70.

9. Dave Rothel, *Those Great Cowboy Sidekicks* (Madison, NC: Empire, 2001), 207.

10. George N. Fenin and William K. Everson, *The Western: From Silents to the Seventies* (New York: Grossman, 1973), 222.

11. Michael Munn, *John Wayne: The Man behind the Myth* (New York: New American Library, 2003).

12. Jerry L. Schneider, *The Ray "Crash" Corrigan Filmography* (Corriganville, CA: Corriganville Press, 2014).

13. George N. Fenin and William K. Everson, *The Western: From Silents to the Seventies* (New York: Grossman, 1973).

14. Michael Munn, *John Wayne: The Man behind the Myth* (New York: New American Library, 2003), 52.

15. George N. Fenin and William K. Everson, *The Western: From Silents to the Seventies* (New York: Grossman, 1973).

16. Dave Kehr, "Tall in the Saddle in 2 Eras at Once," *New York Times* (New York), Sep. 30, 2012.

17. *Ibid.*

18. Jerry L. Schneider, *Corriganville: The Definitive True History of the Ray "Crash" Corrigan Movie Ranch* (Corriganville, CA: Corriganville Press, 2013).

19. Bobby Copeland, *B Western Boot Hill* (Madison, NC: Empire, 1999).

20. Linda Lee Wakely, *See Ya' up There, Baby: The Jimmy Wakely Story* (Shasta, 1992).

21. George N. Fenin and William K. Everson, *The Western: From Silents to the Seventies* (New York: Grossman, 1973), 42.

22. Fred N. Nevins, "Through the Great Depression on Horseback: Legal Themes in Western Films in the 1930s," in *Legal Reelism: Movies as Legal Texts*, ed. Jon Denvir (Urbana: University of Illinois Press, 1996), 67.

23. George N. Fenin and William K. Everson, *The Western: From Silents to the Seventies* (New York: Grossman, 1973), 223.

24. Michael Elliott, "Short and Fun," *IMDB: Internet Movie Data Base*, February 27, 2008, http://www.imdb.com/.

25. Michael O'Keefe, "Fast Paced Western," *IMDB: Internet Movie Data Base*, May 27, 2007, http://www.imdb.com/.

26. Brian Smith, "The 'Duke; Joins the Mesquiteers," *IMDB: Internet Movie Data Base*, February 16, 2001, http://www.imdb.com/.

27. Don Miller, *Hollywood Corral* (New York: Popular Library, 1976), 160.

28. George N. Fenin and William K. Everson, *The Western: From Silents to the Seventies* (New York: Grossman, 1973), 42.

29. Michael Goldman, *John Wayne: The Genuine Article* (San Rafael, CA: Insight, 2015), 110.

30. Louise Brooks, *Lulu in Hollywood* (New York: Alfred A. Knopf, 1985).

31. Louise Brooks, "Duke by Divine Right," in Allen Eyles, *John Wayne and the Movies* (Cranbury, NJ: A.S. Barnes, 1976), 9.

32. Dave Kehr, "Tall in the Saddle in 2 Eras at Once," *New York Times* (New York), Sep. 30, 2012.

33. Louise Brooks, *Lulu in Hollywood* (New York: Alfred A. Knopf, 1985), 9.

34. Jim Tritten, "This One Is a Hoot!," *IMDB: Internet Movie Database*, December 21, 2004, http://www.imdb.com/.

35. Stuthehistoryguy, "The Story behind the Film Alone Is Worth the Viewing," *IMDB: Internet Movie Database*, September 17, 1999, http://www.imdb.com/.

36. Vandino1, "Mesquiteer-Brained Nonsense. *IMDB: Internet Movie Database*, Dec. 8, 2005, http://www.imdb.com/.

37. Louise-14, "One of the Worst Movies I've Seen. *IMDB: Internet Movie Database*, May 13, 1999, http://www.imdb.com/.

38. Jeffrey M. Anderson, "Plane and Simple," *Combustible Celluloid*, (n.d.), http://www.combustiblecelluloid.com/.

39. Bkoganbing, "The Three Mesquiteers," *IMDB: Internet Movie Database*, July 24, 2007, http://www.imdb.com/.

40. Jim Tritten, "This One Is a Hoot!," *IMDB: Internet Movie Database*, December 21, 2004, http://www.imdb.com/.

41. Stuart Galbraith IV, "Santa Fe Stampede," *DVD Talk*, April 23, 2013, http://www.dvdtalk.com/reviews/60214/sante-fe-stampede/.

42. Vandino1, "Mesquiteer-Brained Nonsense. *IMDB: Internet Movie Database*, Dec. 8, 2005, http://www.imdb.com/.

43. Jim Tritten, "This One Is a Hoot!," *IMDB: Internet Movie Database*, December 21, 2004, http://www.imdb.com/.

44. Stuthehistoryguy, "The Story behind the Film Alone Is Worth the Viewing," *IMDB: Internet Movie Database*, September 17, 1999, http://www.imdb.com/.

45. Vandinol, "Mesquiteer-Brained Nonsense. *IMDB: Internet Movie Database*, Dec. 8, 2005, http://www.imdb.com/.

46. Stuthehistoryguy, "The Story behind the Film Alone Is Worth the Viewing," *IMDB: Internet Movie Database*, September 17, 1999, http://www.imdb.com/.

47. Stuart Galbraith IV, "Santa Fe Stampede," *DVD Talk*, April 23, 2013, http://www.dvdtalk.com/reviews/60214/sante-fe-stampede/.

48. Ronald L. Davis, *Duke: The Life and Image of John Wayne* (Norman: University of Oklahoma Press, 1998).

49. Carl Davis, "Santa Fe Stampede," *DVD Talk*, May 1, 2004, http://www.dvdtalk.com/.

50. Brian Smith, "Where's the Stampede?" *IMDB: Internet Movie Data Base*, February 11, 2001, http://www.imdb.com/.

51. Michael Elliott, "Santa Fe Stampede: Good," *IMDB: Internet Movie Data Base*, March 18, 2008 http://www.imdb.com/.

52. Dave Kehr, "Tall in the Saddle in 2 Eras at Once," *New York Times* (New York), Sep. 30, 2012.

53. Emanuel Levy, *John Wayne: Prophet of the American Way of Life* (Metuchen, NJ: Scarecrow Press, 1998),11.

54. Dave Kehr, "Tall in the Saddle in 2 Eras at Once," *New York Times* (New York), Sep. 30, 2012.

55. Steve Haynie, "Four Mesquiteers!," *IMDB: Internet Movie Data Base*, January 16, 2006, http://www.imdb.com/.

56. Stuart Galbraith IV, "Red River Range," *DVD Talk*, October 2, 2012, http://www.dvdtalk.com/reviews/57036/red-river-range/?___rd=1.

57. Michael Elliot, "Early Wayne," *IMDB: Internet Movie Data Base*, February 26, 2008, http://www.imdb.com/.

58. Ronald L. Davis, *Duke: The Life and Image of John Wayne* (Norman: University of Oklahoma Press, 1998), 79.

59. Randy Roberts and James S. Olson, *John Wayne: American* (New York: Free Press, 1005), 141.

Chapter 10

1. Tom Charity, "Go West," *Sight & Sound* 20, no. 8 (2010): 87.

2. David Bosworth, "Saving the Appearances: John Ford's Rescripting of the American Mythos," *The Georgia Review* 64, no. 2 (2010): 302.

3. Michael Munn, *John Wayne: The Man behind the Myth* (New York: New American Library, 2009), 53.

4. Michael Anderson, "Stagecoach," in *100 Greatest Westerns*, ed. Greg Santoro (Leesburg, VA: Weider History Group, 2009), 18.

5. Michael Goldman, *John Wayne: The Genuine Article* (San Rafael, CA: Insight, 2015).

6. *Ibid.*

7. Scott Eyman, *John Wayne: The Life and Legend* (New York: Simon & Schuster, 2014).

8. Michael Munn, *John Wayne: The Man behind the Myth* (New York: New American Library, 2009), 56.

9. Peter Bogdanovich, "Playing John Wayne," *New York Times Book Review* (New York), Mar. 30, 2014.

10. Michael Munn, *John Wayne: The Man behind the Myth* (New York: New American Library, 2009).

11. Allen Eyles, *John Wayne and the Movies* (Cranbury, NJ: A.S. Barnes, 1976).

12. Michael Munn, *John Wayne: The Man behind the Myth* (New York: New American Library, 2009), 57.

13. Ronald L. Davis, *Duke: The Life and Image of John Wayne* (Norman: University of Oklahoma Press, 1998), 83.

14. Mark Ricci, Boris, Zmijewsky, and Steve Zmijewsky, *The Films of John Wayne* (Scausus, NJ: Citadel Press, 1970).

15. Glenn Frankel, *The Searchers: The Making of an American Legend* (New York: Bloomsbury, 2013).

16. Maureen O'Hara and John Nicoletti, *Tis Herself: An Autobiography* (New York: Simon & Schuster, 2004).

17. Mark Ricci, Boris Zmijewsky, and Steven Zmijewsky, *The Films of John Wayne* (New York: The Citadel Press, 1970), 17.

18. Jan Bone and Ron Johnson, *Understanding the film* (Skokie, IL: National Textbook, 1976), 140.

19. *Ibid.*

20. Jed J. Rosebrook and Jeb S. Rosebrook, "John Ford's Monument Valley." *Arizona Highways* 75, no. 7 (July, 1999): 14–21.

21. Fred Cavinder, "John Wayne: How he won the West," *Saturday Evening Post* (July/August, 1979), 58–64.

22. Michael Goldman, *John Wayne: The Genuine Article* (San Rafael, CA: Insight, 2015), 51.

23. Helen Akitt, *Hollywood Westerns: The Movies, the Heroes* (East Bridgewater, MA: World Publications, 2013), 30.

24. Michael Anderson, "Stagecoach," in *100 Greatest Westerns,* ed. Greg Santoro (Leesburg, VA: Weider History Group, 2009), 18.

25. Michael Goldman, *John Wayne: The Genuine Article* (San Rafael, CA: Insight, 2015).

26. C. Taylor, "Stagecoach," *New York Times* (New York), May 2, 2010.

27. Tom Charity, "Go West," *Sight & Sound* 20, no. 8 (2010): 87.

28. Michael Anderson, "Stagecoach," in *100 Greatest Westerns,* ed. Greg Santoro (Leesburg, VA: Weider History Group, 2009), 18.

29. David Bosworth, "Saving the Appearances: John Ford's Rescripting of the American Mythos," *The Georgia Review* 64, no. 2 (2010): 303.

30. Dave Rothel, *Those Great Cowboy Sidekicks* (Madison, NC: Empire, 2001), 132.

31. Michael Munn, *John Wayne: The Man behind the Myth* (New York: New American Library, 2009), 3.

32. Ronald L. Davis, *Duke: The Life and Image of John Wayne* (Norman: University of Oklahoma Press, 1998), 83.

33. Joan Didion, "The Duke: A Love Song," *Saturday Evening Post,* July/August, 1979, 64a.

34. David Bosworth, "Saving the Appearances: John Ford's Rescripting of the American Mythos," *The Georgia Review* 64, no. 2 (2010): 303–304.

35. Michael Munn, *John Wayne: The Man behind the Myth* (New York: New American Library, 2009), 4.

36. *Ibid.,* 1.

37. Dave Kehr, "The Man Who Dared to Fill John Wayne's Boots," *New York Times* (New York), Oct. 16, 2011.

38. Michael Munn, *John Wayne: The Man behind the Myth* (New York: New American Library, 2009), 1.

39. Dave Kehr, "The Man Who Dared to Fill John Wayne's Boots," *New York Times* (New York), Oct. 16, 2011.

40. Ronald L. Davis, *Duke: The Life and Image of John Wayne* (Norman: University of Oklahoma Press, 1998), 82.

41. *Ibid.*

42. George N. Fenin and William K. Everson, *The Western: From Silents to the Seventies* (New York: Grossman, 1973), 188–189.

43. Michael Munn, *John Wayne: The Man behind the Myth* (New York: New American Library, 2009), 4.

44. Marc Eliot, *American Titan: Searching for John Wayne* (New York: HarperCollins, 2014), 83.

45. C. Taylor, "Stagecoach," *New York Times* (New York), May 2, 2010.

46. Gerald Mist, *A Short History of the Movies* (3rd ed.) (Indianapolis: Bobbs-Merrill, 1984), 244.

47. Scott Eyman, *John Wayne: The Life and Legend* (New York: Simon & Schuster, 2014).

48. Marc Eliot, *American Titan: Searching for John Wayne* (New York: HarperCollins, 2014), 90.

49. Dave Kehr, "The Man Who Dared to Fill John Wayne's Boots," *New York Times* (New York), Oct. 16, 2011.

50. C. Taylor, "Stagecoach," *New York Times* (New York), May 2, 2010.

51. Gerald Mist, *A Short History of the Movies* (3rd ed.) (Indianapolis: Bobbs-Merrill, 1984), 243.

52. Richard Schickel, *Keepers: The Greatest Films—and Personal Favorites—of a Movie Going Lifetime* (New York: Alfred A. Knopf, 2915), 116.

53. David Bosworth, "Saving the Appearances: John Ford's Rescripting of the American Mythos," *The Georgia Review* 64, no. 2 (2010): 308.

54. Dave Kehr, "The Man Who Dared to Fill John Wayne's Boots," *New York Times* (New York), Oct. 16, 2011.

55. Allen Eyles, *John Wayne and the Movies* (Cranbury, NJ: A.S. Barnes, 1976), 58.

56. Dave Kehr, "The Man Who Dared to Fill John Wayne's Boots," *New York Times* (New York), Oct. 16, 2011.

57. C. Taylor, "Stagecoach," *New York Times* (New York), May 2, 2010.

58. A. O. Scott, "Films of '62: When Eras Collided," *New York Times* (New York), Oct. 18, 2009.

59. Gerald Mist, *A Short History of the Movies* (3rd ed.) (Indianapolis: Bobbs-Merrill, 1984), 243.

60. Dave Kehr, "The Man Who Dared to Fill John Wayne's Boots," *New York Times* (New York), Oct. 16, 2011.

61. Michael Anderson, "Stagecoach," in *100 Greatest Westerns,* ed. Greg Santoro (Leesburg, VA: Weider History Group, 2009), 18–21.

62. Richard Schickel, *Keepers: The Greatest Films—and Personal Favorites—of a Movie Going Lifetime* (New York: Alfred A. Knopf, 2915), 119.

63. Allen Eyles, *John Wayne and the Movies* (Cranbury, NJ: A.S. Barnes, 1976), 57.

64. Michael Munn, *John Wayne: The Man behind the Myth* (New York: New American Library, 2009), 64.

65. *Ibid.*, 8.

66. Helen Akitt, *Hollywood Westerns: The Movies, the Heroes* (East Bridgewater, MA: World Publications, 2013), 53.

67. Marc Eliot, *American Titan: Searching for John Wayne* (New York: HarperCollins, 2014), 91.

68. Helen Akitt, *Hollywood Westerns: The Movies, the Heroes* (East Bridgewater, MA: World Publications, 2013), 30.

69. Andrew Sarris, *The American Cinema: Directors and Directions* (New York: Da Capo Press, 1996).

70. Tom Charity, "Go West," *Sight & Sound* 20, no. 8 (2010): 87.

71. Fred N. Nevins, "Through the Great Depression on Horseback: Legal Themes in Western Films in the 1930s," in *Legal Reelism: Movies as Legal Texts*, ed. Jon Denvir (Urbana: University of Illinois Press, 1996), 51.

72. Michael Anderson, "Stagecoach," in *100 Greatest Westerns*, ed. Greg Santoro (Leesburg, VA: Weider History Group, 2009), 18.

73. *Ibid.*

74. Marc Eliot, *American Titan: Searching for John Wayne* (New York: HarperCollins, 2014).

75. Patrick McGee, *From* Shane *to* Kill Bill: *Rethinking the Western* (Malden MA: Blackwell, 2007).

Chapter 11

1. Paul Martin, "Big John," *Saturday Evening Post*, July/August, 1979, 57i.

2. Maurice Zolotov, *Shooting Star: A Biography of John Wayne* (New York: Simon and Schuster, 1979).

3. Richard M. Hurst, *Republic Studios: Between Poverty Row and the Majors* (Lanham, MD: Scarecrow Press, 2007), 15.

4. Steve Haynie, "The Three Mesquiteers become Los Capaqueros," *IMDB: Internet Movie Data Base*, April 12, 2006, http://www.imdb.com/.

5. Dave Kehr, "Tall in the Saddle in 2 Eras at Once," *New York Times* (New York), Sep. 30, 2012.

6. *Ibid.*

7. Allen Eyles, *John Wayne and the Movies* (Cranbury, NJ: A.S. Barnes, 1976), 55.

8. Dave Kehr, "Tall in the Saddle in 2 Eras at Once," *New York Times* (New York), Sep. 30, 2012.

9. Kenneth D. Ackerman, *Dark horse: The Surprise Election and Political Murder of James A. Garfield* (New York: Carroll & Graf, 2012).

10. T. Winthrop, "Charles Addison Reavis meet Charles Guiteau," *IMDb: Internet Movie Data Base*, December 9, 2006, http://www.imdb.com/.

11. Donald M. Powell, *The Peralta Grant: James Addison Reavis and the Barony of Arizona* (Norman: University of Oklahoma Press, 1960).; E. H. Cookridge, *The Baron of Arizona* (Milan, IL: John Day Company, 1967).

12. Don Miller, *Hollywood Corral* (New York: Popular Library, 1976), 160.

13. Dave Rothel, *Those Great Cowboy Sidekicks* (Madison, NC: Empire, 2001).

14. *Ibid.* 102.

15. Allen Eyles, *John Wayne and the Movies* (Cranbury, NJ: A.S. Barnes, 1976), 55.

16. Dave Kehr, "Tall in the Saddle in 2 Eras at Once," *New York Times* (New York), Sep. 30, 2012.

17. E. J. Fleming, *Carole Landis: A Tragic Life in Hollywood* (Jefferson, NC: McFarland, 2005), 53.

18. Kenneth Anger, *Hollywood Babylon* (New York: Bantam, 1975).; Eric Gans, *Carole Landis: A Most Beautiful Girl* (Jackson: University Press of Mississippi; Fleming, 2008).

19. *Ibid.*

20. Michael Elliott, "John Wayne," *IMDB: Internet Movie Data Base*, February 26, 2008, http://www.imdb.com/.

21. Don Miller, *Hollywood Corral* (New York: Popular Library, 1976), 160.

22. Allen Eyles, *John Wayne and the Movies* (Cranbury, NJ: A.S. Barnes, 1976), 55.

23. Don Miller, *Hollywood Corral* (New York: Popular Library, 1976), 171.

24. Dave Rothel, *Those Great Cowboy Sidekicks* (Madison, NC: Empire, 2001).

25. Peter Stanfield, *Horse Opera: The Strange History of the 1930s Singing Cowboy* (Urbana: University of Illinois Press, 2002).

26. Kendra Phillips, "A Great Black and White! A Tribute to John Wayne!" *IMDB: Internet Movie Data* Base, January 12, 2008, http://www.imdb.com/.

27. Michael Elliott, "John Wayne," *IMDB: Internet Movie Data Base*, February 26, 2008, http://www.imdb.com/.

28. Don Miller, *Hollywood Corral* (New York: Popular Library, 1976), 171.

29. *Ibid.*

30. Joseph J. DiCerto, *The Saga of the Pony Express* (Missoula, MT: Mountain Press, 2002).

31. Edward Z. Epstein, *Portrait of Jennifer: A biography of Jennifer Jones* (New York: Simon & Schuster, 1995).

32. Don Miller, *Hollywood Corral* (New York: Popular Library, 1976), 171.

33. Wes Connors, "Greener pastures," *IMDB: Internet Movie Data Base*, 2014, http://www.imdb.com/.

Chapter 12

1. Michael Goldman, *John Wayne: The Genuine Article* (San Rafael, CA: Insight, 2015), 56.

2. *Ibid.*, 57.

3. *Ibid.*

4. Terrencce Rafferty, "Building the Duke, Film by Film," *New York Times* (New York), May 20,2007.

5. Joan Didion. "The Duke: A Love Song," *Saturday Evening Post*, July/August, 1979, 64a.

6. Fred Cavinder, "John Wayne: How He Won the West," *Saturday Evening Post*, July/August, 1979, 58.

7. *Ibid.*, 63.

8. John Wayne Enterprises. *John Wayne. The Man. The* Legend, 2016, https://johnwae.com.

9. Jib Fowles, "Mass Media and the Star System," in *Communication in history: Technology, culture and society* (6th ed.), ed. David Crowley and Paul Heyer (New York: Routledge, 2011), 179.

10. *Ibid.*, 180.

11. Scott Eyman, *John Wayne: The Life and Legend* (New York: Simon & Schuster, 2014), 58.

12. Jerry L. Schneider, *The Ray "Crash" Corrigan Filmography* (Corriganville, CA: Corriganville Press, 2014).

13. Alan Young, *Mister Ed and Me* (New York: St. Martin's Press, 1995).

14. Don Graham, *No Name on the Bullet: A Biography of Audie Murphy* (New York: Viking. 1989).; David A. Smith, *The Price of Valor: The Life of Audie Murphy, America's Most Decorated Hero of World War II* (New York: Regnery History, 2015).; Charles Whiting, *American Hero: The Life and Death of Audie Murphy* (J. Whiting Books, 2000).

15. Scott Eyman, *John Wayne: The Life and Legend* (New York: Simon & Schuster, 2014), 4.

16. Michael Goldman, *John Wayne: The Genuine Article* (San Rafael, CA: Insight, 2015), 25.

17. *Ibid.*, 27.

18. *Ibid.*, 62.

19. Scott Eyman, *John Wayne: The Life and Legend* (New York: Simon & Schuster, 2014), 84.

20. Michael Goldman, *John Wayne: The Genuine Article* (San Rafael, CA: Insight, 2015), 56.

21. Jimmy Carter, "The Loyal Opposition," in Goldman, 2015.

22. *Ibid.*, 9–10.

23. *Ibid.*

24. Neal Gabler, "How Barack Obama Killed John Wayne," *Reuters*, November 12, 2012, http://blogs.reuters.com/great-debate/2012/11/14/how-barack-obama-killed-john-wayne/.

25. Scott Eyman, *John Wayne: The Life and Legend* (New York: Simon & Schuster, 2014), 49.

26. Patrick McGee, *From Shane to Kill Bill: Rethinking the Western* (Malden MA: Blackwell, 2007).

27. Philip French, *Westerns* (Manchester, GB: Carcanet Press, 1977), 174.

28. *Ibid.*, 109.

29. Richard Slotkin, *Gunfighter Nation: The Myth of the Frontier in Twentieth-Century America* (New York: Atheneum, 1992).

Bibliography

Abrams, A.J. "A Silly but Very Entertaining Early John Wayne Vehicle." *IMDB: Internet Movie Data Base,* December 23, 2010. http://www.imdb.com/

Ackerman, Kenneth D. *Dark Horse: The Surprise Election and Political Murder of James A. Garfield.* New York: Carroll & Graf, 2012.

Adams, Leslie, and John Howard. "Yak and Eddie Get Wet and Stay Wet." *Imdb: Internet Movie Data Base,* December 9, 2005. http://www.imdb.com/

Akitt, Helen. *Hollywood Westerns: The Movies, the Heroes.* East Bridgewater, MA: World Publications, 2013.

Anderson, Jeffrey M. "Plane and Simple." *Combustible Celluloid.*n.d. http://www.combustiblecelluloid.com/

Anderson, Joan Webster. *Forever Young: The Life, Loves and Enduring Faith of a Hollywood Legend.* Allen, TX: Thomas More, 2012.

Anderson, Michael. "*Stagecoach.*" In *100 Greatest Westerns,* edited by Greg Santoro. Leesburg, VA: Weider History, 2009.

Anger, Kenneth. *Hollywood Babylon.* New York: Bantam, 1975.

Ankerich, Michael G. *Dangerous Curves Atop Hollywood Heels: The Lives, Careers, and Misfortunes of 14 Hard-Luck Girls of the Silent Screen.* Duncan, OK: BearManor Media, 2015.

Armour, Phillip. "Reel Cowboys." *American Cowboy, 21,* no. 6. April/May, 2015, 66–71.

Bogdanovich, Peter. "Playing John Wayne." *New York Times Book Review.* March 30, 2014, 12.

Bone, Jan, and Ron Johnson. *Understanding the Film.* Skokie, IL: National Textbook, 1976.

Boomhower, Ray E. *The Sword and the Pen: A Life of Lew Wallace.* Indianapolis: Indiana Historical Society, 2005.

Boston, John. *Santa Clarita Valley.* Mount Pleasant, SC: Arcadia, 2009.

Bosworth, David. "Saving the Appearances: John Ford's Rescripting of the American Mythos." *The Georgia Review, 64(2),* 2010, 302.

Brooks, Louise. "Duke by Divine Right." In *John Wayne and the Movies,* edited by Allen Eyles. Cranbury, NJ: A.S. Barnes, 1976.

_____. *Lulu in Hollywood.* New York: Alfred A. Knopf, 1985.

Buck, Rinker. *The Oregon Trail: A New American Journey.* New York: Simon & Schuster, 2015.

Canutt, Yakima. *My Rodeo Years: Memoir of a Bronc Rider's Path to Hollywood Fame.* Jefferson, NC: McFarland, 2009.

_____, and Oliver Drake. *Stunt Man: The Autobiography of Yakima Canutt.* Norman: University of Oklahoma Press, 1997.

Carter, Jimmy. "The Loyal Opposition." In *John Wayne: The Genuine Article,* edited by Michael Goldman. San Rafael, CA: Insight, 2015, p. 11

Cavinder, Fred N. "John Wayne: How He Won the West." *Saturday Evening Post,* July/August, 1979, 60.

Charity, Tom. "Go West." *Sight & Sound,* 20, no. 8 (2010), 87.

Clark, Mike. "The Big Trail." *USA Today,* May 16, 2008, 4E.

Cookridge, E.H. *The Baron of Arizona.* Milan, IL: John Day, 1967.

Copeland, Bobby. *B Westerns Boot Hill.* Madison, NC: Empire, 1999.

_____. *Johnny Mack Brown: Up Close and Personal*. Madison, NC: Empire, 2005.

Copeland, Bobby J., and Richard B. Smith, III. *Gabby Hayes: King of the Cowboy Comics*. Madison, NC: Empire, 2008.

Crissman, James K., and Dianne R. Moran. "The Importance of Juvenile Co-Stars in B-western Movies." *Journal of the West*, 50, no. 4 (2011): 17–26.

Davis, Carl. "Santa Fe Stampede." *DVD Talk*, May 1, 2004. http://www.dvdtalk.com/

Davis, Ronald L. *Duke: The Life and Image of John Wayne*. Norman: University of Oklahoma Press, 1998.

Denvir, John. *Legal Reelism: Movies as Legal Texts*. Urbana: University of Illinois Press, 1996.

DiCerto, Joseph J. *The Saga of the Pony Express*. Missoula, MT: Mountain Press, 2002.

Dick, Bernard F. *Hollywood Madonna: Loretta Young*. Oxford: University of Mississippi Press, 2011.

Didion, Joan. "The Duke: A Love Song." *Saturday Evening Post*, July/August 1979, 64a.

Done, Phillip. *The Charms of Miss O'Hara: Tales of* Gone with the Wind *and the Golden Age of Hollywood from Scarlett's Little Sister*. Mountain View, CA: Gateway, 2014.

Donev, Stef. *The Fun of Living Dangerously: The Life of Yakima Canutt*. New York: McGraw-Hill, 2000.

Eliot, Marc. *American Titan: Searching for John Wayne*. New York: HarperCollins, 2014.

Enss, Chris, and Howard Kazanjian. *Cowboy and the Senorita: A Biography of Roy Rogers and Dale Evans*. Guilford, CT: Two Dot, 2005.

Epstein. Edward Z. *Portrait of Jennifer: A Biography of Jennifer Jones*. New York: Simon & Schuster, 1995.

Erickson, Glenn. "The Three Mesquiteers in *Overland Stage Raiders*." *DVD Savant* (N.d.) http://www.dvdsavant.com/

Eyles, Allen. *John Wayne and the Movies*. Cranbury, NJ: A.S. Barnes, 1976.

Eyman, Scott. *John Wayne: The Life and Legend*. New York: Simon & Schuster, 2014.

Fenin, George N., and William K. Everson.

The Western: From Silents to the Seventies. New York: Grossman, 1973.

Fitzgerald, Michael G., and Boyd Majors. *Ladies of the Western*. Jefferson, NC: McFarland, 2009.

Fleming, E.J. *Carole Landis: A Tragic Life in Hollywood*. Jefferson, NC: McFarland, 2005.

Fowles, Jib. "Mass Media and the Star System." In *Communication in History: Technology, Culture and Society*, 6th ed., edited by David Crowley and Paul Heyer. New York: Routledge, 2011, 179.

Frankel, Glenn. *The Searchers: The Making of an American Legend*. New York: Bloomsbury, 2013.

French, Philip. *Westerns*. Manchester, GB: Carcanet, 1977.

Gabler, Neal. "How Barack Obama Killed John Wayne." Reuters, November 12, 2012. http://blogs.reuters.com/great-debate/2012/11/14/how-barack-obama-killed-john-wayne/.

Galbraith, Stuart, IV. "Red River Range." *DVD Talk*, October 2, 2012. http://www.dvdtalk.com/reviews/57036/red-river-range/?___rd=1

_____. "Santa Fe Stampede." *DVD Talk*, April 23, 2013. http://www.dvdtalk.com/reviews/60214/sante-fe-stampede/

Gans, Eric. *Carole Landis: A Most Beautiful Girl*. Jackson: University Press of Mississippi, 2008.

Gardner, Mark Lee. *To Hell on a Fast Horse: The Untold Story of Billy the Kid and Pat Garrett*. New York: William Morrow, 2011.

George-Warren, Holly. *Public Cowboy No.1: The Life and Times of Gene Autry*. New York: Oxford University Press, 2007.

Goldman, Michael. *John Wayne: The Genuine Article*. San Rafael, CA: Insight, 2015.

Graham, Don. *No Name on the Bullet: A Biography of Audie Murphy*. New York: Viking. 1989.

Green, Douglas B. *Singing in the Saddle: The History of the Singing Cowboy*. Nashville: Vanderbilt University Press, 2002.

Hunt, Marsha. *The Way We Wore: Styles of the 1930s and '40s and Our World Since*. London: Fallbrook, 1993.

Hurst, Richard M. *Republic Studios: Be-*

tween *Poverty Row and the Majors.* Lanham, MD: Scarecrow, 2007.

John Wayne Enterprises. *John Wayne: The Legend and the Man.* Brooklyn: power-House, 2012.

Kehr, Dave. "The Man Who Dared to Fill John Wayne's Boots." *New York Times,* October 16, 2011, AR13.

_____. "A Studio Luxuriating in Louche and Lurid." *New York Times,* September 15, 2013, AR13.

_____. "Tall in the Saddle in 2 Eras at Once." *New York Times,* September 30, 2012, AR14.

Larson, T.A. *History of Wyoming,* 2nd ed. Lincoln: University of Nebraska Press, 1990.

Lenberg, Greg. *Classic Western Films Poster Book: 1930–1935.* North Charleston, SC: CreateSpace, 2015.

Levy, Emanuel. *John Wayne: Prophet of the American Way of Life.* Metuchen, NJ: Scarecrow, 1998.

Linet, Beverly. *Ladd: The Life, the Legend, the Legacy of Alan Ladd.* Gettysburg, PA: Arbor House, 1979.

Lovell, Michael. "The Man from Monterey. "*Video Vacuum,* April 5, 2011. http://videovacuum.com/

Maltin, Leonard, and Jerry Beck. *Of Mice and Magic: A History of American Animated Cartoons.* New York: Penguin, 1987.

Martin, Pete. "Big John." *Saturday Evening Post,* July/August 1979, 57c–57i, p. 57e.

Matheson, Sue. "The West-Hardboiled: Adaptations of Film Noir Elements, Existentialism, and Ethics in John Wayne's Westerns." *Journal of Popular Culture* 38 (2005): 888–910.

McCarthy, Todd, and Charles Flynn, eds. *King of the Bs: Working Within the Hollywood System.* New York: E.P. Dutton, 1975.

McCoy, Tim, Ronald McCoy. *Tim McCoy Remembers the West.* New York: Doubleday, 1977.

McGee, Patrick. *From Shane to Kill Bill: Rethinking the Western.* Malden MA: Blackwell, 2007.

McGhee, Richard D. *John Wayne: Actor, Artist, Hero.* Jefferson, NC: McFarland, 1990.

Miller, Don. *Hollywood Corral.* New York: Popular Library, 1976.

Mist, Gerald. *A Short History of the Movies.* 3rd ed. Indianapolis: Bobbs-Merrill, 1984.

Moss, Marilyn Ann. *Raoul Walsh: The True Adventures of Hollywood's Legendary Director.* Lexington: University Press of Kentucky, 2011.

Munn, Michael. *John Wayne: The Man Behind the Myth.* New York: New American Library, 2003.

Nareau, Bob. *The Films of Bob Steele.* Madison, NC: Empire, 1997.

Nevins, Fred N. "Through the Great Depression on Horseback: Legal Themes in Western Films in the 1930s." In *Legal Reelism: Movies as Legal Texts,* edited by John Denvir, pp. 44–46. Urbana: University of Illinois Press, 1996.

Newsom, D. Earl. *The Cherokee Strip: Its History and Grand Opening.* Stillwater, OK: New Forums, 1992.

Nollen, Scott Allen. *Three Bad Men: John Ford, John Wayne, Ward Bond.* Jefferson, NC: McFarland, 2013.

O'Hara, Maureen, and John Nicoletti. *Tis Herself: An Autobiography.* New York: Simon & Schuster, 2004.

Pollack, Allan, and Kim Stephens. *Legendary Locales of the Santa Clarita Valley.* Mount Pleasant, NC: Arcadia, 2012.

Powell, Donald M. *The Peralta Grant: James Addison Reavis and the Barony of Arizona.* Norman: University of Oklahoma Press, 1960.

Rafferty, Terrence. "Building the Duke, Film by Film." *New York Times,* May 20, 2007, AR15.

Rainey, Buck. *The Life and Films of Buck Jones: The Silent Era.* Clearwater, FL: World of Yesterday, 1988.

Ricci, Mark, Boris Zmijewsky, and Steve Zmijewsky. *The Films of John Wayne.* Secaucus, NY: Citadel, 1970.

Roberts, Randy, and James S. Olson. *John Wayne, American.* New York: Free Press, 1995.

Rogers, Ginger. *Ginger: My Story.* New York: Harper, 2008.

Rollyson, Carl. *A Real American Character: The Life of Walter Brennan.* Jackson: University Press of Mississippi, 2015.

Rosebrook, Jeb J., and Jeb S. Rosebrook. "John Ford's Monument Valley." *Arizona Highways* 75, no. 7 (July, 1999): 14–21.

Rothel, David. *Those Great Cowboy Side-kicks*. Madison, NC: Empire, 2001.

Rutherford, John A. *From Pigskin to Saddle Leather: The Films of Johnny Mack Brown*. Waynesville, NC: World of Yesterday, 1987.

Sanford, Henry. "Joseph Kane." In *Close-Up: The Contract Director*, edited by Joe Tusca. Metuchen, NJ: Scarecrow, 1976, 143–187.

Santoro, Greg. "The Big Trail." In *100 Greatest Westerns*, edited by Greg Santoro, pp. 57, 59. Leesburg, VA: Weider History, 2009.

Sarris, Andrew. *The American Cinema: Directors and Directions, 1929–1968*. New York: Da Capo, 1996.

Schickel, Richard. *Keepers: The Greatest Films—and Personal Favorites—of a Movie-Going Lifetime*. New York: Alfred A. Knopf, 2015.

Schneider, Jerry L. *Corriganville: The Definitive True History of the Ray Crash Corrigan Movie Ranch*. Rialto, CA: Corriganville Press, 2013.

_____. *The Ray Crash Corrigan Filmography*. Rialto, CA: Corriganville Press, 2014.

Scott, A.O. "Films of '62: When Eras Collided." *New York Times,* October, 18, 2009, AR1.

Sherman, Robert G. *Quiet on the Set!: Motion Picture History at the Iverson Movie Location Ranch*. Los Angeles: Sherway, 1984.

Simmons, Lee, "The First Action Hero." *Wired* 20, May, 2012, 96.

Slotkin, Richard. *Gunfighter Nation: The Myth of the Frontier in Twentieth-Century America*. New York: Atheneum, 1992.

Smith, David A. *The Price of Valor: The Life of Audie Murphy, America's Most Deco-rated Hero of World War II*. New York: Regnery History, 2015.

Smith, John. M. *The Films of Raoul Walsh: A Critical Approach*. John M. Smith, 2013.

Stanfield, Peter. *Horse Opera: The Strange History of the 1930s Singing Cowboy*. Urbana: University of Illinois Press, 2002.

Stephens, E.J., and Marc Wanamaker. *Early Warner Bros. Studios*. Charleston, SC: Arcadia, 2010.

Stephens, Gail. *Shadow of Shiloh: Major General Lew Wallace in the Civil War*. Indianapolis: Indiana Historical Society, 2010.

Stier, Kenny. *The First Fifty Years of Sound Western Movie Locations (1929–1979)*. Rialto, CA: Corriganville Press, 2006.

Taylor, C. "Stagecoach." *New York Times,* May 2, 2010, MT16.

Wakely, Linda Lee. *See Ya' Up There, Baby: The Jimmy Wakely Story*. Canoga Park, CA: Shasta Records, 1992.

Wallace, Lew. *Ben-Hur: A Tale of the Christ*. New York: Wordsworth, 1995);

Wayne, Ethan. "A Timeless Western Icon." In *John Wayne: The Official Collector's Edition*. New York: Topix Media, 2015, 6.

_____. "The Cowboy Way." In *John Wayne: The Official Collector's Edition*. New York: Topix Media, 2015, 21.

Wellman, William, Jr. *Wild Bill Wellman: Hollywood Rebel*. New York: Pantheon, 2015.

Whiting, Charles. *American Hero: The Life and Death of Audie Murphy*. N.p: J. Whiting, 2000.

Young, Alan. *Mister Ed and Me*. New York: St. Martin's, 1995.

Zolotov, Maurice. *Shooting Star: A Biography of John Wayne*. New York: Simon & Schuster, 1979.

Index